WOMEN AND THE CRIMINAL JUSTICE SYSTEM

Katherine Stuart van Wormer
University of Northern Iowa

Clemens Bartollas
University of Northern Iowa

Allyn and Bacon
Boston • London • Toronto • Sydney • Tokyo • Singapore

Editor in Chief, Social Sciences: Karen Hanson
Series Editorial Assistant: Karen Corday
Sr. Editorial Production Administrator: Susan McIntyre
Editorial Production Service: Nesbitt Graphics, Inc.
Composition Buyer: Linda Cox
Manufacturing Buyer: Megan Cochran
Cover Administrator: Jenny Hart
Electronic Composition: Omegatype Typography, Inc.

Copyright © 2000 by Allyn & Bacon
A Pearson Education Company
160 Gould Street
Needham Heights, MA 02494

Internet: www.abacon.com

Library of Congress Cataloging-in-Publication Data

Van Wormer, Katherine S.
     Women and the criminal justice system / Katherine Stuart van Wormer, Clemens Bartollas.
        p.   cm.
     Includes bibliographical references and index.
     ISBN 0-205-29457-X
     1. Sex discrimination in criminal justice administration—United States.   2. Female offenders—United States.   3. Women prisoners—United States.   4. Women—Crimes against—United States.   5. Women criminal justice personnel—United States.   I. Bartollas, Clemens.
     II. Title.
     HV9950.V38   2000
     364'.082—dc21   99-40317
                                                                              CIP

Printed in the United States of America
10   9   8   7   6   5   4   3   04   03   02   01

Dedicated to Flora Stuart and Natalie Stuart, the sister and niece of Katherine van Wormer, two woman lawyers making a difference

CONTENTS

PREFACE

Women and the Criminal Justice System is unique in at least three respects. The first pertains to the consideration that is given to the effects of the multiple oppressions of gender, race, and class. A fundamental theme of this book is that women are subjected to various forms of discrimination, exploitation, and criminalization. The women who are most likely to experience such oppressions are also poor and from minority groups.

The second innovative feature of this text is the presentation of an empowerment framework within the criminal justice system, a system dominated at every level by men and designed for the incarceration and treatment of hardened male criminals. Whether a woman is in the courtroom as the defendant or lawyer, in prison as an inmate or correctional counselor, or in the police department as an officer or crime victim, she is in alien territory and her special needs and contributions are apt to be overlooked.

Consistent with an empowerment approach—with its stress on solutions rather than problems and on helping people, even in the most dire circumstances, discover their strengths—is a recognition of the reality of racial, gender, and class oppressions. The rhetoric of "welfare reform" is an attack on many of the same women who will enter the justice system or who have returned from it. Our notions of worth and unworthiness regarding "welfare mothers" are the very same notions that criminalize a large portion of the population.

The third innovative feature pertains to the data presented. In a number of chapters, original interviews are presented with women who are offenders, victims, and professionals in the justice system. Interviewees range from women victimized by rape and domestic assault to women offenders on death row and to women who have established law firms against staunch opposition. In addition, in this text are data drawn from the latest governmental and nongovernmental research, including documentation on the nature and frequency of rape (date rape, stranger rape, and prison rape), revelations about wife/partner abuse and how women's shelters are sparing men's lives more than women's, and the incredibly high correlation between early childhood sexual abuse and later addictive behavior in women.

Women and the Criminal Justice System explores not only female offenders and victims, but women on the other side of the law as well: lawyers, police officers, and correctional personnel. In all three of these male-dominated occupations, resistance to women has been profound. The obstacles women still face today mirror the treatment they receive at other levels of the criminal justice system—as victims of crime who seek justice through the law and as offenders facing arrest and prosecution.

A basic premise of this book is that we need to confront sexism and violence against women at multiple levels of our society, on our streets, and in our homes and workplaces. We view traditional crimes against women such as rape and domestic violence not as isolated events but as part and parcel of the denigration of women in the U.S. social structure. A related assumption is that institutional violence on any scale degrades all women and impedes them professionally. Sexual harassment in the workplace, for example, may reinforce women's economic vulnerability and expose them to loss of their livelihood. One sad aspect of oppression is that its victims may blame themselves or others for presumed personal or professional failure. Empowerment, conversely, comes through the realization that the personal is political and that collective action is necessary to change the system. We must travel many miles, however, before we achieve true professional equality.

ORGANIZATION OF THE BOOK

This book is divided into four parts. Part I provides the overview for our study of how the law, social control, and justice have affected women. A discussion of race, gender, and class discrimination is presented from the perspective of feminist theory. Empowerment theory is offered as a guiding framework for the chapters that follow.

Part II brings us into the world of female offenders and their crimes, addictions, and incarceration. The close interconnection of substance abuse, personal involvement with men in the drug world, and the criminal justice process are explored. All the chapters in this part present the latest government statistics on crime prevalence and population profiles.

In Part III women are viewed as victims/survivors. Two forms of victimization, rape and wife/partner abuse, are discussed in terms of male dominance, insecurity, and power (powerlessness). From a strengths approach, we present the cases of women who have "been there" and who reveal how their anger and determination got them through difficult times and how they wrestled with the authorities to get justice and, finally, peace of mind. Guidelines are provided for counselors and victim assistance program providers for working with victims of rape and domestic abuse.

Part IV, Women as Professionals, surveys the field of criminal justice, first by reviewing the history of women in law enforcement, law, and corrections. The contemporary scene is presented through discussion of women's professional progress against a backdrop of discrimination, their contributions to the field, and the empowerment of their clients. The role of sexual harassment as a control mechanism, keeping women out of the "old boys' club," is then explored.

This book was conceived to fill a need in criminal justice and social work for students and practitioners who plan to work in criminal justice and want to "hear it like it is." By presenting a factual knowledge base from official and personal sources, our purpose is to demolish the myths about women victims and offenders (often victims themselves). Accordingly, we delve into areas little explored by other books, for example, date rape on the college campus, women on death row, and sexual abuse of female inmates. Finally, inasmuch as the U.S. criminal justice system is a microcosm of the wider society, the racial, ethnic, and class diversity that characterize that microcosm are a key focus.

ACKNOWLEDGMENTS

Many individuals have contributed to the writing of this book. The authors are profoundly grateful to our spouses. Robert van Wormer edited and typed materials throughout the manuscript. Linda Dippold Bartollas was a constant source of support and encouragement throughout the many phases involved in the publication of this text.

The authors are very grateful to those victims, offenders, and professionals in the justice system who were willing to be interviewed. Special thanks to Hanna Bengston and Jamie Miller for their assistance in typing and photocopying materials and to Betty Heine for all the tasks that she and her staff did to keep the manuscript moving without interruption. We want to acknowledge our appreciation to Peg Markow, Managing Editor of Nesbitt Graphics. As always, we are grateful to Karen Hanson, our editor at Allyn and Bacon. We would also like to thank the following reviewers, whose comments helped shape this book: Anthony Guardino, Tarrant County Junior College; Wendeline Hume, University of North Dakota; and Ida M. Johnson, University of Alabama.

PART I

INTRODUCTION

This introductory chapter provides the social context necessary to examine the "setting in time" of women who are victims of crime, women who are convicted and sentenced for their crimes, and women who work in various agencies of the criminal justice system. This social context is patriarchal society, a society in which males are dominant and females experience oppression in a variety of ways. An examination of sexism, racism, and classism, which begins in this chapter and continues throughout this text, is especially helpful in expressing the multiple marginality that women face in this society and elsewhere.

Feminists are not unified in how women are affected by the oppressions women suffer. Indeed, as Chapter 1 suggests, there are at least four main expressions of feminist theory—liberal feminism, socialist feminism, Marxist feminism, and radical feminism. In terms of the subject matter of this text, feminists have advanced the significance of gender in an alarmingly gender-blind field. Male criminologists have typically written about men and boys and have sometimes totally ignored gender in their analysis of criminological theories. Common themes among feminists are the necessity of women's equality in the courts, the seriousness of sexual harassment in the workplace, and the importance of empowerment in all areas of women's lives.

1

GENDER, PATRIARCHY, AND SOCIAL CONTROL

A major purpose of this text is to empower women who are offenders, victims, and workers in the criminal justice system. Throughout history and across cultures males have typically been allocated power over females in public and in private, in the boardroom and in the bedroom, and in religious institutions and in criminal justice systems. This power is also expressed academically and vocationally, economically and politically, and morally and legally (Money, 1988, p. 69). Money adds to this inequality of power when he says: ". . . insofar as women have had power over men, it has of necessity been achieved deviously by stratagems of obduracy and neglect, conspiracy, seduction, and subterfuge—the sources of the proverbial power behind the throne (Money, 1988, p. 69).

In examining the challenges and obstacles faced by women offenders, victims, and workers in the justice system, this book has developed five underlying feminist themes. First, women offenders, victims, and practitioners experience sexism, racism, and classism on an ongoing basis, and these forms of oppression contribute to the feelings of "multiple marginality" (Chesney-Lind, 1997, p. 4). Second, the effects of the multiple oppressions of gender, class, and race are not merely arithmetic; that is, they are not simply interlocking and piled on each other (Spelman, 1989, p. 123). Thus, "how one form of oppression is experienced is influenced by and influences how another form is experienced" (Spelman, 1989, p. 123). Third, this examination focuses on the social construction of knowledge and how it is typically male oriented. The study of crime itself, as the following discussion reveals, has been written by males about males. The myths concerning female offenders, victims, and practitioners are vivid examples of this social construction of knowledge. Fourth, this examination of women in the justice system heavily emphasizes the importance of social context. In this social context, which is a patriarchal society, women discover how they are expected to think, feel, and act (Spelman, 1989, p. 14). Subcultures within society have varying definitions and expectations of what it means to be a woman, and these norms and values can influence a woman to become a lawyer or a criminal. Finally, the chapters of this text nearly always end with a theme of empowerment. They provide a means or a direction for how women, whether offenders, victims, or practitioners, can move from oppression to empowerment.

Beginning with how the study of crime has been dominated by males and the main feminist theories of criminology, this chapter examines the oppressions that females experience in the social context of the United States and elsewhere. These oppressions take place in a patriarchal society and are reflected in the laws defining women's place; the sexual harassments of women in criminal justice institutions; and the expressions of sexism, racism, and class bias as they affect women offenders, victims, and practitioners.

THE STUDY OF CRIME AND THE MALE PERSPECTIVE

Men commit the majority of crimes. Arrest, self-report, and victimization data all reveal that men and boys commit more frequent and serious crimes than do women and girls. Men also have a virtual monopoly on the commission of corporate, organized, and political crimes (Beirne and Messerschmidt, 1991, pp. 547–548). It is for this reason that "gender has consistently been advanced by criminologists as the strongest predictor of criminal involvement" (Messerschmidt, 1993, p. 1). Yet, as Heidensohn has aptly observed, "most criminologists have resisted this obvious insight with an energy comparable to that of Medieval churchmen denying Galileo or Victorian bishops attacking Darwin" (Heidensohn, 1987, p. 22).

Heidensohn's emphasis on resistance may be somewhat overstated, but it is apparent that major theoretical works written by male criminologists about men and boys have been alarmingly gender-blind (Messerschmidt, 1993, p. 1). Chesney-Lind (2000) has expressed this viewpoint well:

> In my view, the study of crime has been an incontrovertibly male, even "macho," field. Male criminologists have studied other younger men in conflict with an admittedly unequal society and found in their behavior something repellent but also something compelling—witness a major theorist in the area calling the delinquent a "rogue male." Let's face it, male delinquency, particularly gang behavior, is a dramatic form of defiance. Perhaps for that reason, it has been thought of, at least by some criminologists, as the ultimate form of masculinity.
>
> A quick review of the classics in the area will show that my characterization is not all that extreme and that the study of delinquency was almost always the study of male delinquency. In one early work, for example, male delinquency rates were referred to as "delinquency rates"; another 600-page book on gangs spent only one page on the female gangs found by the researcher. Girls were often not even mentioned and occasionally explicitly

eliminated. Delinquency theories, then, stress male experience and male problems. (p. 230)

Chesney-Lind's thesis is that delinquency theories are preoccupied with why males commit delinquent acts. Kathleen Daly and Chesney-Lind also stated that the study of crime and the justice process is shaped by male experiences and understanding of the social world (Daly and Chesney-Lind, 1988). Coramae Richey Mann charged that all the major theorists, including Edwin Sutherland, Albert Cohen, Richard Cloward and Lloyd Ohlin, David Matza, and Travis Hirschi, lacked the development of a female perspective (Mann, 1995). Carol Smart (1976) suggested that a feminist criminology perhaps should be formulated because of the neglect of the feminist perspective in classical delinquency and criminal theories.

FEMINIST THEORIES

There have been two waves of feminism. The first feminist movement was born in 1848 at the Seneca Falls Convention when women demanded the right to vote. Its suffrage emphasis culminated when the Nineteenth Amendment to the Constitution was ratified in 1919. The second feminist movement began in the 1960s. It was sparked by the Equal Pay Act of 1963, which required equal pay for equal work, and Title VII of the Civil Rights Act of 1964, which applied to wages as well as hiring and promotions. Another major influence in the birth of the second feminist movement was the publication of Betty Friedan's *The Feminine Mystique* (1983). Friedan issued a call for housewives to seek their own identity through the development of themselves as full human beings. The second feminist movement has found at least four main expressions of feminist theory: liberal feminism, socialist feminism, Marxist feminism, and radical feminism. Some theories have focused more on juvenile delinquency and adult criminality than others. For example, Chesney-Lind's (1987) radical feminist theory of delinquency, which is examined in Chapter 2, is one of the most exciting efforts to explain delinquent behavior in adolescent females.

Liberal Feminism

Liberal feminism, or egalitarianism, calls for women's equality of opportunity and freedom of choice. Proponents of this theory do not believe that the system is inherently unequal or that discrimination is systematic. Liberal feminists hold that affirmative action, the equal rights amendment, and other opportunity laws or policies provide evidence that men and women can work together to "androgynize" gender roles (blend male and female traits and characteristics) and eliminate discriminatory policies and practices (Simpson, 1989).

Jaggar and Rothenberg (1984) trace liberal feminism to the eighteenth- and nineteenth-century social ideals of liberty and equality (pp. 83–84). Liberal feminists contend that a major reason for the discrimination against women and female adolescents is gender-role socialization. Conventional family patterns, according to this position, structure masculine and feminine identities (Beirne and Messerschmidt, 1991, p. 518).

In 1972, Congress passed the Equal Rights Amendment (ERA). In the campaign to ratify it, many women were mobilized into feminism, and liberal feminists were introduced to the political mainstream. Liberal feminists argued that the physiological differences between men and women fail to justify providing women and men with unequal opportunities. The National Organization for Women (NOW) soon represented what has come to be called liberal feminism or egalitarianism (Rollins, 1996, p. 3).

Liberal feminism has become a reform social movement that has sought to bring about change within the existing social order. By the end of the 1970s, NOW had broadened its stance to include such social issues as lesbian and gay rights, homemakers' rights, the threat of nuclear energy to the species, and legal and economic equality. However, the defeat of the ERA in 1982 ushered in a conservative backlash during which rights previously won by feminists, including affirmative action and legal abortion, were challenged (Rollins, 1996, p. 3).

Socialist Feminism

Socialist feminists, in contrast to other feminists, give neither class nor gender the highest priority. Instead, socialist feminists view both class and gender relations as equal, as they interact with and co-reproduce each other in society. To understand class, socialist feminists argue, it is necessary to recognize how class is structured by gender, and to understand that gender requires that one see how it is structured by class. Crime results from the interaction of these relationships, because it is the powerful who have more legitimate and illegitimate opportunities to commit crime. Low female crime rates, then, are related to women's powerless position in the United States (Rogers, 1973, pp. 223–246).

Socialist feminists challenge both liberal feminists and Marxist feminists. They contend that liberal feminists are fighting for a world in which women pursue self-interest in a capitalist system. Women, then, are pursuing profits, continues this critique, regardless of the good of society. Socialist feminists claim that Marxist feminists have paid insufficient attention to women's issues, neglecting that women have been oppressed as women as well as workers.

Socialist feminists hold that patriarchy predated capitalism. In patriarchy, in U.S. society as well as others, men maintain power over women and exploit their labor in the home as well as in the workplace. MacKinnon (1987) even claims that in socialist feminism sexuality is as central to feminism as work is to Marxism. Accordingly, patriarchy expropriates women's bodies, as is illustrated by rape, pornography, and domestic violence.

Marxist Feminism

Marxist feminists argue that as private property evolved, males dominated all social institutions. Consequently, gender and class inequalities result from property relations and the capitalist mode of production (Beirne and Messerschmidt, 1991). Marxist feminism, sometimes called Marxist feminist radicalism, is based on an anticapitalist premise and, as a reflection of Marxist ideology, sees the oppression of women as arising out of a class society based on private property (Rollins, 1996, p. 5).

According to Marxist radicalism, capitalism makes profits from the low-wage work of women in factories and corporations, both in the United States and elsewhere. The family receives the focus as the means that capitalism uses to conserve and pass on private property and to confine women to domestic slavery. What makes sense from the capitalist perspective, state proponents of Marxist feminism, is that keeping women in a subservient role constitutes the least costly means for a capitalist society to take care of its nonproductive members (Donovan, 1985).

Radical Feminism

Radical feminists view masculine power and privilege as the root cause of all social inequality. The most important relations in any society, according to radical feminists, are found in patriarchy, which pertains to masculine control of labor power and sexuality of women (Beirne and Messerschmidt, 1991, p. 519). Jaggar and Rothensberg (1984), two radical feminists, stated that women were the first oppressed group in history, that women's oppression is so widespread that it exists in virtually every known society, and that women's oppression is so deep that it is the hardest form of oppression to eradicate (pp. 83–84). Radical feminists, especially, focus on sexual violence toward women.

In addition to these traditional four theories of feminism, an African American feminism has developed in recent years. African American feminists are critical of the feminist movement, which they perceive as too oriented to white, middle-class concerns. Instead, they are seeking ways for men and women to work together to eliminate racism, sexism, and class privilege (Rollins, 1996, p. 5). bell hooks (1984), in the following quote, attacks the antimale stance of radical feminists:

> *They were not eager to call attention to the fact that men do not share a common social status; that patriarchy does not negate the existence of class and race privilege or exploitation; that all men do not benefit equally from sexism. They did not want to acknowledge that bourgeois white women, though often victimized by sexism, have more power and privilege, are less likely to be exploited or oppressed, than poor, uneducated, non-white males. (p. 68)*

OPPRESSION, PATRIARCHAL SOCIETY, AND THE CRIMINAL JUSTICE SYSTEM

Each society must grapple with the decision about how to distribute its power, wealth, and opportunities. Sometimes the distribution is fairly egalitarian, and in other cases it is dramatically unequal. Less egalitarian societies have apportioned privilege based on various factors, such as age or race. In the United States and elsewhere, gender has been the determinant. Men and women in U.S. society have been viewed as polar opposites with contrasting abilities and capacities. The very personality traits that are regarded as positive in a man were considered signs of dysfunction in a woman (Rothenberg, 1998). Indeed, as Rothenberg noted, "until very recently, introductory psychology textbooks provided a description of neurosis in a woman that was virtually identical with their description of a healthy male personality" (p. 7).

Social scientists traditionally have distinguished between "sex," which is a biologically based category, and "gender," which refers to the socially constructed meanings that are associated with each sex. The meaning of what is masculine or feminine tends to vary over time. In addition, one culture's perception of masculine or feminine behavior may be the exact opposite of that in another culture. For example, strenuous physical activity is typically considered to be more appropriate for men than for women, but in one society in which women are responsible for such labor, the heaviest load is regarded as being "so heavy only a woman can lift it" (Rothenberg, 1998, pp. 8–9).

It can be argued that the notion of difference between male and female is socially constructed. This social construction of gender's position is based on the assumption that the claimed differences between women and men represent a social and political decision rather than a distinction given in nature (Rothenberg, 1998, p. 9). Rubin (1975) explains it this way:

> *Gender is a socially imposed division of the sexes. . . . Men and women are, of course, different. But they are not as different as day and night, earth and sky, yin and yang, life and death. In fact from the standpoint of nature, men and women are closer to each other than either is to anything else—for instance mountains, kangaroos, or coconut palms. The idea that men and women are more different from one another than either is from anything else must come from somewhere other than nature. (p. 321)*

What is so disturbing about this social construction of gender is that males have assumed the power and control over women in the United States and in most other nations. This is what the term *patriarchial society* means. In their analytic assessment of the patriarchal society, Dobash and Dobash maintain it is comprised of both the structure, or the "hierarchical organization of social institutions and social relations," and the ideology, or the belief system that "is supportive of the principle of a hierarchical order" (Dobash and Dobash, 1979, pp. 43–44). Dougherty adds that it is the way these two ele-

---

BOX 1.1   Decline of Patriarchy

The first and perhaps most profound transition is due to the slow and reluctant but inevitable decline of patriarchy. The time span associated with patriarchy is at least three thousand years, a period so long that we cannot say whether we are dealing with a cyclical process because the information we have about prepatriarchal eras is far too tenuous. What we do know is that for the past three thousand years Western civilization and its precursors, as well as most other cultures, have been based on philosophical, social, and political systems in which men—by force, direct pressure, or through ritual, tradition, law and language, customs, etiquette, education, and the division of labor—determine what part women shall or shall not play, and in which the female is everywhere subsumed under the male.

The power of patriarchy has been extremely difficult to understand because it is all-pervasive. It has influenced our basic ideas about human nature and about our relation to the universe—"man's" nature and "his" relations to the universe, in physical language. It is the one system which, until recently, had never in recorded history been openly challenged, and whose doctrines were so universally accepted that they seemed to be laws of nature; indeed, they were usually presented as such. Today, however, the disintegration of patriarchy is in sight. The feminist movement is one of the strongest cultural currents of our time and will have a profound effect on further evolution.

Source: Fritjof Capra, *The Turning Point: Science, Society, and the Rising Culture* (New York: Bantam Books, 1988), pp. 29–30.

ments of structure and ideology are dynamically related "that makes the patriarchal organization of society such an effective means of oppressing women" (Dougherty, 1993, p. 95). In Box 1.1, Capra reveals what the consequences are for women who live in patriarchal societies.

Laws Defining Women's Place

The oppression of women under patriarchy is first seen through the laws of that society. Early in the history of this nation, the men who wrote and interpreted the law saw that it was necessary to secure the safety of women to protect the family and the community. Kanowitz (1973) aptly expressed this position: "That God designed the sexes to occupy different spheres of action, and that it belonged to men to make, apply, and execute the laws, was regarded as an almost axiomatic truth" (p. 44). The creators of the law, then, made certain that women could enter certain areas of life only under carefully controlled circumstances. This means of protecting womanhood and motherhood sought by legislators and judges actually harmed women by restricting their ability to work and earn a living on an equal basis with men. Such protections, especially, have made having careers in criminal justice difficult for women (Feinman, 1994, p. 7).

This belief that women had to be protected from the sordid nature of life led to their exclusion from jury duty. In 1879 the U.S. Supreme Court lent its support to the common-law exclusion by deciding that states had the constitutional right to limit jury duty to men only. The Civil Rights Act of 1957 gave women the right to serve on federal juries, but some states continued to impose restrictions. Despite the 1975 U.S. Supreme Court decision in *Taylor v. Louisiana* that women could not be excluded from jury duty because of sex, four states continued to provide automatic exemptions for women (Feinman, 1994, pp. 8–9).

The law that was quick to protect the proper woman was equally quick to punish women who were offenders. The Muncy Act of Pennsylvania is an example of discriminatory legislation that was developed to punish women offenders. This act stated that any female pleading guilty to or convicted of a crime punishable by imprisonment of one year or more "must" be sentenced to the state prison for women and that her sentence "shall be merely a general one" and the court "shall not fix or limit the duration thereof" (Kanowitz, 1969, p. 59).

Eventually, as with those prohibiting women on juries, laws similar to the Muncy Act were declared unconstitutional. In *Commonwealth v. Daniel,* Jane Daniel was convicted in Pennsylvania of robbery, an offense that carried a maximum sentence of ten years. After sentencing her to one to four years in the county prison, the judge brought Daniel back to court for resentencing under the Muncy Act, which required an indeterminate term of up to ten years at the state prison for women. Daniel won her appeal to the Pennsylvania Supreme Court in a precedent-setting case, and the Muncy Act was declared unconstitutional (*Commonwealth v. Daniel*).

In *State v. Costello,* Mary A. Costello argued that her constitutional right to equal protection under the Fourteenth Amendment had been violated when she received an indeterminate sentence of not more than five years for pleading guilty to a gambling offense. Under New Jersey law, a man convicted of a similar offense would have received a sentence of not more than two years and not less than one year. The New Jersey Supreme Court ruled: "These distinctions, in essence, form the basis of defendant's claim of denial of equal protection because of discrimination on the basis of sex" (*State v. Costello,* 1971).

Sexual Harassment of Women in Criminal Justice Institutions

The sexual harassment of women emerged as a critically important issue in the 1980s and 1990s. Contributing to the attention given sexual harassment is the number of notorious cases catapulting sexual harassment onto the front pages of newspapers and magazines and onto television news programs. Sportswriter Lisa Olsen claimed that she was sexually harassed by players on the New England Patriots football team, who displayed their body parts in close proximity to her face while she attempted to conduct interviews in the players' locker room (Webb, 1994, p. 4). Dr. Frances Conley, a well-known neurosurgeon, left her position at Stanford University because of "ongoing verbal and physical harassment by her fellow surgeons" (p. 4). Three months later, the nation watched as law professor Anita Hill accused Supreme Court nominee Clarence Thomas of creating a hostile working environment "laden with inappropriate sexual overtones" (p. 4). The alleged conduct occurred when they both worked for the Equal Employment Opportunity Commission in the 1980s (p. 4). Three weeks before the Thomas-Hill hearing, the military's biggest sex scandal unfolded, involving aviators at the Navy's annual Tailhook Association Convention (Rifkind and Harper, 1994, p. 487). The convention generated nearly 150 complaints of harassment (Petrocelli and Repa, 1994). Finally, accusations of harassment continue to hound Bill Clinton. Sexual harassment clearly became one of the most important employment issues of the nineties (Lee and Greenlaw, 1995, p. 357).

G. Patrick Gallagher (1996) defines employee harassment as "any explicit or implicit ridicule, mocking, derision, or belittling of any person or sexual harassment . . ." (p. 21). This inappropriate attitude toward sworn and civilian personnel in an agency "in general will lead to and encourage sexual harassment, because both emanate from the same source—an absence of respect for the individual . . ." (p. 21). Gallagher concludes, ". . . any form of harassment imposes tremendous liabilities on the organization" (p. 21). It does this by reducing productivity, mutual respect, departmental values, philosophical bases for the agency's working relationship with the community, officers' safety, and the organizational climate (p. 21).

The National Advisory Council on Women's Education Programs has categorized sexual harassment into five levels:

1. The first level includes generalized sexual remarks and behavior that are directed at a person because of his or her gender, rather than designed to elicit sexual activity. Examples might include comments about women's supposedly lesser cognitive abilities and their mythical propensity to be vindictive, jealous, and seductive.
2. The second level includes situations that make actual sexual references. What distinguishes this level from the first level is the introduction of the request for sexual encounters, which is often accompanied by some sort of touching. These situations do not need to be blatantly offensive, just inappropriate, and take place where the woman is the subordinate and the man is the superior.
3. The third level includes a solicitation for sex and the promise of some reward. Explicit threats may be absent, but the harasser uses some kind of organizational or institutional authority to "make payment" for a sexual favor.
4. In the fourth level the notion of punishment is introduced for failure to comply with the request for sexual favors. This is generally thought of as the quintessential type of sexual harassment and is illustrated by a failing grade in class, a negative job performance review, or dismissal from work.

5. The final type includes such extreme behaviors as indecent exposure, gross sexual imposition, and outright sexual assaults. Probably the least common type of sexual harassment, this behavior is usually the most devastating to victims. (Erez and Tontodonato, 1995, pp. 231–235)

Through interviewing 106 female officers, Connie Fletcher (1995) observed an underlying theme: women in law enforcement consistently felt that the system failed to protect them against enemies or harassers within the organization, while it views most male officers as neutral or even encouraging to their female counterparts (p. xi). The interviews were not scientific, random samples of the women police officer population but rather officers referred to Fletcher, yet she does provide insightful observations. She continues:

I was surprised by the almost universal picture of police work that emerged from these very diverse sources: Policing is a club for men . . . the club still operates in a culture of socializing and informal contacts impervious to legislation; people who are not wanted in the club may be harassed, ostracized, denied desired assignments, days off, shifts, or promotion; speaking or "grieving" (filing a grievance) about what happens within the club breaks the code and, thereafter, breaks the officer. This is a club where harassers can get away with virtually anything because no one, male or female, can afford the punishments that follow ratting on a fellow cop. And this is a club where you can get killed if people don't like you. (pp. xix–xx)

Women who are lawyers, as well as those who are probation, parole, or correctional officers, also face discrimination and sexual harassment. It was a long uphill battle for women to be accepted into law school, then to find jobs as lawyers and to be appointed as judges and, more recently, to be employed in the most desirable law firms and legal positions. Even today, women lawyers face various forms of discrimination and harassment. Women who enter corrections also have found discriminatory barriers placed before them and, on overcoming these barriers, have faced sexual harassment in one form or another. It is these forms of sexual harassment that have prevented probation and parole officers from achieving supervisory positions or being appointed directors of agencies and that have limited the upward mobility of women in correctional institutions. The antiwomen sentiment that is sometimes present in correctional institutions for men is revealed in the following quote from a female correctional officer:

I expected a negative reaction and thought I was prepared for it. But on my very first day, before I had even been assigned to a post, this male guard came up to me and asked what I was doing there. He said that women don't belong in men's prisons and told me that he would do anything he could to make my life miserable and force me to leave. (Zimmer, 1986, p. 94)

GENDER, CLASS, AND RACE AND WOMEN
IN THE CRIMINAL JUSTICE SYSTEM

Women grow up in a particular social context of domination and control by males. In this patriarchal society, troublesome females are quickly subjected to various forms of discrimination, exploitation, and criminalization. These forms of oppression are expressions of sexism, racism, and classism.

Leonard is one of those who argues that the new theoretical efforts to understand women's crime must include analysis of the links among gender, race, class, and culture (Leonard, 1995, p. 54). Spelman accused some feminists of ignoring racial, class, ethnic, religious, and cultural differences among women. It is through examining sexism, racism, and classism, according to Spelman, that oppression against women can be more clearly grasped and understood (Spelman, 1989, p. ix).

Chesney-Lind (1997) further extended this argument when she said that adolescent females and women are victims of "multiple marginality" because their gender, class, and race have placed them at the economic periphery of society (p. 4). To be labeled a delinquent takes place in a world, Cheseny-Lind charges, "where gender still shapes the lives of young people in very powerful ways. This means that gender matters in girls' lives and that the way gender works varies by the community and the culture into which the girl is born" (p. 121). Chesney-Lind also makes the point that the social context of this world is not fair to women and girls, especially to those of color and those with low incomes (p. 133). For a review of the emerging context of class, race, and gender analysis, see Box 1.2 on page 14.

Gender, class, and race receive the focus of attention in this text. Yet sexuality cannot be ignored and, at times, will be included with gender, class, and race. Culture also becomes a critical component of understanding the criminal justice system's resistance to women pursuing a police career, to women lawyers gaining employment at leading law firms, and to women correctional officers finding acceptance in prisons for men.

Also emphasized is that the total of gender, race, and class is greater than its parts. Spelman (1989) states that "it isn't easy to think about gender, race, and class in ways that don't obscure or underplay their effects on one another" (p. 115). The most common approach focuses on gender and sexism and then considers how gender and racism are related to race and racism and to class and classism and "obscures the way in which race and class identity may be intertwined with gender identity" (pp. 112, 115).

Daly (1993) summarized this argument by saying that "unless you consider all the key relations of inequality—class, race, gender (and also age and sexuality)—you have considered none." She added that "unless you consider the inseparability of these relations in the life of one person, you do not understand what we are saying" (p. 65). This perspective suggests that gender, class, and race are interlocking forms of oppression and that the whole is greater than the parts. Thus, women offenders, victims, and workers in the

BOX 1.2   Historical Context of Class-Race-Gender Analysis

Two sources seem to be largely accountable for the class-race-gender analysis: experiences of African American women in the 1960s and curriculum-integration projects in higher education that were organized by women's studies faculty members.

The actual inspiration for class-race-gender analysis was the experiences of African American women in movement activities in the 1960s. From their experiences came an analysis of sexism in the civil rights and black nationalist movements and of racism in a predominantly white women's feminist movement.

Their first wave of publications in the 1970s focused on black women's experiences in movement politics and their relationships with white women. In the mid to late 1970s,

their analyses became more focused on the development of black feminist thought.

The curriculum-integration projects that were largely organized by women's studies faculty members in higher education were what consolidated and popularized class-race-gender analysis. By 1985, at least eighty projects had been launched to examine how women's studies should be "redefined and reconstructed to include us all." It was not long before the class-race-gender construct was being widely articulated in women's studies, African American studies, cultural and multicultural studies, sociology, anthropology, English and American studies, and history. This became a popular and widely used phrase "to signal a way that theory and research ought to be done."

Source: Kathleen Daly, "Class-Race-Gender: Sloganeering in Search of Meaning," *Social Justice 20* (1993): 56–57.

system suffer the consequences of multiple oppression as more than some form of simple additive experience (p. 65).

An examination of the gender, class, race, and sexuality literature reveals six common themes. First, gender, race, class, and sexuality are contextual. They undergo change as part of the emergence of new political, economic, and ideological processes, events, and trends. Second, gender, race, class, and sexuality are socially constructed. The meaning of these social constructs develops out of group struggles over socially desired resources. Third, and perhaps most important, gender, class, race, and sexuality are power relationships that are historically specific and socially constructed hierarchies of domination. They are power hierarchies in which one group (males) exerts control over another (females), securing a position of dominance and assuming control over such material and nonmaterial resources as income, wealth, and access to health care and education. Fourth, gender, class, and race have meaning at the micro level of individuals' lives as well as the macro level of community and social institutions. Understanding the significance of the constructs of gender, class, race, and sexuality requires grasping the meaning in both contexts. Fifth, gender, class, race, and sexuality simultaneously exist in every social situation. This fact suggests that almost everyone experiences both dominant and subordinate positions at some time and that, therefore, there are no pure oppressors or oppressed in the United States or other industrial nations. Finally, gender, race, class, and sexuality scholarship consistently emphasizes the interdependence of knowledge and activism. This process is dynamic, continually moving from understanding oppression to seeking social change and social justice (Weber, 1998, pp. 16–25).

THE EMPOWERMENT PERSPECTIVE

An understanding of the race-gender-class interactionist configuration is essential to a study of the criminal justice system. The feminist and empowerment perspectives view power and powerlessness related to race, gender, and class as central to the experiences of women in poverty and women of color. *Empowerment theory,* sometimes called the *strengths approach* because of its positive approach in helping people, sees individual problems as arising not from personal deficits, but from the failure of society to meet the needs of all the people (Gutiérrez, 1991).

Central to the empowerment approach is the concept of power, which is viewed as an attribute with consequences that may be negative or positive. Negative consequences arise from powerlessness, power imbalances in relationships, and an inability to make choices about one's life or livelihood. The subordination of women is a factor that creates violence, whether institutionally (for example, against women in prison) or within the family system. From a positive standpoint, power can be a liberating force. Gaining a sense of personal power can be a first step in assuming personal responsibility for change and in moving, as Gutiérrez states, from apathy and despair to positive social action.

Of special relevance to criminal behavior, and without which change is unlikely, is the taking of personal responsibility for one's actions and for one's life. The counseling relationship can serve as a powerful tool for helping clients change cognitive misconceptions that result in self-destructive thoughts and behavior. Even in a life crushed by circumstances of time and place, there nevertheless exists the potential for actions other than those characteristically taken. This belief in potential is at the core of a healthy, therapeutic relationship.

An empowerment approach focuses on oppression and on those who suffer from its consequences. Oppressed individuals are not devoid of personal or moral strengths or resources. Help in tapping into those resources often is needed. For all of us, a sense of control over our lives and relationships is crucial. McWhirter (1991) captures the essence of empowerment in her inclusive definition:

> *Empowerment is the process by which people, organizations, or groups who are powerless (a) become aware of the power dynamics at work in their life context, (b) develop the skills and capacity for gaining some reasonable control over their lives, (c) exercise this control without infringing upon rights of others, and (d) support the empowerment of others in their community. (p. 224)*

Until recently, the empowerment perspective has been absent from the criminal justice literature. A computer search of the criminal justice abstracts index (as of February 1999) reveals no listing for articles under the headings *strengths approach* or *strengths perspective*. The word *empowerment* does appear in the computer index as a progressive term for work with juveniles, female victims, and occasionally, female offenders. Writing about probation, Clark (1998) calls for a new paradigm to focus on offenders' strengths rather than their faults and failures. This perspective, borrowed from social work, is gaining ground, according to Clark. Barajas (1996), similarly, refers to a paradigm shift in corrections, "a quiet, grassroots, seemingly unobtrusive, but truly revolutionary movement" (p. 32) that reflects a renewed emphasis on rehabilitation rather than punishment. A focus on solutions rather than problems is empowering to clients and corrections workers alike.

Empowerment theory, with its focus on personal, social, educational, and political dimensions, offers a useful framework for addressing the needs of women at all the various levels of the criminal justice hierarchy. Just as a woman in prison or on probation can be empowered through understanding that her situation is not just a personal problem but one related to gender, class, and racial oppression, so too can female correctional officers and lawyers be informed by a macro view that explains why affirmative action programs may be a necessary but not sufficient requisite to success.

The personal is political and the political is personal. This, in a nutshell, is the underlying theme of the feminist empowerment approach. The view of humanity underlying this approach is that humans are unique, multifaceted beings with the potential to make a contribution to their community (Kelley, 1996). This contribution can be made quietly or through public consciousness-raising and networking, for example, through membership in various self-help groups or specialized professional associations. Sharing in writing and receiving newsletters is an example of educational empowerment. Political empowerment can occur through activities such as lobbying politicians and mass media campaigns. Issues relevant to women in criminal justice are lobbying for victims rights, working toward legislative changes to protect women in prison from sexual abuse, and working to enhance affirmative action programs to increase the female-to-male ratio in policing. The empowerment of professional women in the field of criminal justice should have a ricocheting effect on women at every level of the criminal justice system.

SUMMARY

bell hooks (1998) states that "we live in a world in crisis—a world governed by politics of domination, one in which the belief in a notion of superior and inferior, and its concomitant ideology—that the superior should rule over the inferior—affects the lives of all people everywhere, whether poor or privileged, literate or illiterate" (p. 579). She reminds us that "systematic dehumanization, worldwide famine, ecological devastation, industrial contamination, and the possibility of nuclear destruction are realities that remind us daily that we are in crisis" (p. 579). The origin of this crisis, according to some feminist thinkers, is sexual politics. bell hooks adds that these feminist thinkers believe that "differentiation of status between females and males globally is an indication that patriarchal domination of the planet is the root of the problem" (p. 579).

This chapter provided an overview of how male domination affects women victims, offenders, and workers in the criminal justice system. Women have experienced the domination of men in terms of such matters as the right to own property; to vote; to serve on a jury; and to be protected from predators, fathers, and husbands. Sexual harassment has been a special problem for women who become police officers, lawyers, and corrections workers. This chapter also briefly examined the categories of gender, class, and race and how they intersect in the lives of women victims and offenders. As one of the six major themes, an analysis of gender, class, and race guides the discussion throughout the remainder of this book.

Moreover, this chapter has proposed that there is consensus among feminist theorists on at least two beliefs. First, social context, especially patriarchal society, is vitally important in understanding the oppression of women. But a contextual analysis, in turn, requires an examination of politics, economics, law, and culture on both macro and micro levels. Second, feminist ethics is guided by two principles: "that it is wrong to hurt anyone, and that it is right to sustain human relationships" (McDermott, 1993, p. 37).

Finally, this chapter has suggested that there is no single feminist perspective on the victimization of women. Feminist theories have been categorized as liberal, radical, socialist, and Marxist. But, even within perspectives, there are differences. These differences may vary in the extent to which feminist theorists advocate for victims, identify with victims, or emphasize offender rights and treatment. Women, adds Bernat (1995), do not make up a homogenous entity (p. 7). As she aptly puts it, "we have a community of differences which need to be:

> Celebrated,
> > Uncovered,
> > > Legitimated,
> > > > Taught,
> > > > > Understood,
> > > > > > Respected, and
> > > > > > > Embraced." (p. 7)

REFERENCES

Barajas, E. (1996). *Community justice: Striving for safe and just communities.* Washington, D.C.: U.S. Institute of Corrections, 1996.

Beirne, P., and Messerschmidt, J. (1991). *Criminology.* San Diego: Harcourt Brace Jovanovich.

Bernat, F. P. (1995). Opening the dialogue: Women's culture and the criminal justice system. *Women and Criminal Justice 7:* 1–7.

Chesney-Lind, M. (2000). Interview in Clemens Bartollas, *Juvenile Delinquency,* 5th ed. Needham Heights: Allyn & Bacon, 2000, p. 214.

Chesney-Lind, M. (1987). Girls' crime and woman's place: Toward a feminist model of female delinquency. Paper presented at the Annual Meeting of the American Society of Criminology. Montreal, Canada, November 10–14, 1987.

Chesney-Lind, M. (1997). *The female offender: Girls, women and crime.* Thousand Oaks, Calif.: Sage.

Clark, M. D. (1998, June). Strength-based practice: The ABC's of working with adolescents who don't want to work with you. *Federal Probation 62,* 46–53.

Commonwealth v. Daniel, Appellant 430 Pa. 642.

Daly, K., and Chesney-Lind, M. (1988). Feminism and criminology. *Justice Quarterly 5:* 497–538.

Daly, K. (1993). Class-race-gender: Sloganeering in search of meaning. *Social Justice 20:* 56–71.

Dobash, R. E., and Dobash, R. (1979). *Violence against wives: A case against the patriarchy.* New York: Free Press.

Donovan, J. (1985). *Feminist theory: The intellectual traditions of American feminism.* New York: Frederick Ungar.

Dougherty, J. (1993). Women's violence against their children: A feminist perspective. *Women and Criminal Justice 42:* 91–114.

Erez, E., and Tontodonato, P. (1992). Sexual harassment in the criminal justice system. In *The changing roles of women in the criminal justice system: Offenders, victims, and professionals* (pp. 227–252), 2nd ed. Prospect Heights: Waveland Press.

Feinman, C. (1994). *Women in the criminal justice system,* 3rd ed. Westport, Conn.: Praeger Publishers.

Fletcher, C. (1995). *Breaking and entering: Women cops talk about life in the ultimate men's club.* New York: Harper/Collins.

Friedan, B. (1983). *The feminine mystique.* New York: Norton.

Gallagher, G. P. (1996, November and December). When will the message about harassment be acted upon. *The Law Enforcement Trainer 11.*

Gutiérrez, L. (1991). Empowering women of color: A feminist model. In M. Bricker-Jenkins, N. R. Hooyman, and N. Gottlieb (eds.), *Feminist social work practices in clinical settings* (pp. 271–303). Newbury Park, Calif.: Sage.

Heidensohn, F. (1987). Women and crime: Questions for criminology. In P. Carlen and A. Worrall (eds.), *Gender, crime, and justice* (pp. 16–27). Philadelphia: Open University Press.

hooks, b. (1984). *Feminist theory: From margin to center.* Boston: South End Books.

Jaggar, A. M., and Rothenberg, P. (eds.). (1984). *Feminist frameworks.* New York: McGraw-Hill.

Kanowitz, L. (1973). *Sex roles in law and society: Cases and materials.* Albuquerque: University of New Mexico Press.

Kanowitz, L. (1969). *Women and the law: The unfinished revolution.* Albuquerque: University of New Mexico Press.

Kelley, P. (1996). Narrative theory and social work treatment. In F. Turner (ed.), *Social work treatment: Interlocking theoretical approaches* (pp. 461–479). New York: Free Press.

Lee, R. D., and Greenlaw, P. S. (1995, July). The legal revolution of sexual harassment. *Public Administration Review 55:* 357–364.

Leonard, E. (1995). Theoretical criminology and gender. In B. R. Price and N. J. Sokoloff (eds.), *The criminal justice system and women: Offenders, victims, and workers* (pp. 54–70), 2nd ed. New York: McGraw-Hill.

MacKinnon, C. (1987). *Feminism unmodified: Discourses on life and law.* Cambridge, Mass.: Harvard University Press.

Mann, C. R. (1995). Women of color and the criminal justice system. In B. R. Price and N. J. Sokoloff (eds.), *The criminal justice system and women: Offenders, victims, and workers* (pp. 118–135). New York: McGraw-Hill.

McWhirter, E. H. (1991). Empowerment in counseling. *Journal of Counseling and Development 69*(3), 222–227.

Messerschmidt, J. W. (1993). *Masculinities and crime: Critique and reconceptualization of theory.* Lantham, Md.: Rowman & Littlefield.

Money, J. (1988). *Gay, straight, and in-between: Sexology of erotic orientation.* New York: Oxford University Press.

Petrocelli, W., and Repa, B. K. (1994). *Sexual harassment on the job,* 2nd ed. Berkeley, Calif.: Nolo.

Price, B. R., and Sokoloff, N. J. (1995). The criminal law and women. In B. R. Price and N. J. Sokoloff (eds.), *The criminal justice system and women: Offenders, victims, and workers* (pp. 11–29). New York: McGraw-Hill.

Rifkind, L., and Harper, L. (1994, September). Conflict management strategies for the equal opportunity difficult person in the sexually. . . . *Personnel Management 23.*

Rogers, K. O. (1973). For her own protection . . . Conditions of incarceration for female juvenile offenders in the state of Connecticut. *Law and Society Review 7:* 223–246.

Rollins, J. H. (1996). *Women's minds, women's bodies: The psychology of women in a biosocial context.* Upper Saddle River, N.J.: Prentice-Hall.

Rothenberg, P. S. (1998). *Race, class, and gender in the United States: An integrated story,* 4th ed. New York: St. Martin's Press.

Rubin, G. (1975). The traffic in women. In R. R. Reither (ed.), *Toward an anthropology of women* (p. 179). New York: Monthly Review Press.

Simpson, S. S. (1989, November). Feminist theory, crime, and justice. *Criminology 27:* 605–622.

Spelman, E. V. (1989). *Inessential woman.* Boston: Beacon Press.

State v. Costello. New Jersey State Supreme Court 59, 1971.

Webb, S. L. (1994). *Shockwaves: The global impact of sexual harassment.* New York: MasterMedia.

Weber, L. (1998). A conceptual framework for understanding race, class, gender, and sexuality. *Psychology of Women Quarterly 22:* 13–32.

Zimmer, L. (1986). *Women guarding men.* Chicago: University of Chicago Press.

PART II

WOMEN CRIMINALS

Racial, ethnic, and class diversity come together in compelling ways in the chapters of this part. Here we concentrate on the female offender, often a drug addict/alcoholic with a long history of sexual and physical abuse. The typical adjudicated female offender is a woman of color and mother of small children. Their stories reveal how social control of already oppressed people is carried out by the state and legitimized through the mass media. The ultimate inequality of U.S. society is revealed in a visit to the nation's prisons.

How do women get caught up in violating the law? Which crimes do they commit? Are women committing more crimes today, or are they being arrested and prosecuted more diligently than in the past? What is the nature of addiction and the abuse/crime connection? These are among the questions considered in Chapter 2. The focus on substance abuse is timely in light of recent government data indicating substance abuse involvement in the backgrounds of 80 percent of prison inmates, both male and female.

Despite being a small portion of the entire U.S. prison population, women, and especially women of color, have shown the greatest increase in state and federal imprisonment for drug-related crimes. Their numbers have doubled and tripled in recent years, creating drastic overcrowding and a boom in prison construction across the states. Modeled on medium-security prisons for dangerous men, women's prisons are not hospitable places. Research shows that behind bars women's treatment needs—in the areas of substance abuse, mental health, and prior victimization—are not being met. Many of the incarcerated women could lead productive lives in the community and at tremendous savings to the state if alternative intensive supervision programs were provided.

Chapter 3, Women in Prison, contains shocking documentation of the widespread sexual abuse of female inmates by male correctional officers. The facts, still not widely known, have been kept secret until recently revealed in court documents and international reports. Findings show that a terrifying situation exists for many women in prison, who are vulnerable to sexual abuse by men against whom they dare not complain. Compared to the controversy over sexual harassment of women in the military, the U.S. media have been remarkably reticent on this subject.

The personal side of the harsh sentencing practices is reified for us in this chapter through personal narratives from female inmates, a prison chaplain, and others who are in the system at the present time. Their comments, many of which are surprisingly uplifting, provide diverse viewpoints and experiences. The empowerment theme emerges as some inmates reveal how they have been empowered through innovative treatment programs and caring counselors and how their lives literally have been turned around. Chapter 3 ends with a consideration of several exemplary correctional programs in the United States as well as in Western Europe and Canada.

2

WOMEN IN CRIME

In the midst of a great deal of indifference toward women offenders, Freda Adler's *Sisters in Crime* (1975) contended that a new woman criminal had arrived on our social horizons. She argued that the rise in crime among adult women and juvenile females is clearly linked to opportunity. Adolescent girls and adult women, according to Adler, face the plight because they are instilled with almost boundless ambition but lack opportunities to achieve their desired goals. The end result is that female adults and juveniles strive for the same goals as males and adopt male roles to achieve them. Accordingly, they are becoming involved in more aggressive and violent acts. Adler contended that the rise in official rates of female crime reflects the changes brought about by the liberation of women. The rise in female crime, then, is directly related to females becoming more competitive with males, more aggressive, and more "masculine" in general. As she reported:

> "I know it's happening but I'll be damned if it still doesn't shock me when I see it," explained one exasperated sergeant who was slumped in the chair of a district precinct house in Washington, D.C. He was talking about the new problems which girls have created for police. "Last week, for instance, we got a call of a disturbance at the high school. A fight . . . after school. So we get down there and pull up and here is a hell of a crowd yelling and screaming at the kids in the center, who are fighting. I push my way through the crowd—they're going crazy like it is really a mean fight and when I get to the middle . . . I like to fell over. Here are two husky broads, and they are fighting . . . now I don't mean any hair-pulling face-scratching kind of thing; I mean two broads squared off and duking it out. Throwing jabs and hooking in at each other and handling themselves like a couple of goddamned pro sparring partners. I mean, I got to ask myself, what the hell is going on? What in the name of God is happening to these girls anymore?" (pp. 96–97)

Laura Crites (1976) was one of many who found fault with Adler's women's liberation thesis. She pointed out that female offenders most often come from minority groups. They are frequently unemployed and usually are responsible for their own support and often for that of any children. In addition, their employment potential is limited because more than half have not graduated from high school and their work experience has generally been in low-wage, low-status occupations. Crites reasons that the psychological independence and expanded economic opportunities of the women's rights movement are almost meaningless for this group; instead of being concerned with the ideological constructs of the women's liberation movement, the typical female offender is caught up in a struggle for economic, emotional, and physical survival (pp. 36–39).

Yet, even though Adler's thesis of the women's liberation movement has received little support, it has contributed in a major way to stimulating interest in the extent and nature of women's crime. The vast amount of recent literature on female delinquents and women criminals has also appeared in part because of a desire to offset the preponderance of theories and studies centered on males and in part as a response to the perceived "dramatic increases" in the amount and versatility of involvement in delinquency by juvenile girls and in criminal behavior by adult women.

Beginning with the various explanations of why females commit unlawful activities, this chapter also considers the extent of female crime, the types of crimes females commit, and the processing of female offenders through the criminal justice system.

EXPLANATIONS OF FEMALE CRIME

Feminist criminologists are quick to agree that adolescent females have different experiences from adolescent males. They generally support that females are more controlled than males, enjoy more social support, are less disposed to crime, and have fewer opportunities to commit certain types of crimes (Office of Juvenile Justice and Delinquency Prevention, 1998). Some evidence also exists that "high self-esteem discourages definitions favorable to risk-taking among females but encourages these definitions among males" (Heimer, 1994, p. 164). Moreover, juvenile justice research tends to support that young women's patterns of offending differ in scope and motivation from those of their male counterparts (Office of Juvenile Justice and Delinquency Prevention, 1998). Finally, Meda Chesney-Lind (1997) argues that female adolescents are frequently the victims of violence and sexual abuse at home and this abuse is a chief reason that they choose to run away (pp. 25–26).

However, among feminist criminologists are three vastly different opinions about how the commonly accepted male-oriented approach to delinquency and criminology should be handled. Some feminist theorists emphasize that feminist research should be presented in textbooks "as a seamless whole rather than as a separate chapter" (Daly, 1995, pp. 447–448). These feminist theorists question the need for separate discussions on female delinquency or women in crime, because little evidence to date suggests that separate theories are needed to account for female and male delinquency and criminality. Moreover, they claim that latent structural analysis shows that female delinquency and women in crime tend to operate through the same factors as male delinquency and male criminality. Empirical studies generally reveal that much more variation exists within each gender than between the sexes (McDonough and Selo, 1980, pp. 333–343; Hagan, Gillis, and Simpson, 1985, pp. 1151–1178; Smith and Paternoster, 1987, pp. 140–172).

In contrast, other feminist theorists argue that new theoretical efforts are needed to understand female delinquency and women's involvement in adult crime. Carol Smart (1976) and Dorie Klein (1973), two early criminologists, suggested that a feminist criminology should be formulated because of the neglect of the feminist perspective in classical delinquency theories. Klein's 1973 article ended in a call for "a new kind of research on women and crime—one that has feminist roots and a radical orientation. . . ." (p. 46). In a 1995 update, Klein contributed that the feminist critique of such subjects as women, crime, and justice "has exploded in volume and advanced light-years in depth, and interest. . . ." (p. 48). Daly and Chesney-Lind (1988) defined a feminist perspective as one "in which women's experiences and ways of knowing are brought to the fore, not suppressed" (p. 498).

Eileen Leonard (1995) further questioned whether anomie, labeling, differential association, subculture, and Marxist theories can be used to explain the crime patterns of women. She concluded that these traditional theories do not work and that they are basically flawed. Chesney-Lind's application of the male-oriented theories to female delinquency has determined that existing delinquency theories are inadequate to explain female delinquency. She suggested that there is a need for a feminist model of delinquency, because a patriarchal context has shaped the explanations and handling of female delinquents and status offenders. Therefore adolescent females' sexual and physical victimizations at home and the relationship between these experiences and their crimes have been systematically ignored (1989, pp. 5–29; 1995, pp. 71–88).

A third feminist position, presented in Chapter 1, argues that the structural categories of gender, class, and race are more helpful than individual or sociopsychological explanations in understanding women's involvement in crime. Based on the assumption that gender, class, and race are interlocking forms of oppression, this position suggests that an adequate explanation of why women commit crime requires an examination of the total effects of not only each of these factors but also the combined effect of these forces of oppression on women's lives. This position poses a rhetorical question: How is being viewed as a female delinquent in U.S. society influenced by a particular social context? It answers this question by proposing that the particular social context is patriarchal society and that discrimination, exploitation, and oppression take place on the basis of sex or gender and are critical factors in explaining why females become involved in criminal behavior.

Sexism and Female Crime

The biological, psychological, and sociological explanations for why females become involved in crime are examined in this section. Early explanations of female crime focused on biological and psychological factors, but more recent explanations have placed much greater emphasis on sociological factors.

Biological and Constitutional Explanations

In *The Female Offender*, initially published in 1903, Cesare Lombroso deals with crime as atavism, or the survival of "primitive" traits in female offenders. First, he argued that women are more primitive, or lower on the evolutionary scale, because they are less intelligent and have fewer variations in their mental capacities than men: "even the female criminal is monotonous and uniform compared with her male companion, just as in general women are inferior to men." Second, Lombroso contended that women are unable to feel pain and, therefore, are insensitive to the pain of others and lack moral refinement. He stated:

> *Women have many traits in common with children; that their moral sense is deficient; that they are revengeful, jealous. . . . In ordinary cases these defects are neutralized by piety, maternity, want of passion, sexual coldness, weakness, and an undeveloped intelligence. (p. 151)*

Third, he argued, women are characterized by a passive and conservative approach to life. Although he admitted that women's traditional sex roles in the family bind them to a more home-centered life, he insisted that women's passivity can be directly traced to the "immobility of the ovule compared with the zoosperm" (p. 109).

Lombroso (1920) contended that because most women are born with "feminine" characteristics, their innate physiological limitations protect them from crime and predispose them to live unimaginative, dull, and conforming lives. But women criminals, he argued, have inherited male characteristics, such as excessive body hair, moles, wrinkles, crow's feet, and abnormal craniums. He added that the female criminal, being doubly exceptional as a woman and as a criminal, is likely to be more vicious than the male criminal (pp. 150–152).

With the recent biosocial revival in criminology, biological or physiological explanations for crime and delinquency have regained some popularity. In a 1968 study, Cowie, Cowie, and Slater (1968) presented data on an English approved school (training school) sample that emphasize genetic factors as the major cause of delinquency. These researchers even proposed that these genetic factors might be specific enough to determine the types of crimes the sexes will commit (p. 17). T. C. N. Gibbens (1971) also reported a high rate of sex chromosomal abnormalities in delinquent girls (pp. 279–286). Furthermore, Cowie and colleagues (1968) noted the above-average weight of their institutional sample and suggested that physical overdevelopment tends to draw a girl's attention to sex earlier in life, resulting in sexual promiscuity. In addition, they claimed that menstruation is a distressing reminder to females that they can never be males and that this distress makes them increasingly prone to delinquent acts.

In sum, the viewpoints of Lombroso and other supporters of biological explanations for female criminality can be regarded as merely a foolish testimony to the historical chauvinism of males. Unfortunately, the study of female criminality has not yet fully recovered from the idea "that the cause of a socially generated phenomenon might be reduced to a genetically transmitted biological unit" (Campbell, 1981, p. 46).

Psychological Explanations

The claimed "innate nature" of women is the basis of much of the literature on psychological explanations of female crime. W. I. Thomas, Sigmund Freud, and Otto Pollak are among those who addressed this "innate" female nature and its relationship to deviant behavior.

Thomas's works marked a transition from physiological explanations to more sophisticated theories embracing physiological, psychological, and social structural factors. In *Sex and Society* (1907), he suggested that there are basic biological differences between the sexes. Maleness, according to Thomas, is "katabolic," from the animal force that involves a destructive release of energy and allows the possibility of creative work through this outward flow, but femaleness is "anabolic"—motionless, lethargic, and conservative. Thomas's underlying assumptions are physiological ones, for he credits men with higher amounts of sexual energy that lead them to pursue women for sexual pleasure. In contrast, he attributes to women maternal feelings devoid of sexuality, so they exchange sex for domesticity.

In his 1923 work *The Unadjusted Girl,* Thomas dealt with female delinquency as a "normal" response under certain social conditions. He argued that a girl is driven by four wishes or ambitions: new experiences, security, response, and recognition. He assumed that the delinquent girl's problem is not criminality but immorality, and he confined himself almost exclusively to a discussion of prostitution. According to Thomas, the major cause of prostitution rested in the girl's need for love, and a secondary factor is her wish for recognition or ambition. Thomas maintained that it is not sexual desire that motivates delinquent girls, because they are no more passionate than non-delinquent girls, but that they are using male desire for sex to achieve their own ultimate needs (Thomas, 1923).

The beginning of delinquency in girls is usually an impulse to get amusement, adventure, pretty clothes, favorable notice, distinction, freedom in the

larger world. . . . The girls have usually become "wild" before the devel-
opment of sexual desire, and their casual sex relations do usually awaken
sexual feelings. Their sex is used as a condition of the realization of other
wishes. It is their capital. (Thomas, 1923, p. 109)

The sad commentary on the state of theory regarding female criminalityis that until recently the psychoanalytic writings of Sigmund Freud have represented the most pervasive theoretical position. The structure of the personality and the psychosexual stages of development of the child are the two major concepts from which most of Freud's theories have evolved.

The most controversial and ridiculous aspects of Freud's theory had to do with his assumption that women's sex organs make them anatomically inferior to men. Freud (1949) contended that a little girl assumes she has lost her penis as punishment and, therefore, feels traumatized and grows up envious and revengeful. A woman becomes a mother to replace the "lost penis" with a baby. The delinquent girl or woman criminal, in the Freudian perspective, is one who is attempting to be a man. Her drive to accomplishment is the expression of her longing for a penis (p. 278).

The Freudian orientation is not limited to penis envy in its explanation of female crime, because it suggested that at any state of psychosexual development, faulty mechanism, fixations, and other problems may occur. Freud also argued that women are inferior because they are concerned with personal matters and have little social sense. Women, according to Freud (1933), have weaker social interests than men and less capacity for the sublimation of their interests (p. 183).

Otto Pollak's *The Criminality of Women* (1950) advanced the theory that women are more criminal than is usually believed, but that their crimes are largely unreported or hidden. Pollak credited the nature of women themselves for the traditionally low official rates of female crime, because women are inherently deceitful and, therefore, act as instigators rather than perpetrators of criminal activity. The roles played by women are a factor in hidden crimes as well because such roles as domestics, nurses, teachers, and housewives enable them to commit undetectable crimes. Pollak further advances the "chivalry factor" as a root cause of hidden crime; that is, the police and the court forgive a girl for the same act for which they would convict a boy (p. 8).

Pollak (1950) also suggested two factors that influence adolescent females to become juvenile delinquents. First, he said, early physical development and sexual maturity allow a female more opportunities to engage in immoral or delinquent behavior. Second, a female's home life, especially one who has criminal parents or grows up in a broken home, may cause her to seek outside substitutes for that poor home life. She is likely to seek the company of other maladjusted females, and they will eventually become involved in a life of petty crimes (pp. 125–139).

In sum, psychological studies of female crime shifted in the 1950s from the psychoanalytical to the familial-social type. Considerable research continues to perpetuate the notion that personal maladjustment characterizes the female criminal: She has a psychological problem, is unable to perform her proper sex role adequately, or suffers from the ill effects of a bad home life (Giordano and Cernkovich, 1979, p. 24).

Sociological Explanations

Beginning in the late 1970s, several studies proceeded from the assumption that sociological processes traditionally related to males could also affect the antisocial involvement of females. Juvenile delinquency researchers who examined the sociological themes of blocked opportunity theory, social control theory, masculinity hypothesis, power-control theory, and labeling theory found that they offered much more promise than biological or psychological causes. But Leonard, who focused on other sociological theories, was much less convinced of the value of sociological factors in explaining criminality among women offenders.

Sociological Explanations for Female Delinquent Behavior.   The role of blocked or limited opportunity has received considerable attention in the sociological analysis of male delinquency. The usefulness of such variables in studying female delinquency has been largely ignored because males are seen as concerned with achieving short- and long-term status and economic success, whereas juvenile females are commonly viewed as possessing no such aspirations but, instead, as being satisfied to occupy a role dependent on males (Parsons, 1942; Coleman, 1961; Rittenhouse, 1963).

Yet Datesman and colleagues (1975) found that perception of limited opportunity was more strongly related to female delinquency than it was to male delinquency. Both African American and white female delinquents regarded their opportunities less positively than did nondelinquents in their sample. Status offenders also perceived their opportunities as being less favorable than did nondelinquents (p. 120). Figueira-McDonough and Selo's (1980) formulation of feminist opportunity theory contended that similar levels of strain (arising from high success aspirations and low legitimate opportunities) lead to similar antisocial patterns by both genders, provided that they are equal in their knowledge of and access to illegitimate means (pp. 333–343).

Proponents of social control theory contend that females are less involved in crime than males because sex-role socializations result in a greater tie to the social bond for females than for males. In addition, females may have less opportunity to engage in delinquent behavior because in general they are more closely supervised by parents. Adolescent females are also more dependent on others, whereas adolescent males are encouraged to be more independent and achievement oriented. Consequently, differences in sex-role socialization supposedly promote a greater allegiance to the social bond among females, and this allegiance insulates them from delinquency more than it does males. This position infers that females require a greater "push" to become involved in delinquent and criminal acts.

Anderson, Holmes, and Ostresh (1998) found from a survey of adolescent males and females confined in the Wyoming boys' and girls' training schools that there were no differences in males' and females' levels of attachment when parents' attachment and attitude toward school were controlled. Yet some gender differences in the effects of the various attachments on the severity of delinquency were found. Although attachment to parents reduced the severity of males' delinquency, attachment to peers and schools reduced the severity of females' delinquency.

Freda Adler argued in *Sisters in Crime* (1975) that both adult women and adolescent females are imitating males in their desire for the same goals and their adoption of male roles to achieve them. Because of this merging of gender roles, adolescent females, as well as their older counterparts, engage in more violent crime. Adler contended that as females become more male-like and acquire more "masculine" traits, they become more criminal.

Cullen, Golden, and Cullen (1977) found that the more male and female adolescents possessed "male" personality traits, the more likely they were to become involved in delinquency, but the relationship between masculinity and delinquency was stronger for males than for females (pp. 87–104). Thornton and James (1979) found a moderate degree of association between masculine self-expectations and delinquency but concluded that males were still more likely to be delinquent than females, regardless of their degree of masculinity (pp. 225–241).

Hagan and colleagues proposed a power-control theory to explain female delinquency (Hagan, Simpson, and Gillis, 1987, pp. 788–816; Hagan, Gillis, and Simpson, 1985, pp. 1151–1178). Using a Marxian framework and data collected in Toronto, Canada, they contended that as mothers gain power relative to their husbands, usually by employment outside the home, daughters and sons alike are encouraged to be more open to risk taking. Parents in egalitarian families, then, redistribute their control efforts so that daughters are subjected to controls more like those imposed on sons.

In contrast, daughters in patriarchal families are taught by their parents to avoid risks (Hagan, Simpson, and Gillis, 1987, pp. 791–792). Hagan and colleagues concluded that "patriarchal families will be characterized by large gender differences in common delinquent behavior while egalitarian families will be characterized by smaller gender differences in delinquency" (p. 793). Power-control theory thus concludes that when daughters are freed from patriarchal family relations, they more frequently become delinquent (pp. 813–814).

In evaluating power-control theory, Singer and Levine (1987) contended that it is unclear in what ways work relationships produce more egalitarian home environments. The balanced class categories of egalitarian households may still reflect unbalanced work situations; the husband and wife may both be managers, but the husband is likely to make a higher income and to have more authority at work. Chesney-Lind (1987), in an even more stinging criticism, stated that power-control theory is a variation of the earlier liberation hypothesis, but it claims that mothers' liberation causes daughters' crime.

Bartusch and Matsueda (1996), in assessing whether an interactionist model can account for the gender gap in delinquency, used data from the National Youth Survey. Based on a symbolic interactionist model of delinquency, they argued that "delinquency is determined in part by the self as conceived by symbolic interactionists, which in turn is determined by a process of labeling by significant others" (p. 145). They did find some gender interactions. Parental labeling and reflecting appraisals had a larger effect on male delinquency, and parents were more likely to falsely accuse male delinquents.

Other Sociological Theories and Female Criminality.   Leonard (1995) contends that sociological theories in general inadequately explain adult women's involvement in crime. She argues that anomie theory is unworkable in analyzing the crimes that occur among women. It "fails to explain why women deviate the way they do or what type of strain leads to each outcome. The theory applies largely to men and mainly to the goal of financial success" (p. 57). Leonard also finds a number of difficulties in applying labeling theory to women. She claims that labeling theory fails to explain female criminality because it lacks an analysis of why people engage in crime in the first place, does not examine the impact of positive and negative labeling, and fails to analyze the structures of power as they impinge on women. Furthermore, Leonard finds differential association theory inadequate in explaining female criminality. She argues that this theory fails "to explain not only how certain behavior is transmitted but why such patterns exist in the first place and why they vary so much from one group to another" (p. 61). She adds that this theory deemphasizes "wider historical and structural changes and the responses of women to these changes" (p. 61). Moreover, Leonard charges that the male orientation of subcultural theories makes them inapplicable to females. Each of the sociocultural theories "is viewed primarily in terms of male success goals" (p. 64).

Evaluating the Explanations of Female Crime.   A discussion of female delinquency and adult criminals readily leads to the conclusion that biological explanations are the least predictive factors. Assumptions of sexual inferiority appear to be tied more to the historical context of male chauvinism than to the reality of female delinquency. Personal maladjustment hypotheses may have some predictive ability in determining the frequency of crime in girls and women, but these variables, too, have been overemphasized in the past. Sociological explanations appear to be far more predictive of female crime. Used much more in explaining female delinquency and crime in adult women, strain theory, social control theory, power-control theory, labeling and symbolic interactionist theory, and feminist theory all have received some support.

Some feminists argue, using the empirical support found in the above studies relating sociological explanations of male and female delinquency, that little evidence to date suggests that separate theories are needed to account for female and male delinquency, that female delinquency tends to operate through the same factors as male delinquency, and that empirical studies generally reveal much more variation within gender than between the sexes.

However, Leonard (1995) has written an insightful article evaluating the ability of the major sociological theories of crime to explain the crime patterns of females. She concluded that the traditional theories do not work and therefore are basically flawed. She made the case, in both her original article published in the early 1970s, as well as in its 1995 revision, that new theoretical efforts are needed to understand female crime, efforts that take into account not only gender but also race, class, and culture.

Feminist Theory of Delinquency

The feminist theory of delinquency, an expression of radical feminism, contends that girls' victimization and the relationship between that experience and girls' crime have been systematically ignored. Chesney-Lind (1987), one of the main proponents of this position, stated that it has long been understood that a major reason for girls' presence in juvenile courts is their parents' insistence on their arrest. But what researchers, as well as those who work with female status offenders, are discovering today is that a substantial number are victims of both physical and sexual abuse.

Chesney-Lind (1987, 1995) proposed that a feminist perspective on the causes of female delinquency includes the following propositions: First, girls are frequently the victims of violence and sexual abuse (estimates are that three-quarters of sexual-abuse victims are girls), but girls' victimization, unlike that of boys, and their response to that victimization are shaped by their status as young women. Second, their victimizers (usually males) have the ability to invoke official agencies of social control to keep daughters at home and vulnerable. Third, when girls run away from abusive homes characterized by sexual abuse and parental neglect, they are forced into the life of an escaped convict. Unable to enroll in school or take a job to support themselves because they fear detection, female runaways are forced to engage in panhandling, petty theft, and occasional prostitution to survive. Finally, it is no accident that girls on the run from abusive homes or on the streets because of impoverished homes become involved in criminal activities that exploit their sexuality. Because U.S. society has defined physically "perfect" young women as desirable, girls on the streets, who have little else of value to trade, are encouraged to utilize this resource. Not surprisingly, the criminal subculture also views them from this perspective. In Box 2.1 Meda Chesney-Lind expands on this notion of the feminist theory of delinquency.

Chesney-Lind does more than develop an alternative theory to explain female delinquency. She places her theory in the context of the gender roles of girls in a patriarchal society and includes class (poverty) and race (minority status) as part of the oppression and victimization of girls.

BOX 2.1   Meda Chesney-Lind on the Need for a Feminist Theory of Delinquency

The question now is whether the theories of "delinquent behavior" can be used to understand female crime, delinquency, and victimization. Will the "add women and stir" approach be sufficient to rescue traditional delinquency theories? My research convinces me that it will not work. Gender stratification or the patriarchal context within which both male and female delinquency is lodged has been totally neglected by conventional delinquency theory. This omission means that a total rethinking of delinquency as a social problem is necessary.

The exclusion of girls from delinquency theory might lead one to conclude that girls are almost never delinquent and that they have far fewer problems than boys. Some might even suspect that the juvenile justice system treats the few girls who find their way into it more gently than it does the boys. Both of these assumptions are wrong.

Current work on female delinquency is uncovering the special pains that girls growing up in a male-dominated society face. The price one pays for being born female is upped when it is combined with poverty and minority status, but it is always colored by gender. Consequently, sexual abuse is a major theme in girls' lives, and many girls

on the run are running away from abusive and violent homes. They run to streets that are themselves sexist, and they are often forced to survive as women—to sell themselves as commodities. All of this is shaped by their gender as well as by their class and their color.

You might ask: How about the system's response to girls' delinquency? First, there has been almost no concern about girls' victimization. Instead, large numbers of girls are brought into juvenile courts across America for noncriminal status offenses—running away from home, curfew, truancy, etc. Traditionally, no one in the juvenile justice system asked these girls why they were in conflict with their parents; no one looked for reasons why girls might run away from home. They simply tried to force them to return home or sentenced them to training schools. The juvenile justice system, then, has neglected girls' victimization, and it has acted to enforce parental authority over girls, even when the parents were abusive. Clearly, the patterns described here require an explanation that places girls' delinquent behavior in the context of their lives as girls in a male-dominated society—a feminist model of delinquency if you will.

Source: Interview conducted in 1988 and contained in Clemens Bartollas, *Juvenile Delinquency,* 5th ed. (Boston: Allyn and Bacon, 2000), p. 214.

Gender, Class, and Race

The application of gender, class, and racial analysis to women and class leads to a number of findings.

Gender Relations

The importance of gender among adult women is seen by their subordinate position in the creation and implementation of law. Conflict theorists have long argued that women, racial/ethnic minorities, and the poor benefit far less from the law than others in society. The most influential in creating laws, according to this perspective, is rich white men and those who work in their interests. The intent of framers of the law, as previously suggested, was to protect both men and their property. Much of the criminal law is written by state legislatures and the U.S. Congress, both of which are overwhelmingly male. Thus, this conflict position, which has gained increased acceptance among mainstream political theorists, contends that states, their legal systems, and criminal laws operate in the interests of the dominant male class in U.S. society (Price and Sokoloff, 1995, p. 14).

Gender is further related to the themes of domination and subordination. Those who are subordinate in a society experience inequality of many resources but chiefly of status and power. Women in a patriarchal society, as in the United States, are placed in subordinate categories. In analyzing the treatment given to women offenders, victims, and practitioners, it is useful to question what happens in situations of inequality and what forces are set in motion (Miller, 1998, p. 73). Wife battering, incestuous attacks on female adolescents by fathers or father substitutes, and rape are crimes of domination against women that take place in situations of inequality (Caputi and Russell, 1995, p. 272).

Influence of Class

Class oppression is another facet of multiple marginality experienced by women in U.S. society. In a number of ways, powerful and serious problems of childhood and adolescence related to poverty set the stage for females' entry into homelessness, unemployment, drug use, survival sex and prostitution, and, ultimately, even more serious criminal acts (Chesney-Lind, 1997, p. 4). Even adolescent females from middle-class homes may be thrust into a situation of economic survival if they choose to run away from abusive environments.

Traditional theories also fail to address the life situations of females on the economic and political margins, because researchers typically fail to study or talk with these females. For example, almost all urban females identified by police as gang members have been drawn from low-income groups (Chesney-Lind, 1993, p. 338). Lee Bowker and Malcolm Klein's (1983) examination of data on females in gangs in Los Angeles stated the importance of classism as well as racism:

> We conclude that the overwhelming impact of racism, sexism, poverty, and limited opportunity structures is likely to be so important in determining the gang membership and juvenile delinquency of women and girls in urban ghettos that personality variables, relations with parents, and problems associated with heterosexual behavior play a relatively minor role in determining gang membership and juvenile delinquency. (pp. 750–751)

Eleanor Miller's *Street Women* (1980), which is based on intensive interviews with sixty-four Milwaukee prostitutes, contended that prostitution evolves out of the profound social and economic problems confronting females, especially young women of color. For African American women, constituting over half of Miller's sample, movement into prostitution occurred as a consequence of exposure to deviant street networks. Typically recruited by older African American males with lengthy criminal records, these women organized themselves into "pseudo families" and engaged chiefly, but not exclusively, in prostitution. They viewed prostitution as an alternative to boring and low-paying jobs and as a means to relieve the burdens of pregnancy and single motherhood. (The young women interviewed had a total of eighty-one children). Although they were attracted by the excitement and money involved in prostitution, they soon found that the life was not nearly as glamorous and remunerative as they had anticipated.

Social class also affects adult women's contacts with the system. Lower-class women are more likely to be victimized than are middle- and upper-class ones. Part of the reason for this is that middle-class women usually live in better neighborhoods and are less exposed to the violence of street gangs, to drug trafficking, and to armed robbers and house break-ins. In addition, the lower-class woman must deal with greater areas of indefensible space, in which her likelihood of victimization increases dramatically.

Lower-class women are also more likely to be subjected to domestic abuse. Middle- and upper-class women usually have the advantage of greater economic resources, as well as educational credentials, making it easier for them to leave an abusive situation. But for lower-class women, who are both fearful of their husbands and in need of financial assistance to care for their children, leaving an abusive situation can seem much more like an unmanageable problem. Staying in these situations, of course, increases the likelihood that either the wife or the children will experience a fatal injury from the out-of-control husband, or the wife may in desperation kill her husband.

Middle-class women who commit crimes are also more likely to receive the benefits of chivalry than are lower-class lawbreakers. They tend to be treated with more respect at time of arrest, to be given mental health placements more often than are lower-class offenders, to spend less time in jail, to be given probation more frequently, to be sentenced to residential programs less often than lower-class offenders, and, if sentenced to residential facilities, to spend less time in these placements. Moreover, they are sentenced to prison much less frequently than are lower-class offenders.

Many reasons explain this preferential treatment of middle- and upper-class women. They, of course, are able to privately retain attorneys who can provide legal help superior to that of the public defender services offered the poor. They also have the financial resources to seek out counseling, private therapeutic settings, and other diversionary programs that help avoid criminal justice processing. Further they are less likely to become involved in crimes of violence, drug trafficking, prostitution, and crimes of larceny, including shoplifting.

Racial Discrimination

Young women of color, as well as other minority girls, often grow up in contexts much different from those of their white counterparts. Signithia Fordham's 1993 article, "Those Loud Black Girls," showed that young African American women resisted accepting the Anglo norm of femininity by being loud or otherwise asserting themselves through their voices. Yet this behavior led to negative school experiences, and it does not take long for these juvenile females to discover that it is the quiet ones who do well in school. Some of this population decided to "pass for white" or to adopt more acceptable norms of femininity to be successful in school. Others refused to adopt this survival strategy, and their tool for liberation contributed to isolating or alienating them from school success (Fordham, 1993).

Because racism and poverty often go hand-in-hand, females from these backgrounds are forced to deal early and on a regular basis with problems of abuse, drugs, and violence. They also are likely to be attracted to gang membership (Chesney-Lind, 1997). H. C. Covey, S. Menard, and R. Franzese (1997) summarized the effect of ethnicity on gang membership:

> *Racial differences in the frequency of gang formation such as the relative scarcity of non-Hispanic, white, ethnic gangs may be explainable in terms of the smaller proportion of the non-Hispanic European American population that live in neighborhoods characterized by high rates of poverty, welfare dependency, single-parent households, and other symptoms that characterize social disorganization. (p. 240)*

Mann (1995) has documented how the criminal justice system has widened the net for women of color and particularly for African American and Latina women. In examining the pretrial treatment and sentencing of women of color, Mann found the disproportionality in prison sentencing in California, Florida, and New York by comparing arrest rates with sentencing rates. She also presented data documenting the dramatic increase in jail incarceration rates for minority women, whereas rates for white women decreased slightly (p. 118).

The specific needs and concerns of African American rape victims, including poverty, homelessness, unemployment, violence in the community, difficulties in feeding their children, racism, and fear of the police, have discouraged them from talking about their rapes to crisis centers. For local anti-rape or crisis centers to intervene successfully in the victimization of these women, their primary needs and problems must be addressed. The extent of these primary concerns makes women of color reluctant to report their rapes and to file charges against those who have violated them (Matthews, 1995, pp. 216–217).

The Total Is Greater Than Its Parts

Lewis (1977) has noted that because feminist theories of women's inequality "focused exclusively upon the effects of sexism, they have been of limited applicability to minority women subjected to the constraints of both racism and sexism" (p. 339). Lewis further noted that "black women . . . tended to see racism as a more powerful cause of their subordinate position than sexism and to view the women's liberation movement with considerable mistrust" (p. 339).

The Combahee River Collective's statement in 1977 about African American feminism was also an important contribution. The group stated that it is committed to challenge all forms of "racial, sexual, heterosexual, and class oppression" (p. 157). This group's multifaceted commitments reflected that it viewed these relations as inseparable:

> *We believe that sexual politics under patriarchy is as pervasive in black women's lives as are the politics of class and race. We also often find it difficult to separate race from sex oppression because in our lives they most often are experienced simultaneously. We know that there is such a thing as racial-sexual oppression which is neither solely racial nor solely sexual, e.g., the history of black women by white men as a weapon of political repression. (p. 365)*

EXTENT AND NATURE OF FEMALE CRIME

This section examines the extent and nature of female crime. Beginning with the extent of female crime, this section discusses the trends in violence of women offending and women and drug violations. The importance of drug violations is that they have become the most significant reason that the rates of arrests among women have increased and that more women are being incarcerated.

Is Female Crime Increasing?

Two views have been expressed about the issue of changing patterns of female crime: (1) the perspective, usually based on official statistics, that female participation in crime has increased significantly, particularly in areas that traditionally have been considered "masculine" crimes and (2) the argument that not much has changed.

Official Statistics

Arrests for both girls under eighteen and adult women have dramatically increased in recent years. In 1988, the police arrested 1,430,974 females, and in 1997, the number of females arrested was 2,000,818, a 39.8 percent increase over ten years. In 1988, 284,928 girls under eighteen were arrested, and in 1997, 455,211 girls were arrested, a 59.8 percent increase over 1988 (Federal Bureau of Investigation, 1998, p. 227).

With adult women, the major areas of increase between 1988 and 1997 included (Federal Bureau of Investigation, 1998):

- aggravated assault (32,743 to 61,582; 88.1 percent)
- other assaults (85,778 to 181,415; 111.5 percent)
- offenses against family and children (7,430 to 21,446; 188.6 percent)
- drug abuse violations (104,848 to 170,886; 63 percent)
- curfew and loitering law violations (10,648 to 35,522; 233.6 percent)

Candace Kruttschnitt (1992, p. 227) argues that such statistics do not give an accurate picture of female crime. On one level, she notes that arrest rates represent only a fraction of the crimes known to the police and that the crimes known by the police represent only a fraction of the total volume of crime. In addition, the courts' reliance on plea bargaining may result in conviction data that bear little resemblance to the actual charges brought against criminal defendants. In examining a stratified random sample of females convicted of assault, forgery, petty theft, and drug law violations in northern California in 1976, Kruttschnitt (1992) discovered a wide degree of discrepancy between the offenses for which women were convicted and those for which they were arrested. In this study, women were arrested most frequently for theft, drunkenness, drug law violations, disorderly conduct, and assaults. However, three of the top five offenses for which women were convicted—forgery, fraud, and drunken driving—failed to appear on the most-frequent arrest list. To explain this discrepancy, Kruttschnitt identified visibility of conduct, deviance processing priorities, and the use of plea bargaining. On further analysis, the defendant's race and income bracket, the respectability of her associates, and the nature of the official conduct seemed to be more important characteristics within a crime category than the crimes themselves (p. 92).

Feinman (1994) notes that the major changes in the extent of women's arrests took place from 1960 to 1991, but from 1980 to 1991 the increase was small for both men and women. She offers several possible explanations for the increased numbers of arrests of women over men. First, she observes that the official statistics must be interpreted in light of events taking place in the United States in this time. For example, during the 1960s, many men of the age of risk were drafted for the Vietnam War. If these men had remained in the community, Feinman surmises, the increase in the number of arrests of men might have been proportionally similar to or even larger than that of women. Second, Feinman notes that the drug epidemic and the "War on Drugs" and mandatory sentencing laws for convicted drug offenders affected female offenders as much as it did male offenders. Third, as a result of technological improvements in law enforcement, contributed largely because of the Law Enforcement Assistance Administration (LEAA) monies, more female offenders were arrested. These technological improvements, for the first time, provided the resources and ability to record arrests of women separately from those of men. Finally, victims of crime committed by women, especially shoplifting and employee theft, seemed to be more willing than in the past to report these crimes to authorities (pp. 23–24).

Steffensmeier (1995) analyzes national arrest data from the *Uniform Crime Reports* for the thirty-year period of 1960 to 1990. In basic agreement with Kruttschnitt and Feinman, Steffensmeier found that analysis of the data failed to reveal that female crime became similar to male crime in either type or amount. In acknowledging that some increases in female crime emerged, he cautions against giving these increases too much attention, because female arrest rates have traditionally been very low compared with men's rates. This increase in rates over time occurred for both genders, particularly for fraud, larceny, drug and liquor violations, and assault. Yet the arrest profile for women, in comparison with men, has not changed: women's involvement is relatively high in such minor property crimes as larceny, forgery, and fraud and low in "masculine" or serious property and violent crimes (pp. 89–104).

Crime Patterns and Race

Mann's (1995) examination of official statistics in California, Florida, and New York in 1990 revealed somewhat different crime patterns based on race/ ethnicity. Aggravated assault and other assaults were higher for women of color than for white women. White women showed higher rank orders for fraud, whereas women of color showed higher rank order for burglary, forgery, and other thefts. White women tended to exceed women of color, except for Native American women, in the rank ordering of alcohol-related offenses: liquor law violations, drunkenness, and driving under the influence (DUI). Drug violations and prostitution were the distinguishing arrest offenses within the public order offense category for African Americans. Indeed, Mann found that drug offenses were the second most frequent cause of arrests for African American women in all three states. For Latina women in the three states, arrests for public order crimes were the most frequent, followed by arrests for property offenses and arrests for violent crimes (p. 123).

The Female Chronic Offender

Wolfgang, Figlio, and Sellin's (1972) cohort study in Philadelphia identified that 6 percent of the total sample had been arrested five times or more. In a second cohort study, which included female offenders, Tracy and Figlio (1982) were able to identify only 1 percent of the females as chronic offenders. These female offenders were involved in significantly less serious crimes than the males of the cohort. Yet, similar to males of both cohorts, the more the female offenders were arrested and the more serious their court's disposition, the more likely they were to be arrested again.

Danner, Blount, Silverman, and Vega (1995) examined female chronic offenders from data on file for 1,076 incarcerated female offenders in Florida. They found that female chronics in comparison with female nonchronics were more likely to be younger, of minority status, substance abusers, single, and involved in spouse abuse as well as to have committed the crimes alone. In comparing the female chronics to female nonchronics, it was found "that the process of becoming a female chronic offender appeared to be more complex than for males in that more criminogenic forces were required to overcome the crime-inhibiting effects of female socialization" (pp. 45–46). Furthermore, they found that the core variables that discriminated most strongly between the female chronics and nonchronics were age at first adult arrest, offense seriousness, substance abuse, and minority group status.

Trends in Violent Crimes among Women Offenders

The amount of violence committed by female offenders has attracted a great deal of attention over the past twenty-five years. Many assume that women are committing more violent and aggressive crimes than they have in the past.

Several factors converged in the mid 1970s to convince the public that women were definitely involved in more violent crimes. The activities of the Symbionese Liberation Army brought Patty Hearst, Emily Harris, and other female offenders into the public eye. Television showed news clips of armed women pulling a bank robbery and tough-looking women engaging in guerrilla warfare. Sara Jane Moore and Lynette "Squeaky" Fromme were each charged with attempted assassination of President Gerald Ford. No longer arrested merely for shoplifting or passing bad checks, women now were making the FBI's most-wanted list. Finally, Freda Adler's *Sisters in Crime* (1975) appeared, seemingly in answer to the public's bewilderment over what to make of the new female criminal. In her book, Adler offered a plausible answer: violent, aggressive female criminals were now committing crimes traditionally committed only by males. Adler's appearance on several television programs gave her views nationwide publicity. She stated:

> *Women are no longer behaving like subhuman primates with only one option. Medical, educational, economic, political, and technological advances have freed women from unwanted pregnancies, provided them with male occupational skills, and equalized their strength with weapons. Is it any wonder that, once women were armed with male opportunities, they should strive for status, criminal as well as civil, through established male hierarchical channels? (pp. 10–11)*

Little evidence shows, however, that women in the 1970s were more violent than they had been previously or that they became more violent in the

1980s or 1990s. In a study of crime among women in Washington, D.C., Rita Simon (1975) found that in 1974 and 1975, 82 percent of the women arrested for violent crimes had attacked someone they knew. Slightly more women than men used weapons when they committed violent acts: 79 percent of women arrested for crimes against persons versus 79 percent of men in 1974, and 84 percent of women versus 78 percent of men in 1975. In 1974, 16.7 percent of those arrested for violent crimes in Washington, D.C., were women, compared with 14.1 percent nationally (pp. 69–70). Thus, the typical violent female offender, as she is revealed in this study, arms herself against a known person: her husband, her lover, or a pimp. She differs only slightly from the stereotype of an enraged women stabbing her husband with a carving knife. Such women, Simon argues, are less desperate and more rational in their violence than ever before.

Meda Chesney-Lind (1995), in examining the dramatic rise in the number of women imprisoned (from 12,300 in 1980 to 43,800 in 1990), considers various possible causes: greater amount of crime by women, more dangerous and tougher women offenders, and a change in the response of the criminal justice system to women offenders (pp. 105–117). Chesney-Lind is quick to dismiss the more dangerous or violent female offender. She observes that the percentage of women incarcerated for violent offenses declined during the 1980s from 49 to 41 percent in prisons and from 21 to 13 percent in jails. Instead of a more violent offender, Chesney-Lind argues that the data reflect: (1) that the justice system is imprisoning more women for drug offenses; (2) that mandatory sentencing laws have reduced the amount of discretion available to judges, which has increased the numbers and lengths of sentences for both men and women; and (3) that women are caught up in the societal mood of "getting tough on crime," driven in part by violent male criminals "getting away with murder" (p. 105).

Thus, researchers generally challenge the popular assumption that women are becoming more violent in their crimes. They say, in effect: Women may be hungrier, greedier, or unhappier, but, as a group, they do not appear to be any more violent than they were in the past.

Homicide by Women

About one of every nine or ten persons arrested for homicide in the United States is a woman. Compared to men, research has revealed that women arrested for homicide are less likely to have previous criminal histories; are more likely to have committed the offense alone; are more likely to have killed an intimate, especially a spouse; and are more likely to have killed as the result of domestic conflict (Brownstein, Spunt, Crimmins, Goldstein, and Langley, 1994). As Simpson aptly expresses it, "The female offender is an anomaly—both in the United States and cross-culturally.... On those rare occasions when women are violent, their victims tend to be intimates" (Simpson, 1991, p. 116).

By the 1980s, there was strong support for the finding that women who killed their male partners were likely to have been battered women whose abuse by their partner had influenced, if not resulted in, the killing (Bannister, 1991; Walker, 1989). This research suggested that violent offending by women, especially lethal violent offending, was the response of victims to subordination in a patriarchal society (DeKeseredy and Hinch, 1991). These women had been abused by their partners and, therefore, were responding to the abuse and the patriarchal society that perpetuated it. These victims were not merely mimicking the aggressive criminal behavior of violent men but were responding as violent victims being forced out of their passive states (Brownstein, Spunt, Crimmins, Goldstein, and Langley, 1994, p. 101).

Recent evidence indicates that women involved in familial homicide are involved in other types of homicide as well. That is, they are not only husband killers, but are also killers of other victims (Goetting, 1988). Indeed, "there appears to be a growing proportion of women involved in the killing of strangers, or at least of people with whom they have no known emotional ties" (Brownstein, Spunt, Crimmins, Goldstein, and Langley, 1994, p. 102).

Women's Violence against Their Children

Feminists have been reluctant to venture into what they define as the problematic waters of child abuse research (Dougherty, 1991). Washburne (1983), a feminist scholar, attempts to clarify what is at stake in formulating a feminist understanding of women's violence against their children:

> Feminists have recognized that women are on occasion violent toward men and understand that violence as a direct result of societal and interpersonal pressures on women. Women's violence toward children needs to be recognized and discussed in the same context. Women's abuse of children stems directly from their own oppression in society and within the family. (p. 291)

Dougherty argues that ultimately, if one is serious about unlocking the secrets of maternal child abuse, the key is found in a feminist perspective that reveals needed insight into the lives of women who live in a patriarchical society. The patriarchal nature of society provides the social context for the oppression of women. The toxicity of this oppression is determined largely by how effective the socialization process has been in internalizing a negative self-concept among women. Women are encouraged by the patriarchy to accept the belief that it is inappropriate for them to struggle against their powerlessness. At the same time, the burden of child care is placed nearly solely on women's shoulders. Women's violence against their children, then, represents their rage and their own abuse of power (Dougherty, 1993, pp. 108–109).

Wilczynski (1991) examined the images of women who kill their children, dividing infanticidal women into the "mad" and the "bad." Women who are defined as "mad" are typically perceived as mentally ill. Ms. B. was one such defendant who appeared before an English court in 1988. While she was severely depressed she suffocated her 11-month-old child and then tried to commit suicide. The judge, who gave Ms. B. a three-year probation, said:

> *You are in need of help and not of punishment. It is quite clear to me that no useful purpose would be served by sending you to prison.*
>
> *Yours is a very sad case. . . . You not only loved that child but love all children because one of the ironies of this case is that in your will you left the residue of your estate to N.S.P.C.C. [National Society for the Prevention of Cruelty to Children]. (pp. 78–79)*

"Bad" women, in contrast, are "viewed as ruthless, selfish, cold, callous, neglectful of their children or domestic responsibilities, violent or promiscuous" (p. 78). These women, according to Wilczynski, are viewed as "monsters" who neglect their infants, fail to protect them from harm, show no remorse for what they have done to their children, and are perceived as "whores" who have strong and inappropriate instinctual sexual drives (p. 80).

In the 1990s, pregnant mothers who used drugs were increasingly identified by the state as "bad." Kasinsky (1994) identifies the state's reaction to pregnant, drug-using mothers today as having major continuities with the Progressive Era's response to mothers accused of child abuse. In both historical periods, the child savers have imposed their class, ethnic, and racial biases on immigrant, poor, and African American women. During the Progressive Era, those mothers who did not conform to a cultural ideal of maternal care were labeled as "unfit" and needing state control. In the modern era, physicians have joined with social workers and prosecutors to prosecute pregnant mothers who use drugs through the use of mandatory reporting laws along with drug tests (p. 97).

The medicalization of pregnant women drug users has led to an increasing number of women being sanctioned by the state. Sanctions include having newborn infants taken away and placed in foster homes; the placement of other, older children in foster homes; the loss of such welfare benefits as eligibility for subsidized housing; and being arrested and prosecuted. In 1992, according to the Center for Reproductive Law and Policy, 164 women in twenty-six states were arrested on criminal charges because of their behavior during pregnancy (Kasinsky, 1994, pp. 110–111). Some of the women have been sentenced to short- or long-term confinement in correctional institutions (Callahan and Knight, 1992).

Callahan and Knight state three objections to the legal sanctions that have been used or are proposed to be used against pregnant women to prevent prenatal harm. First, they define these sanctions as "morally unjustified" even where they might be legal. Second, they argue that these sanctions "are morally and legally unacceptable because they violate important moral values captured in our legal system." Finally, they contend that the sanctions "are morally unacceptable and would make bad law because they would contribute to the harm they would be instituted to prevent" (p. 5).

WOMEN AND DRUG OFFENSES

The discussion in this chapter has suggested that as Alida V. Merlo (1995) aptly puts it: "The typical female offender is not a corporate or computer criminal, a terrorist, a burglar, or a murderer. Instead, she is likely to engage in theft, fraud, drug offenses, forgery, embezzlement, and prostitution" (p. 119). Merlo goes on to say that an important dimension in understanding female criminality as we begin the twenty-first century is the female offender's use of drugs. She adds: "Female drug-related activity merits closer scrutiny as an important element in female criminality. It warrants concern and social policy implications" (p. 119).

The impact of the U.S. War on Drugs on the criminal justice system is substantial. The number of female inmates grew by 9.1 percent during 1996, nearly double the male increase (*Corrections Today*, 1997). Worldwide, Canada is second only to the United States in the number of drug arrests per capita

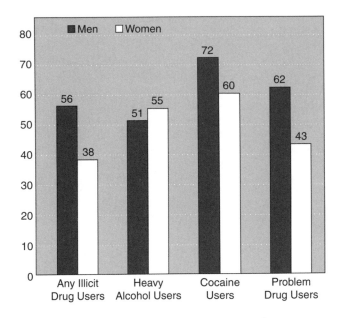

FIGURE 2.1   **Percent of Past-Year Substance Users Reporting Past-Year Criminal Activities, by Gender, Types of Substance, and Level of Substance Use**

Source: Substance Abuse and Mental Health Services Administration, *Substance Use among Women in the United States.* Rockville, Md.: Department of Health and Human Services, 1997.

(Marron, 1996). Women offenders, especially in the younger age brackets, are arrested at increasingly high rates for drug offenses, and women of color have had the greatest overall increase in criminal justice supervision, including imprisonment. The unequal impact of mandatory and determinant sentencing requirements on nonviolent female offenders, unfortunately, has not been matched by a commensurate investment in substance abuse programs to meet these special needs. See Figure 2.1 to gauge the crime/substance abuse link.

In a national self-reported survey of the general population concerning substance abuse issues, the Substance Abuse and Mental Health Administration (1997) discovered a significant amount of criminal activity among substance abusers. Their report, *Substance Use among Women in the United States*, records the results of past-year substance users who reported criminal activities (see Box 2.2).

BOX 2.2   How Does the Relationship between Crime and Substance Use Vary by Gender?

Among both men and women, substance users were much more likely than nonusers to report criminal justice involvement or criminal activities (theft, assault, etc.). For example, among adult women who had not used *any* illicit drug in the past year, only .2 percent reported having been arrested in the past year, compared with 4 percent among women who had used *any* illicit drug in the past year. Similarly, while 38 percent of drug-using women reported committing *any* criminal activity during the past year, only 5.5 percent of women not using drugs did so.

A significantly lower proportion of women than men who used *any* illicit drug or cocaine in the past year or who were past-year problem drug users reported that they had been involved in criminal activities in the past year. However, female *heavy* alcohol users were just as likely as male *heavy* alcohol users to report any criminal activity: 55 percent for females and 51 percent for males (the difference was not statistically significant). Similarly, nearly half (47 percent) of female *heavy* alcohol users reported that they

had driven under the influence of alcohol or drugs in the past year, while a comparable proportion of male *heavy* alcohol users (44 percent) reported driving under the influence of alcohol or drugs in the past year.

The association between illicit drug use and crime remained significant for both women and men, after statistically controlling for age, race/ethnicity, education, marital and employment status, household members' receiving welfare assistance, and age at substance use initiation. Adult women who used *any* illicit drug in the past year were six times as likely as women who had not used *any* illicit drug to have been arrested in the past year, and four times as likely to have committed *any* criminal activity in the past year. Among men, the relationship between past-year illicit drug use and crime was similar, although male illicit drug users were only three times as likely as males who did not use illicit drugs to report having been arrested in the past year. This suggests that the association between drug use and crime is stronger for women than for men.

Source: Substance Abuse and Mental Health Administration (1997). *Substance Use among Women in the United States*. Rockville, MD: Department of Health and Human Services, Chapter 8, pp. 9, 12.

Women in the Illegal Drug Economy

Morgan and Joe (1997) compared women's experiences in the illicit drug economy of San Francisco, San Diego, and Honolulu and found that these women had diverse drug-use careers. In this study, female users tended to fall within four categories, and many women shifted from one category to another during different periods of their drug-using careers. First, "social outlaws" were deeply immersed in a deviant and marginal lifestyle. Of this category, one group lived "on the edge" and was on the lowest level of economic and social status, but another group was able to maintain some control over their lives. Second, "welfare moms" were on welfare, living in poor suburban areas and married or had children at a young age. Methamphetamine was used partly as a survival strategy to cope with daily hardships and social disaster. Third, "floaters" were women who went in and out of mainstream life. For a while, they held a regular job, then quit to live with a boyfriend or to engage in full-time drug dealing. They generally maintained a respectable image, managing to escape from long-term participation in deviant or criminal lifestyles. Finally, "citizens" were women who lived within mainstream society. They were able to retain a measure of stability and respectability, as they resided in good neighborhoods and had money and often a husband and family (pp. 93–94).

Dunlap, Johnson, and Maher (1997) examined female crack sellers in New York City. They found that most of their social and occupational roles were confined to low-level sales and distribution activities. These women did move in and out of various roles at the street level in a way similar to male distributors (p. 52). They summarized the experiences of the female crack sellers:

> *Collectively, these women's experiences illustrate the multiplicity of roles by which females currently participate in the drug economy. While they occupy a minority status in the sense of being women in a male-dominated labor market, these women have the capacity to change and shape this world insofar as they can be seen to exhibit considerable innovation, role variation, and a number of different patterns of involvement. (p. 52)*

Treatment and Drug Use

Eighty percent of people behind bars were involved in some way with alcohol or other drugs at the time of their crime, according to the report by the National Center on Addiction and Substance Abuse at Columbia University (reported by Fields, 1998). This finding is mirrored for women interviewed in a 1996 National Council on Crime and Delinquency Study (Acoca, 1998). In other words, inmates committed crimes while they were high, stole property to buy drugs, have a history of drug or alcohol abuse, or are in jail for violating drug or alcohol laws.

Analysis of state-level data reveals that 45 percent of the women prisoners require treatment for chronic substance abuse, compared with 22 percent of men requiring such treatment. These people, women as well as men, are not psychopaths, according to the article, but alcoholics and drug addicts. According to a survey conducted by the Bureau of Justice Statistics (1999), one in four inmates participated in drug treatment programs, the majority of which were of the self-help group nature. Only 4 percent received professional counseling. Little variation by gender was revealed in these studies.

Substance abuse, especially of alcohol, cocaine, and methamphetamine, is not only directly linked to criminality due to the drug laws themselves, but is also related to crimes of violence such as robbery and homicide (Mann, 1990). Other addictions, such as gambling and spending addiction, are also associated with the commission of economic crimes such as embezzlement. Therefore, one of the most effective crime prevention interventions is substance abuse treatment.

Kaplan and Sasser (1996) recommend that the United States follow the lead of the Netherlands in alleviating the conditions that increase people's vulnerability to drug use while aggressively seeking out drug addicts for treatment.

Nevertheless, in the United States, where the War on Drugs seems to have become a war on minority and poor women, punishment comes before treatment. Treatment interventions for women, accordingly, tend to be linked to criminal justice sanctions or perhaps to child protective services investigations. The majority of women offenders in the system, approximately three out of four, are on probation, and the remainder are in jail or prison or on parole.

In the United States, there is a lack of coordination of service agencies even within a state, much less across states. Comprehensive assessments based on empirically validated research are done to some extent within the U.S. federal system, but female offenders, if they are assessed (i.e., for risk and treatment needs) at all, are assessed on the basis of tools that have been developed for use with males. In Canada, in contrast, the intake and periodic assessment of female offenders are done based on empirically validated classification instruments. Psychological and chemical use assessments are tailored to the offender for the purpose of approximate treatment interventions as well as for security classification within the Canadian correctional system (Blanchette, 1997). The United States can learn a great deal from Canadian female programming, which has undergone sweeping changes over the last few years in order to place women's concerns at the center, rather than the periphery, of correctional planning.

PROCESSING OF FEMALE OFFENDERS

The issue of discrimination within the criminal justice system has long interested social scientists. They have particularly attempted to identify and explain the disparity in sentences imposed on defendants representing various social classes and racial groups. More recently, as they have analyzed the treatment of male and female defendants, social scientists have reached somewhat contradictory conclusions (Spohn and Spears, 1997). Some have found women to be more likely than men to be released on their own recognizance or on bail, to have their cases dismissed before trial, to be less likely than men to be convicted, to receive less severe sentences, or to be incarcerated. However, other researchers have found that females are treated no differently from males, especially with respect to decisions to prosecute, to plea bargain, or to convict (pp. 30–31).

Yet despite these contradictory findings, the bulk of the evidence has indicated more lenient treatment of female defendants, especially at the sentencing stage. It is generally concluded that this preferential treatment reflects paternalism or chivalry. According to this view, women are treated more leniently than men because criminal justice officials feel that women are physically weaker than men and therefore must be protected from the harshness of the justice system or that women are less dangerous, less culpable, or less likely to recidivate than men and, accordingly, deserve less punitive treatment (Spohn and Spears, 1997, p. 31).

In examining the differences in felony court processing, Farnworth and Teske (1995) express the three most frequently claimed hypotheses concerning women offenders and chivalry. First, the "typicality" hypothesis contends that "women are treated with chivalry in criminal processing, but only when their charges are consistent with stereotypes of female offenders." Second, "selective chivalry" argues that "decision makers extend chivalry disproportionately to white females." Third, "differential discretion" views disparity as "most likely in informal decisions such as charge reduction rather than in formal decisions at final sentencing" (p. 23). Farnworth and Teske found from data of 9,966 felony theft cases and 18,176 felony assault cases disposed in California in 1988 that gender disparity was more frequently found with females with no prior record, who were more likely than similar males to receive charge reductions; this, in turn, enhanced females' chances of receiving probation. The only selective chivalry found was a tendency to change charges of assault to nonassault more frequently among white female defendants than among minority females. They further found that pivotal decisions concerning charge reduction provided some support for the notion of differential discretion, but that the findings provided no clear support for the typicality hypothesis (pp. 23–24).

Spohn and Spears (1997) used data on male and female defendants charged with violent felonies to examine the effects of gender on case processing decisions (1997). They found that female defendants were more likely than male defendants to have all the charges against them dismissed and that females were sentenced less harshly than males. But, as with other researchers, Spohn and Spears found that gender and race interacted and highlighted the importance of testing an interactive model incorporating the effects of both gender and race (p. 29).

SUMMARY

This chapter presented a basic agreement and several disagreements among feminists concerning crime and women in the United States. The basic area of agreement, among feminists as well as most nonfeminists, is that delinquency/ criminology theories are preoccupied with why males commit delinquent acts. A major disagreement among feminists relates to whether separate theories are needed to explain female delinquency/criminality among women. On one hand are those feminists who argue that separate theories are not needed to account for female and male delinquency and female and male criminality. On the other hand, other feminists charge that existing delinquency/criminology theories are inadequate to explain female delinquency and female criminality. These theories, adds this position, represent an androcentric perspective that cannot encompass the empirical results of available research.

We conclude that both positions are essentially correct. Considerable evidence supports the finding that female delinquency and female criminality operate through the same sociological factors as male delinquency and male criminality and that more variation exists within each gender than between the sexes. This position also charges that proposing new, separate theories of female crime and delinquency actually falls into a brand of reductionism by assuming that the experiences of women are universal and distinct from those of men. Yet a sound argument can be made that adolescent females' sexual and physical victimizations at home and the relationship between these experiences and their later adult crimes have been ignored, and that, therefore, new theoretical efforts are needed to deal with these experiences. The second position is also justified; new theoretical efforts are needed to examine the "multiple marginality" of adolescent females and female criminals.

The problems of sexism, racism, and class and their implications have been generally ignored by criminologists. As a result, writers on female delinquency and female criminality have been more concerned with the adjustment of the adolescent female or adult woman to society than with the extent and consequences of oppression in her life. An examination of how the categories of gender, class, and race are interlocked will lead to needed insight about what the female delinquent and female criminal faces in U.S. society. As Dorie Klein (1995) has indicated, "[T]he road from Lombroso to the present is surprisingly straight" (p. 33).

The progress recently made in understanding female delinquency and female criminality promises that this area of inquiry may be a fruitful one in the future. For example, much more research is needed into sociological explanations, such as blocked opportunity, the influence of peers, and the impact of labeling. In addition, although adult women and adolescent female offenders appear to have much in common, the significant differences between them need further examination. Moreover, cross-cultural comparisons that show similar patterns of female delinquency and female criminality in the United States and in other cultures should be used more fully.

REFERENCES

Acoca, L. (1998). Defusing the time bomb: Understanding and meeting the growing health care needs of incarcerated women in America. *Crime and Delinquency 44:* 49–69.

Adler, F. (1975). *Sisters in Crime.* New York: McGraw-Hill.

Anderson, B. J., Holmes, M. D., and Ostresh, R. (1998, March). Males' and females' delinquent attachments and the effects of attachments on severity of self-reported delinquency. Paper presented to the Annual Meeting of Criminal Justice Sciences in Albuquerque, New Mexico.

Bannister, S. A. (1991). The criminalization of women fighting back against male abuse: Imprisoned battered women as political prisoners. *Humanity and Society 15:* 400–416.

Bartusch, D. J., and Matsueda, R. L. (1996, September). Gender, reflected appraisals, and labeling: A cross-group test of an interactionist theory of delinquency. *Social Forces 75:* 145.

Blanchette, K. (1997, January). Classifying female offenders for correctional interventions. *Forum in Corrections 9:* 1–8.

Bowker, L. H., and Klein, M. W. (1983). The etiology of female juvenile delinquency and gang membership: A test of psychological and social structural explanations. *Adolescence 18:* 739–751.

Brownstein, H. H., Spunt, B. J., Crimmins, S., Goldstein, P. J., and Langley, S. (1994). Changing patterns of lethal violence by women: A research note. *Women and Criminal Justice 5:* 99–118.

Bureau of Justice Statistics. (1999). *Substance abuse and treatment, state and federal prisoners, 1997.* Washington, D.C.: U.S. Department of Justice.

Callahan, J. C., and Knight, J. W. (1992). Prenatal harm as child abuse? *Women and Criminal Justice 3:* 5–33.

Campbell, A. (1981). *Girl delinquents.* New York: St. Martin's Press.

Caputi, J., and Russell, D. E. H. (1995). Femicide: Sexist terrorism against women. In B. R. Price and N. J. Sokoloff (eds.), *The criminal justice system and women: Offenders, victims, and workers* (pp. 272–279). New York: McGraw-Hill.

Chesney-Lind, M. (1987, November 10–14). Girls' crime and woman's place: Toward a feminist model of female delinquency. Paper presented at the Annual Meeting of the American Society of Criminology, Montreal, Canada.

Chesney-Lind, M. (1995). Girls, delinquency, and juvenile justice: Toward a feminist theory of young women's crime. In B. R. Price and N. J. Sokoloff (eds.), *The criminal justice system and women: Offenders, victims, and workers* (pp. 71–88). New York: McGraw-Hill.

Chesney-Lind, M. (1993). Girls, gangs, and violence: Reinventing the liberated female crook. *Humanity and Society 17:* 321–344.

Chesney-Lind, M. (1997). *The female offender: Girls, women, and crime.* Thousand Oaks, Calif.: Sage Publications.

Chesney-Lind, M. (1995). Rethinking women's imprisonment: A critical examination of trends in female incarceration. In B. R. Price and N. J. Sokoloff (eds.), *The criminal justice system and women: Offenders, victims, and workers* (pp. 89–104). New York: McGraw-Hill.

Coleman, J. S. (1961). *The adolescent society.* New York: Free Press.

Combahee River Collective. (1979). The Combahee River Collective statement. In Z. Eistenstein (ed.), *Capitalist patriarch and the case for socialist feminism* (pp. 362–372). New York: Monthly Review Press.

Corrections Today. (1997, August). U.S. prison population rises. *Corrections Today,* p. 12.

Covey, H. C., Menard, S., and Franzese, R. (1997). *Juvenile gangs,* 2nd ed. Springfield, Ill.: Charles C Thomas.

Cowie, J., Cowie, B., and Slater, E. (1968). *Delinquency in girls.* London: Heinemann.

Crites, L. (1976). Women offenders: Myth vs. reality. In Laura Crites (ed.), *The female offender* (pp. 36–39). Lexington, Mass.: Lexington Books.

Cullen, F. T., Golden, K. M., and Cullen, J. B. (1977). Sex and delinquency: A partial test of the masculinity hypothesis. *Criminology 15:* 87–104.

Daly, K. (1995). Looking back, looking forward: The promise of feminist transformation. In B. R. Price and N. J. Sokoloff (eds.), *The criminal justice system and women: Offenders, victims, and workers* (pp. 447–448). New York: McGraw-Hill.

Daly, K., and Chesney-Lind, M. (1988). Feminism and criminology. *Justice Quarterly 5:* 497–538.

Danner, T. A., Blount, W. R., Silverman, I. J., and Vega, M. (1995). The female chronic offender: Exploring life contingency and offense history dimensions for incarcerated female offenders. *Women and Criminal Justice 6:* 45–66.

Datesman, S. K., Scarpitti, F. R., and Stephenson, R. M. (1975). Truancy: An application of self and opportunity theories. *Journal of Research in Crime and Delinquency 12:* 120.

DeKeseredy, W. S., and Hinch, R. (1991). *Woman abuse—Sociological perspectives.* Toronto: Thompson Educational Publishing.

Dougherty, J. (1993). Women's violence against their children: A feminist perspective. *Women and Criminal Justice 4:* 91–114.

Dunlap, E., Johnson, B. D., and Maher, L. (1997). Female crack sellers in New York City: Who they are and what they do. *Women and Criminal Justice 8:* 25–55.

Farnworth, M., and Teske, R. H. C. Jr. (1995). Gender differences in felony court processing: Three hypotheses of disparity. *Women and Criminal Justice 6:* 23–44.

Federal Bureau of Investigation. (1998). *Crime in the United States: Uniform crime reports 1997.* Washington, D.C.: U.S. Government Printing Office.

Feinman, C. (1994). *Women in the criminal justice system,* 3rd ed. Westport, Conn.: Praeger Publishers.

Fields, G. (1998, January 9). Study links drugs to 80% of incarcerations. *USA Today,* p. 2A.

Figueira-McDonough, J., and Selo, E. (1980). A reformulation of the equal opportunity explanation of female delinquency. *Crime and Delinquency 26:* 333–334.

Fordham, S. (1997). "Those loud black girls": (Black) women, silence and gender "passing" in the academy. In M. Seller and L. Weis (eds.), *Beyond black and white: New faces and voices in U.S. schools.* Albany: University of New York Press.

Freud, S. (1949). *An outline of psychoanalysis,* trans. James Strachey. New York: Norton.

Freud, S. (1933). *New introductory lectures on psychoanalysis.* New York: Norton.

Gibbens, T. C. N. (1971). Female offenders. *British Journal of Hospital Medicine 6:* 279–286.

Giordano, P. C. (1978). Girls, guys and gangs: The changing social context of female delinquency. *Journal of Criminal Law and Criminology 69.*

Giordano, P. C., and Cernkovich, S. A. (1979, February 28). Changing patterns of female delinquency. A research proposal submitted to the National Institutes of Mental Health.

Goetting, A. (1988). Patterns of homicide among women. *Journal of Interpersonal Violence 3:* 3–20.

Hagan, J., Simpson, J., and Gillis, A. R. (1987, January). Class in the household: A power-control theory of gender and delinquency. *American Journal of Sociology 92:* 788–816.

Hagan, J., Gillis, A. R., and Simpson, J. (1985). The class structure of gender and delinquency: Toward a power-control theory of common delinquent behavior. *American Journal of Sociology 90:* 1151–1178.

Heimer, K. (1994). Gender, race, and the pathways to delinquency. In J. Hagan and R. Peterson (eds.), *Crime and inequality* (p. 164). Stanford, California: Stanford University Press.

Hirschi, T. (1969). *Causes of delinquency.* Berkeley: University of California Press.

Juvenile female offenders: A status of the states report. (1998). Washington, D.C.: Office of Juvenile Justice Delinquency Prevention.

Kaplan, M. S., and Sasser, J. E. (1996). Women behind bars: Trends and policy issues. *Journal of Sociology and Social Welfare 23:* 43–46.

Kasinsky, R., and Goldsmith. (1994). Child neglect and "unfit" mothers: Child savers in the progressive era and today. *Women and Criminal Justice 6:* 97–129.

Klein, D. (1995). The etiology of female crime: A review of the literature. In B. R. Price and N. J. Sokoloff (eds.), *The criminal justice system and women: Offenders, victims, and workers* (pp. 30–53). New York: McGraw-Hill.

Kruttschnitt, C. (1985). "Female crimes" or legal labels? Are statistics about women offenders representative of their crimes? In I. L. Moyer (ed.), *The changing roles of women in the criminal justice system* (pp. 81–97), 2nd ed. Prospect Heights, Ill.: Waveland Press.

Leonard, E. (1995). Theoretical criminology and gender. In B. R. Price and N. J. Sokoloff (eds.), *The criminal justice system and women: Offenders, victims, and workers* (pp. 54–70). New York: McGraw-Hill.

Lewis, D. K. (1977). A response to inequality: Black women, racism, and sexism. *Signs: Journal of Women in Culture and Society 3:* 339–361.

Lombroso, C. (1920). *The female offender.* New York: Appleton.

Mann, C. R. (1990). Female homicide and substance abuse: Is there a connection? *Women and Criminal Justice 1:* 87–109.

Mann, C. R. (1995). Women of color and the criminal justice system. In B. R. Price and N. J. Sokoloff (eds.), *The criminal justice system and women: Offenders, victims, and workers* (pp. 118–135). New York: McGraw-Hill.

Marron, K. (1996). *The slammer: The crisis in Canada's prison system.* Toronto: Doubleday Canada.

Matthews, N. A. (1995). Surmounting a legacy: The expansion of racial diversity in a local anti-rape movement. In B. R. Price and N. J. Sokoloff (eds.), *The criminal justice system and women: Offenders, victims, and workers* (pp. 216–227). New York: McGraw-Hill.

Merlo, A. V. (1995). Female criminality in the 1990s. In A. V. Merlo and J. M. Pollock (eds.), *Women, law, and social control* (pp. 119–134). Boston: Allyn and Bacon.

Miller, E. M. (1986). *Street woman.* Philadelphia: Temple University Press.

Miller, J. B. (1998). Domination and subordination. In P. S. Rothenberg (ed.), *Race, class, and gender in the United States* (pp. 73–89), 4th ed. New York: St. Martin's Press.

Morgan, P., and Joe, K. A. (1997). Uncharted terrain: Contexts of experience among women in the illicit drug economy. *Women and Criminal Justice 8:* 85–109.

Norland, S., and Shover, N. (1977). Gender roles and female criminality: Some critical comments. *Criminology 15:* 87–104.

Office of Juvenile Justice and Delinquency Prevention. (1998). Addressing female development in treatment. In *Juvenile female offenders: A status of the states report* (pp. 1–3). Washington, D.C.: U.S. Justice Department.

Parsons, T. (1942, October). Age and sex in the social structure of the United States. *American Sociological Review 7.*

Pollak, O. (1950). *The criminality of women.* Philadelphia: University of Pennsylvania Press.

Price, B. R., and Sokoloff, N. J. (1995). The criminal law and women. In B. R. Price and N. J. Sokoloff (eds.), *The criminal justice system and women: Offenders, victims, and workers* (pp. 11–29). New York: McGraw-Hill.

Rittenhouse, R. (1963). A theory and comparison of male and female delinquency. Ph.D. dissertation, University of Michigan, Ann Arbor.

Rogers, K. O. (1973). For her own protection . . . conditions of incarceration for female juvenile offenders in the state of Connecticut. *Law and Society Review 7:* 223–246.

Sarri, R. C. (1976). Juvenile law: How it penalizes females. In L. Crites (ed.), *The juvenile offender* (pp. 68–69). Lexington, Mass.: Lexington Books.

Simon, R. J. (1995). *Women and crime.* Lexington, Mass.: Heath.

Simpson, S. (1991). Caste, class, and violent crime: Explaining differences in female offending. *Criminology 29:* 115–135.

Singer, S. I., and Levine, M. (1987, November). Re-examining class in the household and a power-control theory of gender and delinquency. A paper presented at the Annual Meeting of the American Society of Criminology.

Smart, C. (1976). *Women, crime and criminology: A feminist critique.* Boston: Routledge and Kegan Paul.

Spohn, C. C., and Spears, J. W. (1997). Gender and case processing decisions: A comparison of case outcomes for male and female defendants charged with violent felonies. *Women and Criminal Justice 8:* 29–59.

Steffensmeier, D. (1995). Trends in female crime: It's still a man's world. In B. R. Price and N. J. Sokoloff (eds.), *The criminal justice system and women: Offenders, victims, and workers* (pp. 89–104). New York: McGraw-Hill.

Terry, R. (1967). Discrimination in the police handling of juvenile offenders by social control agencies. *Journal of Research in Crime and Delinquency 14.*

Thomas, W. I. (1907). *Sex and society.* Boston: Little, Brown.

Thomas, W. I. (1923). *The unadjusted girl.* New York: Harper.

Thornton, W. E., and James, J. (1979, July). Masculinity and delinquency revisited. *British Journal of Criminology 19:* 225–241.

Tracy, P., and Figlio, R. (1982). "Chronic recidivism in the 1958 birth cohort. In L. Shannon (ed.), *Assessing the relationships of adult criminal careers to juvenile careers: A summary* (pp. 742–775). Washington, D.C.: U.S. Department of Justice.

Walker, L. E. (1989). *Terrifying love—Why battered women kill and how society responds.* New York: Harper and Row.

Washburne, C. K. (1983). A feminist analysis of child abuse and neglect. In D. Finkelhor, et al. (eds.), *The Dark Side of Families* (pp. 289–292). Beverly Hills, Calif: Sage Publications.

Wilczynski, A. (1991). Images of women who kill their infants: The mad and the bad. *Women and Criminal Justice 2:* 71–88.

Wolfgang, M. E., Figlio, R. M., and Sellin, T. (1972). *Delinquency in a birth cohort.* Chicago: University of Chicago Press.

3

THE PRISON ENVIRONMENT

In the United States, the thrust toward prison reform and rehabilitation is in decline. The public mood, fired up by mass media rabid for stories, cries out for vengeance against people perceived as a threat—specifically, inner-city males engaging in street crime and illegal drug users. Paradoxically, women of color are bearing the brunt of the "lock 'em up and throw away the key" mentality. The war against single mothers on welfare in the "free world" is matched by an increasing severity in the treatment of women within prison walls. This pattern is echoed in Birmingham, England, as well as Birmingham, Alabama; a harshness against women offenders is seen in Tokyo, Japan, as well. Throughout the world, the antifeminist backlash is palpable: If women want to be equal to men, or so the thinking goes, they can be punished like men—put on chain gangs, in boot camps, and even executed. And, at the employee level, if female guards can be assigned to a full range of duties in men's prisons (because of affirmative action mandates), then male guards can operate unrestricted in women's prisons as well.

The major purpose of this chapter is to present the reality and context of life for women in confinement so that budding correctional and social workers and other treatment providers will be prepared, intellectually, at least, for the major challenges awaiting them in this line of work.

We begin to explore the topic of women in prison with a brief history of the imprisonment of women and of theoretical frameworks concerning their criminality. We then construct a profile of the typical female inmate based on statistics involving race, ethnicity, drug involvement, and other demographic criteria available from government sources. Turning our attention to the *internal* dynamics of prison society, we ponder the way in which women of various ages and ethnicities construct a social world that is unique in itself. A related discussion on prison "play" families and sexual role-playing follows. One grim topic—women on death row—and one positive topic—innovative treatment programs—conclude this chapter.

The theme that binds these seemingly disparate topics is that of empowering feminism. *Empowering feminism* is the term we use for a perspective that engenders pride in women through recognition of their special needs, gifts, and vulnerabilities. Another major theme is the War on Drugs, which has become a war against African American and Latina women. A third major theme, equally disturbing, is the susceptibility of women behind bars to sexual abuse and harassment by male guards.

HISTORY OF THE WOMEN'S PRISON

To the extent that prisons do indeed represent a social barometer of a nation's health and level of civilization, as Dostoevsky (1864) believed they did, the punishment of female offenders can be viewed as a mirror for the treatment of women in a society. If we view female offenders' treatment historically, as well as culturally, we will realize the connection between the punishment of women who deviated from the norms of society and the patriarchal social structure of the day. In a book written in her prison cell, Jean Harris (1988) summarized the history of women's prison succinctly: "From a woman depraved, to a woman wronged, to a woman who now says she wants to be treated equally with men, we've spanned two hundred years, and we're more ambivalent today than we ever were" (p. 40).

In the early days of prison history, women—like men—suffered in filth, overcrowding, and hard conditions. They were confined in separate quarters in men's prisons (Kurshan 1996). In the 1920s, at Auburn Penitentiary in New York, women were lodged together; they were subject to beating and sexual abuse by the male guards. African American and poor women were, as always, disproportionately incarcerated in all parts of the United States. Following the passage of strict Jim Crow laws in the Southern states, which were designed to keep blacks "in their place," Southern prison populations became almost all black overnight.

Despite retrogressive laws and harsh punishments affecting women as well as men, the roots of feminism lie deep within the prison reform movement. Even before the end of slavery, Quaker abolitionists and suffragists were at the forefront of this movement. Elizabeth Fry of England helped organize the women confined at London's Newgate Gaol in the early 1800s. Her brave and innovative work at Newgate with incarcerated women and their children was testimony to the fact that, with decent treatment, women convicts were redeemable, that a single light could dispel the darkness. She challenged the rampant sexual abuse of institutionalized women, advocated as one of her key principles that women should be under the authority of women and in their own institution, and sought to substitute the Quakers' system of absolute silence with one in which inmates could communicate with each other and help each other reform. Working indefatigably until her death in 1845 to transform the lives of inmate women, Fry managed to instill hope and dignity where there was only despair (American Friends Service Committee, 1971, p. 16). Today, in Canada, the Elizabeth Fry associations play an active role in exposing abuses in prisons for women.

On becoming matron of the woman's prison at Sing Sing in 1844, Eliza Farnham stirred up controversy with the new techniques that she implemented and with her articulate defense of them. Farnham strove in many ways to brighten the tone of inmate life during the period of her tenure (Lewis, 1965, pp. 230–255).

The first separate prison for women, the Indiana Women's Prison was founded by a Quaker couple and opened in 1873. Massachusetts followed four years later with the building of an all-female state reformatory. Another American Quaker cited by Jean Harris (1988) helped found the progressive women's reformatory at Bedford Hills. Gradually, other states followed, until unisexual institutions for men and women became the basic, though not exclusive, pattern. Fry's program, which consisted of women helping women and emphasized rehabilitation, obedience, and religious education, became instituted throughout North America. In the ensuing "matriarchy in corrections," the staffs, architectural designs, and programs reflected the culturally valued norms for women's behavior (Feinman, 1994, p. 44). At the administrative level, the women's prison was to remain, for a considerable time, a domain of female guidance for control and leadership.

Many significant aspects of contemporary corrections were, in fact, pioneered by female administrators in charge of institutions for female offenders (Allen and Simonsen, 1995). Correctional innovations such as educational instruction, work release programs, and vocational activities were initiated in an atmosphere that was female. Women's prisons, as Walker (1980) notes, became a testing ground for the new penology: prison reformers regarded women as good candidates for rehabilitation, probably because they were considered less dangerous than their male counterparts (p. 21).

To speak only of the reformatory tradition in women's prisons and to neglect the existence of harsh, disciplinary institutions, such as the State Prison for Women at Auburn, New York, is to overlook the origins of what is the women's prison as we know it today, a wall built around society's problems. In 1844, New York prison authorities voiced little concern for their charges:

> *The opinion seems to have been entertained, that the female convicts were beyond the reach of reformation, and it seems to have been regarded as a sufficient performance of the object of punishment, to turn them loose within the pen of the prison and there leave them to feed upon and destroy each other. (Lewis, 1965, p. 159)*

And then there was the racial factor. Chivalry for white women figured into the picture in the form of "cottage-style" reformatories, establishments that proliferated during the Progressive Era as an alternative to the harsh custodial institutions. Whereas the custodial (mainly African American) prisons were characterized by filth and violence inflicted by male guards, "reformatories" were usually staffed by women and stressed correcting women's moral behavior. There were no comparable reformatories for men. Women were sentenced to these prisons for various sexual offenses, including unwed pregnancies and unlawful sexual intercourse (Kurshan, 1996). By 1935, the Progressive Era was over, and the reformatories and custodial prisons were merged. The legacy of the "cottage system" still prevails at the women's federal prison at Alderson, West Virginia, and in many state prisons, such as Bedford Hills in New York State.

The 1960s and 1970s, that period of civil rights awareness and protest by various oppressed groups in the society—minorities, women, gays, and lesbians—was also a time of much feminist reformist zeal concerning women in prison. Although compassion was expressed for women who had killed their husbands in self-defense and were charged with murder, there was also a huge outcry over political prisoners, such as Angela Davis and Joan Little. Davis was charged with abetting a violent prisoner escape, and Little was tried for killing her jailer in the act of rape. Within prison walls, similarly, this period marked the beginning of much prisoner-generated litigation (mostly initiated from men's prisons), protesting inhumane conditions and the violation of human rights.

The period of retrenchment of social services and the War on Drugs, which got under way in the 1980s and continues at the turn of the century, parallels a mass media campaign dramatizing crimes of violence. Women of color have been the most adversely affected by the new mandatory drug-sentencing laws, namely, the harsh sentencing for crack cocaine, the drug associated with inner-city drug abuse and violence. In Canada, native women (3 percent of the population) are disproportionately locked up (20 percent of federally sentenced women are aboriginal), as are minorities of African and Latin American origin. A further factor affecting all prisoners, as Chesney-Lind (1997) indicates, is the vested interest of major corporations, the *prison industrial complex,* which has become a component of many local communities that depend on the building and maintenance of prisons for economic stability. The new surge in prison privatization has made the operation of prisons, as well as their construction, a typical capitalist venture. It is difficult, therefore, to alter priorities, such as, for example, to put money into substance abuse treatment and subsidized housing to prevent crime, when the dividends of crimes are so profitable to outside interest groups.

In summary, if women at times have been given special consideration throughout correctional history by virtue of their gender, they also have been treated badly. They have been simultaneously protected and punished. A temporal perspective emphasizes that women in society at large, like women in criminal justice, have been thought of in terms of the Madonna/whore duality so aptly spelled out by Feinman (1994).

The women-centeredness of the early women's prisons no longer exists under the influence of the twin forces of women's equality and the new punitiveness in North American society. In the nation's imagination, a criminal is a criminal, but the strict mandatory penalties are usually set with a hardened male street criminal in mind. Whereas women in prison are significantly less violent than men in prison, women's prisons are constructed on a correctional model based on assumptions about violent men (Le Blanc, 1996). Male gangs thrive in prison; women create small families. Men are territorial and fight to maintain positions of power. Women fight because of jealousy, but more often they take out their hostility on themselves through self-mutilation. Men tend to congregate by race; women create their "families" across racial lines. Women relate to each other, too, across security-level lines, whereas men's prisons are divided by classification of dangerousness of crime and criminality. The women are all incarcerated in one location and, for the most part, mix freely.

THE POPULATION PROFILE

The influx of women filling America's prisons now eclipses the male incarceration increase. Since 1980, the number of women in prison has increased fivefold (Dowling, 1997). Whereas women were only 4 percent of the incarcerated population in 1980, today they account for 6.4 percent. Women also make up 10 percent of the total jail population.

State and county departments of corrections are no longer focused on rehabilitation but are forced to warehouse people and to worry over finding the next cell. Jail and prison construction has become the major expense in counties across the United States. Ironically, the prison building boom is occurring at the same time that the crime rate is steadily decreasing, especially the rates of the crimes of violence so often sensationalized in the news. The more prisons that are built, inevitably the more people will be sentenced to fill them. "Build them and they will convict" is the common refrain. States that once managed with one or no prisons for women now are building several.

The repercussions of the upsurge in women's incarceration will be felt well beyond prison walls. Experts point, in particular, to the children of inmates who are far more likely than other children to end up in the juvenile justice system or prison (Gaouette, 1997). Today, two-thirds of the 137,000 women behind bars are mothers and most often single parents.

About 75 percent of women prisoners in the United States are serving time for nonviolent offenses because of mandatory drug sentencing laws. During the period of 1991 and 1997, the number of female inmates serving time for drug offenses doubled, but the number of comparable males increased by only 55 percent (Bureau of Justice Statistics, 1998b). Mandatory minimum sentences provide the same punishments for conspiracy to commit crimes, such as driving the getaway car, as for the instigator of the crime itself. Accordingly, almost half the women in prison today under these mandatory sentencing laws have been convicted of conspiracy (Siegal, 1998). This is an example of what we might call "equality with a vengeance," an equality of punishment meted out to women who violate the law.

In Canada, property crimes bring most women to prison. Canada relies heavily on short sentences for women offenses such as for public intoxication, shoplifting, and theft. Almost 40 percent of the sentences are for 14 days or less (Shaw, 1994). The lack of alternative sentencing options seems to be a factor in these brief incarcerations. The high percentage of women who have small children is similar to that south of the border (National Crime Prevention Council, 1995). Poor women locked in Canadian prisons often have been driven into "underground economies," such as prostitution and drug dealing as a way to make ends meet.

The United States' War on Drugs, combined with the backlash against affirmative action, sometimes is played out in the form of "zero tolerance" for women who violate drug use laws. Mandatory minimum sentencing laws tie the hands of judges who personally might favor probation in sympathetic cases. In the political world, Meda Chesney-Lind (1995) suggests, there seems to be a return to the imagery of depraved women, women whose crimes put them outside the ranks of "true womanhood." The new hostility signaled by the bringing of child-abuse charges against women who use drugs, even before the birth of their children, is a case in point provided by Chesney-Lind. A recent development in South Dakota is illustrative: Drinking while pregnant has recently been criminalized as a form of child abuse (Aamot, 1998).

Because of the intergenerational costs of locking up mothers and paying for foster care for their children, women are far more expensive to the state to imprison than men. Such a willingness to spend millions of dollars incarcerating women stands, of course, in stark contrast to the paucity of resources made available to other women's programs (Chesney-Lind, 1995).

When a mother is imprisoned, often merely held in jail awaiting trial, the separation from her children can be traumatic for them all. Prisons, and especially women's prisons, generally are located in remote, rural areas far away from home and community. Family ties, over time, are broken. Yet prisoner's family relationships are very important not only for mental health considerations but also in terms of postrelease success (Hairston, 1995). Martin's examination of mothers who were incarcerated in the Minnesota correctional facility at Shakopee in 1985 established that their commitment to parenthood was deeply tenacious (Martin, 1997). When these mothers were followed up five years later, most of them had sustained continuous and primary parenting education from within prison and had reunified with their children when released from prison (p. 1). Nevertheless, internal prison policies as well as traditional public policies, as Hairston indicates, have provided minimal support for the maintainance of family relationships for individuals involved in the criminal justice system.

Prisoner and jail inmate profiles can be best revealed through recent studies from the U.S. Bureau of Justice Statistics (BJS) (1998a, 1998b) and the

National Crime Prevention Council Canada (1995). From these government sources we learn that:

- Almost half the female inmates in U.S. jails, compared to 13 percent of jailed men, have been abused sexually or physically; 27 percent of the women and 3 percent of the men have been raped. In the Canadian federal system, 53 percent of the women report they have experienced sexual abuse.
- Only 9 percent of women in state prisons get visits from their minor children.
- The female jail inmate population has grown by 9.5 percent a year since 1983, compared to 6.2 percent for men. The female prison population's annual growth rate has averaged 11.2 percent since 1985.
- Since 1980, the number of African American female prisoners per 100,000 African American females has increased fourfold.
- Males are nine times more likely than females to go to prison in their lifetimes; African American women, however, have almost the same chance of going to prison as do white men.
- Among women, African Americans are more than twice as likely as Hispanics and seven times more likely than whites to go to prison in their lifetimes.
- Children of inmates are five times more likely to be imprisoned in adulthood than other children.
- Over 60 percent of state inmates have not finished high school; over 50 percent were unemployed at the time of their arrest.
- HIV positive rates for women in prison are almost double those of men; the rate is 6.8 percent for Latinas, 3.5 percent for African Americans, and 1.9 percent for non-Hispanic whites.
- Incarcerated Canadian Native women have an exceptionally high suicide rate.
- More often than not, the women in U.S. facilities are guarded by men.

These statistics, gathered from government services, provide documentation of the racism, sexism, and classism that exists in contemporary society. The racism is revealed in the harsh sentencing practices for involvement with drugs such as crack cocaine, associated in the public mind with inner-city crime. Mandating minimum sentencing for dealing and conspiring to deal in these kinds of drugs is filling up jail cells with African American and Latina women. Sexism is played out in the harsh sentencing of women and their transportation to prisons far from home. Classism is evidenced in the poor educational backgrounds and high poverty rates of these women.

Approximately 80 percent of women in U.S. prisons and almost two-thirds of women in Canadian prisons have a serious problem with drugs or alcohol, and substance abuse is associated with their crime in some way. Related problems are eating disorders, other mental health problems such as depression and high anxiety, and self-mutilation.

Reports from the United Kingdom (Bennetto, 1997) reveal almost identical circumstances for British women prisoners, mainly because of overcrowding and a shortage of professionally trained personnel. Many women are in jail "on remand," awaiting trial for which most will not be sentenced to prison. Conditions at Holloway jail in London are so bad, in fact, that they triggered a walkout by official inspectors in 1995. The female prison population has risen 76 percent in the last four years—twice the rate of men. Nearly two-thirds of women interviewed in the Bennetto study were mothers, nearly half said that they had been physically or sexually abused earlier in life, and two-thirds reported having used illegal drugs. Self-mutilation is a constant problem at Holloway, especially by psychologically disturbed women, who instead of being given the psychotherapy and/or medication they need, find themselves shut away in solitary confinement (Carlen and Tchaikovsky, 1996).

A recent outcry reported in the British press concerns the hundreds of girls under age 18 serving time in adult prisons, many for minor offenses such as shoplifting (Hugill, 1997). Britain lacks any young offenders' institutions for girls, such as exist for boys. Carlen and Tchaikovsky (1996) argue convincingly that women's imprisonment is different from men's and that their special needs have been systematically ignored by prisoner advocates as well as prison administrators. As elsewhere, the major stumbling block in substantial reform is the new punitiveness, which is an outgrowth of a climate of fear and resentment toward the deviant poor and nonworking single mothers living on welfare. Disproportionate numbers of ethnic minorities are members of this group and are especially prominent among those sentenced to prison.

One reason for the increasingly multicultural composition of prison populations is the result of the international War on Drugs. In England, Canada, and elsewhere, women who have been convicted for their work as "mules" in international drug trafficking are being held in countries far from home. Women are forced or talked into doing this work by international drug smugglers. Because they are generally ignorant of the overall operations and criminal justice policies, women often plead guilty and receive extensive mandatory minimum sentences (Pollock, 1998). The sex-neutral Draconian sentences, as Pollock argues, do not take into account that many of the seemingly deep-end female criminals may have been acting on behalf of male drug traffickers, who are often their boyfriends and partners. In conjunction with the high profits in the drug trade, increasing numbers of female drug smugglers are caught while passing through customs in Washington, D.C., New York, and London. In private correspondence, Kim Pate (1998) of the Elizabeth Fry Association of Canada, describes the situation befalling foreign women in Canada:

We have a few Latina women in prison, but more women from the Caribbean, and increasingly, women from Southeast Asia for drug importation and/or trafficking charges. Most have no contact with their families for fear of repercussions on them if it is known that their sister/mother/daughter/etc. is in prison abroad. They are terribly isolated as a result, all the more so if they

do not speak English or French. We used to be able to try to get them early pa-
role for the purposes of deportation, but legislative changes in 1992 stopped
this. . . . Now the women have to serve their entire prison sentences prior to
deportation.

PRISON STRUCTURE

Because women are such a small percentage of the U.S. prison population, they inherit a system designed for men, men who are defined as a high security risk to society. Yet it was for the sake of controlling a population of violent male predators that the whole correctional apparatus, this military-style system of command run by officers given the ranks of lieutenant, captain, and sergeant, was set up. This framework, designed for the 93 percent or so majority of (male) prisoners, was superimposed on the female minority, for whom its suitability is questionable. Some allowance is made for women's special needs, admittedly, such as the establishment of nurseries for inmate children in a few select places; to date no one has argued for placing a nursery in a men's prison.

The formal structure of the women's prison in many ways belies the informal treatment women receive within the prison walls. At the personal level, women are treated not as tough men, but as children; they are infantilized. Harsh punishments are meted out for cursing, disrespect, and other minor violations (Pollock, 1998). Called "girls" by staff or "ladies" as at New Bedford (as the title of Harris's book, *They Always Call Us Ladies* indicates), but never "women," female prisoners are encouraged to display "good" passive behavior by prison officials. See Box 3.1. Independent thinking, much less

---

BOX 3.1   They Treat Us Like Children

[Being in] the penitentiary is the most humiliating thing I have ever experienced. For instance, if a matron wants you to strip down to bare skin, you must do so or face disciplinary action for disobeying a direct order. If you are sick and would like to rest for the day, you must get the nurse's permission. If they can't come up with a conclusion about your ailment immediately and you decide to rest anyway, then you will be locked up in your room the entire day. They say that I'm a mature adult, yet they tell me my every move and treat me as a child.

I don't feel that the penitentiary is the right place to learn and grow. I know more about crime now than when I came here. Being here makes you more of a criminal. That is why people may spend years incarcerated and are not reformed.

Source: Interviewed by Clemens Bartollas in October 1995 and contained in Clemens Bartollas and
John P. Conrad, *Introduction to Corrections,* 2nd ed. (New York: HarperCollins, 1991), p. 468.

grassroots organizing for social change, is severely punished. Appropriately, Watterson (1996) refers to women's prison as "inside the concrete womb," a phrase that serves as the subtitle of her book. On the subject of sex, Watterson comments, "It seems sex for prisoners is considered dessert in our culture—too special and rare a treat for bad children" (p. 285).

The Social World of the Women's Prison

The complex and diverse histories of women incarcerated in prison produce a prison culture that is itself complex and diverse in many ways (Owen, 1998). We now consider three critical dimensions of life that constitute the culture of women's prisons: the social and cultural background of the women themselves, the cliques or families that develop in prison, and prison sexuality.

Any attempt to comprehend the social organization of prisons must address the contemporary prisoner experience in light of what John Irwin (1980) calls the "cultural baggage" that inmates import into the prison setting with them. Much of this cultural baggage today is the end product of the drug wars on the streets and the War on Drugs in society. Caught up in the War on Drugs are minority women involved with male gang members (Latino and African American), foreigners arrested at airports as drug "couriers" for international syndicates, and the usual array of violent and nonviolent offenders arrested for crimes that are indirectly related to drug use. Race and class intersect in predictable ways to ensure that the persons most feared and resented by society will be those who are shut away. Today, as Chesney-Lind (1997) suggests, street crime has become a code word for *race*. And racial tensions in the community lay the groundwork for ethnic differences and resentments behind prison bars.

Sometimes the resentments, as Jean Harris (1988) reports, are taken out on "honkie," or white, correctional officers. Sometimes prisoners take them out on each other. In at least one prison, as reported by Feinman (1994), observers note that overt problems occur more often between African American and Hispanic women than between white and African American women. More studies are needed to confirm this phenomenon throughout the prison system. Research does tell us that the kind of race wars and gang warfare that characterize the social structure in men's prisons seem to have no counterpart in women's institutions (Pollock, 1998). Two aspects of the social structure with which we are concerned here are prison homosexuality and kinship ties, parts of the female prison culture that, although addressed separately in the literature, are inextricably linked.

Prison Families

Often located in rural areas miles away from their own families, and inaccessible in any case because of financial and legal restrictions, women in prisons tend to develop their own networks for familial ties. In sharp contrast to the male prison society organized around power, women prisoners, at least in the United States, often replicate the family patterns they knew on the outside for life on the inside. "Married" couples may head such families and even occasionally include a father figure. Prison "mamas" keep their "children" in line and provide emotional support (see Giallombardo, 1966; van Wormer, 1987). Although these inmates generally live in a world dominated by pettiness, gossip, and much regressive behavior, a lot of love and nurturing goes on in such a society of women; care and respect for the elderly and mothering of the very young (or retarded) are common themes.

Considerable controversy surrounds the viability of these family forms and whether or not they even exist. As Pollock (1998) suggests, "Although it seems clear that women do form affectional ties that have some similarity to familial relationships, it is not clear that the extensive kinship networks were or are anywhere near as defined as one might believe reading the early studies" (p. 38). Faith (1993) concurs in the view that early researchers exaggerated the centrality of family forms. See Box 3.2 for early studies describing family forms in women's prisons.

Among recent witnesses to the prison "kinship" scene are Owen (1998), who studied the subculture on the prison yard in a California institution; Jean Harris (1988), who spent eight years in residence at Bedford Hills, New York; and Watterson (1996), a journalist, who reports that she would occasionally be introduced to an inmate's entire prison family, including the wife, son, daughter-in-law, and daughter.

Because there has never been any consensus concerning the percentage of inmates involved in prison play-families, it is hard to conclude whether they are, in fact, on the decline, as contemporary writers such as Fox (1984), Harris (1988), and Diaz-Cotto (1996) contend. Diaz-Cotto argues that the degree to which family groupings are growing less common may be the result of increasing access to family, friends, and outside volunteers. Her description of the Latina prisoners' active involvement in these adoptive families and of the tremendous emotional investment in these relationships is consistent with descriptions in the classic studies. A difference is the ethnic cliquishness of these bondings. Because Latina inmates come from families with strong extended kinship ties and they are in many cases incarcerated in a foreign country logically increases their need to recreate familiar role relationships.

As long as women are shut away from the outside world and from the close, caring (and scolding) relationships to which they are accustomed, the argument can be made that the old, familiar pattern will be replayed with a different cast. The functions of prison families are many: They offer mutual support and protection in a strange and often bewildering environment; they provide a mutual aid network in an atmosphere of deprivation; they are often encouraged by the administration for their social control aspect—keeping family members out of trouble; and above all, they create situations for fun and laughter (Hart, 1995).

BOX 3.2   Pseudo-Families in Women's Prisons

In their 1965 study of the Frontera Correctional Institution in California, David A. Ward and Gene G. Kassebaum found that women attempted to deal with the painful conditions of confinement by establishing homosexual alliances. These prison love affairs appeared unstable, short-lived, and explosive, and they involved strict role differentiation between the butch and the femme. The butch, who plays the dominant, or male, role, is expected to pursue the femme and to always be strong, in control, and independent.

However, in the 1966 study of the Federal Reformatory for Women at Alderson, West Virginia, Rose Giallombardo discovered that the major difference between male and female prisons is that the women's inmate society establishes a substitute world in which women can identify or construct family patterns similar to those in the free world, whereas male prisoners design a social system to combat the social and physical deprivations of imprisonment. Family life—with "mothers and fathers," "grandparents," and "aunts and uncles"—was at the very center of inmate life at Alderson. Giallombardo also notes that membership in kinship groups took place more frequently than participation in homosexual activity and occurred

earlier than sexual involvements. Providing a sense of belonging and identification, she adds, enabled inmates involved in "family affairs" to do easy time.

L. LeShanna's 1969 investigation at the Maryville Correctional Institution in Ohio also discovered the presence of the fictive family. Unlike Giallombardo's findings, most of the Maryville families were matricentric—they did not center around a mother and father united in a homosexual marriage. LeShanna further observed that the mother was the most frequently reported and influential role at Maryville.

The 1972 research of E. Heffernan at the District of Columbia Women's Reformatory in Occoquan, Virginia, also supported the hypothesis that fictive kinship structures are present in women's prisons. Heffernan, along with Giallombardo, emphasized the concept of latent cultural identity as a factor in the formation of the fictive family. This refers to the preinstitutional identity that the female offender brings with her into the prison setting. Heffernan argues that the reason women construct the kinship structure is that females are socialized to conceive of themselves, their needs, and their peer relations primarily in terms of family roles and situations.

Sources: R. Giallombardo, *Society of Women: A Study of a Women's Prison* (New York: Wiley, 1966); E. Heffernan, *Making It in Prison: The Square, the Cool, and the Life* (New York: Wiley-Interscience, 1972); Richard S. Jones, "Coping with Separation: Adaptive Responses of Women Prisoners," *Women & Criminal Justice* 5 (1993), pp. 71–97; L. LeShanna, *Family Participation: Functional Responses of Incarcerated Females.* Unpublished master's thesis, Bowling Green State University, 1969; and D. A. Ward and G. G. Kassebaum, *Women's Prison: Sex and Social Structure* (Chicago: Aldine Publishing, 1965).

Another possible advantage of clearly defined family roles for women who live in close quarters is that relationships can become very intimate and include touching and hugging without taking on sexual connotations. In same-sex institutions, where sexual tensions often are played out as homophobia, a clarification of one's relationship in terms of sister-to-sister and mother-to-daughter ties can serve to legitimize the bonding between unrelated women (see van Wormer, 1987).

Prison Sexuality

In men's prisons, homophobia is played out in a different way. A men's prison is a world of untempered masculinity where the strong preserve their sense of manhood through sexual conquest of the weak. Sexual threats, taunting, and assault dominate the scene into which the new inmate is initiated. Under a ruthless inmate code that enables carefully executed schemes of smuggling and escape to go undetected, predators subdue their prey. Young men, especially nonstreetwise white males, are especially vulnerable to sexual harassment and physical attack. In the male prison society, rape or the threat of rape serves as a form of peer group social control exerted by the aggressors and leaders in the facility. While the rapist wields power and respect, the victim is shamed and feminized. The aggressor is never considered anything other than heterosexual; his "punk" is a mere woman substitute. Among men, rape is about power and dominance as well as sexual gratification. Once victimized, a man is ranked as a target for sexual exploitation and subject to gang rapes; one escape avenue is to become more or less a prostitute to one "protector" (Donaldson, 1995; *Prison Legal News,* 1995). Interestingly, a similar pattern prevailed among the convict laborers in colonial Australia as described in disturbing detail in the epic history, *The Fatal Shore* (Hughes, 1987).

Behind bars, women recreate a world of the familiar. Many seek out strong types of women with whom to relate and to play their accustomed roles. The father or brother role in the family is usually assumed by the studs or butches; these "players" are not lesbians but women playing at being men. Their popularity in a house of femmes exceeds all expectations. Referred to by the pronouns "he" and "him," butches are sought after by male-starved women who provide them with cigarettes and all kinds of other enticements. It is a myth perpetuated in Hollywood B grade movies that butches have to resort to force against unwilling parties.

Butches tend disproportionately to be African American and the females white. Jean Harris (1998) describes the role-playing at the New York State facility:

> Many of the butches make a concentrated effort to emulate the behavior of young black males, the hip-walking, cool-talking model of masculinity. Some cut their hair short or shave their heads. . . . I've watched many a woman wash, iron, and cook for her "butch," "dike," "bulldagger," and I've heard one stand outside a cell door, begging forgiveness for some wrongdoing she couldn't identify. Inside, as well as outside, it's the woman who pays. (pp. 136, 139)

In personal correspondence with Katherine van Wormer, Kathy Tyler (1998), who was sentenced to life at the Iowa Correctional Institution for Women at Mitchellville, shares her reactions to the author's earlier research:

I was rather astonished to learn of the mother/sister/brother/cousin, whatever, that you have researched. I have not seen that at all here. What I have seen, and sadly, lots of it is the homosexual relationships. I find them sad because they are so counterproductive in many ways. First, the women fight—it is strange relationships, almost like they fight between each other to ease the boredom. Secondly, I think the relationships prevent them from doing things they would otherwise do because they always do things in tandem. And thirdly, they are transient, and each time a breakup occurs and a new one takes the place, I think something is lost within each of them. (pp. 1–2)

The prison sex role-playing, even though it says more about female heterosexuality than about homosexuality, in all probability makes the homophobia that much worse by increasing sexual tensions in crowded institutions. Hence, as we have seen, one finds the tendency throughout the prison system for women to define themselves as kin—as sisters, mainly, or as mother/daughters. As kin, they can maintain a certain closeness while avoiding all the gossip that would flow from a less clearly defined relationship. The prison counselor is well advised to recognize the centrality of family relationships to women and to advocate for strengthening family ties with relatives on the outside. A good example is found at Bedford Hills, one of comparatively few prisons in the United States to permit family visits overnight. Trailers on the prison grounds make such extended visits possible.

In summary, taken together, these dimensions—ethnicity, prison family construction, and sexual relationships—compose the prison culture typical of many U.S. prisons for women. An inmate's participation in this culture is determined by many factors, as Owen (1998) informs us, including time spent in prison, social and cultural background, and commitment to a deviant law-breaking lifestyle.

ATTITUDES TOWARD WOMEN IN PRISON

It is now clear to all researchers, as it was always clear to feminist theorists, that the notion that Women's Liberation was associated with a new type of female criminal was false (Crites, 1976; Erez, 1988; Watterson, 1996; Weisheit and Mahan, 1988). The now exponential increase in the numbers of women in prison is a political fact, a result of a societal backlash against poor and minority women who become involved with drugs, often through their men. Typically, these women get caught up in legal violations, through drug possession, drug transporting, or drug trafficking. Far from being liberated, such women are doubly dependent—dependent on drugs and dependent on the men who supply them.

Despite women inmates' relatively low level of criminality (compared to male offenders), female correctional officers are very often biased against their female charges. They see "the girls" they supervise as immature, overemotional, and quarrelsome. It has been van Wormer's experience in her prison study, confirmed by Faith, that female correctional officers overwhelmingly prefer to work with male offenders, who are considered less difficult. The negative attitude is often mutual (Erez, 1988). Women inmates resent female officers enforcing rules, many of them quite petty. Correspondents writing to van Wormer list the following rules, which are especially oppressive:

Shirts must be tucked in
No Q Tips
No lending, borrowing, or trading
No giving gifts to each other
No hugging
No writing to people in other institutions
No tank tops or sleeveless shirts

In Canada during the 1980s, women's groups succeeded in persuading criminal justice agencies to refer to convicted female lawbreakers as "women in conflict with the law," as a less pejorative term (Faith, 1993). Nevertheless, the prejudice against women offenders persists. Women in Canadian as in U.S. prisons are punished much more readily than men for minor offenses such as disrespect and use of strong language, as Faith indicates.

The Bad Mother Image

One of the most painful stigmas attached to imprisonment is that of being a bad mother. Incarcerated mothers are often blamed for their forced separation from their children (Watterson, 1996). For prison mothers, visits with children are rare; no touching is generally a rule, and access to the telephone is limited. Whether out of shame or to keep children from "blabbing" about where their mothers are, small children are often told, especially by their grandparents, that the prison they are visiting is a hospital. If the children are in foster care, there is little incentive to take them for what could be a disturbing institutional visit.

Especially in divorce proceedings, women are often declared to be unfit mothers by virtue of their imprisonment. If they retain custody, after they serve their time their role as mother is difficult in every way. Among the major challenges are children who feel abandoned, foster parents or grandparents who may not want to let go, and a society that has little compassion for a woman who took drugs or stole or killed, much less a mother who did these things.

Females convicted of infanticide occupy the lowest status in the female convict world. Because most women in prison are mothers who sincerely miss their children, they have little understanding of a mother who would harm her baby. Women who take the lives of their young are often highly suicidal and act out of extreme hopelessness. In a personal interview, Chaplain Kay Kopatich (1998) of the Iowa Correctional Institution for Women, informs us:

They [mothers convicted of killing their children] are subject to discrimination and to cruel words. I don't think that they are beaten up in women's prison like they might be in a men's prison, but there is mental cruelty. They might be going through the food line and somebody might, an inmate who is serving her might whisper, "baby killer."

DEGRADING PRACTICES

The history of women in conflict with the law is the history of male oppression. Society is afraid of both the feminist and the female criminal, for each of them in her own way tests society's established boundaries (Jones, 1980). The interconnectedness of feminist advances and harsh punishment of female criminality noted by Ann Jones in her book, *Women Who Kill* (1980) is even more apparent today than when it was written, because of current sentencing practices. Not surprisingly, the political interests of feminist and criminal, therefore, sometimes coincide. The sexual harassment of women in prison by male guards is clearly a women's political issue, however reluctant women prisoners are to unite their cause with that of "liberated" women on the outside.

Increased sexual harassment of women prisoners has come about, ironically, because of the push for women's equality to work as correctional officers in men's prisons and to engage in body-pat frisks and other close contact searches the same as men do. This has led to a situation in which men are allowed the same responsibilities in female institutions. Because of men's greater proclivity than women to be sexually aroused by visual stimuli, the results are about what one would expect (Moir and Jessel, 1991).

Whether the guard is a man or a woman, loss of control over privacy and the most intimate access to one's body are among the most disturbing aspects of imprisonment for women. So disturbing that they can be defined as sexual abuse are invasive body cavity searches, use of strip searches for punishment, women giving birth in chairs and leg shackles, gynecological medical neglect, gynecological procedures performed with male guards present, and women's susceptibility to sexual abuse by male guards.

What Erving Goffman (1961) said about the functions of degradation ceremonies and mortification of the self in total institutions as a means of establishing control certainly rings true in women's prisons. The prisoner must surrender again and again to degrading rituals in which the state has taken ownership of the body/self (Faith, 1993). Prisoners who do not submit readily to body-part searches, which may be performed by male guards, typically are forced to strip for more thorough searches. This is how power is negotiated, how the new prisoner is moved into the status of "nonperson" as a passive recipient of whatever the guards choose to mete out. This is not to impugn the motives of the prison employees but rather to show, in the Goffman tradition, how a total institution keeps its charges in line.

One in six women entering U.S. prisons is pregnant (Bureau of Justice Statistics, 1994). Pregnancy poses special difficulties. Delivery is often an ordeal for women who, if drug addicted, commonly are deprived of sufficient pain medication and who may deliver while shackled to the delivery table and then be whisked back to the prison away from the baby and health care (Watterson, 1996). This shoddy medical care of women in childbirth is duplicated in all areas of health care. Gynecologic care, for example, is poor to nonexistent.

Taking into account that about half the women in U.S. and Canadian prisons have been victimized sexually in the past, the forced body searches are especially disturbing. Indeed, as Albor (1997) tells us, for many women, prison literally recalls the arbitrary, self-eroding terror of life in previous violent relationships. Inmates may be stripped naked at any time and made to kneel on all fours for rectal/vaginal searches. Male or female guards are often required by institutional policy to probe inmates' body cavities for contraband.

The public got a rare look at the racist and sexist brutality in the women's federal prison when the Canadian Broadcasting Company aired a videotape of male guards roughing up crying women in a forced strip search. The outcry that ensued and the resulting follow-up investigations have done a lot to force the prison to take remedial action and to get the women removed to regional institutions (Dreidger, 1997).

Prison Sexual Abuse

All rape is an exercise in power, but some rapists have an edge that is more than physical; they operate within an institutionalized setting (Brownmiller, 1975). Rape in slavery, rape in the military, and rape in prison are three such examples.

The scandal involving sexual harassment of women in the military has been highlighted in the mass media. Relatively little attention has been paid until recently to the sexual assaults on female prisoners by their male guards. In 1996, extensive documentation was provided by the Human Rights Watch Women's Rights Project (1996), an international nongovernmental organization, which revealed that the extent of guard-on-inmate abuse behind the closed doors of prisons is staggering. This 347-page report, drawn from first-hand interviews, court records, and records of guards' disciplinary hearings, is astonishing in its graphic detail of everyday experiences of women in our state prisons. As one would expect of a cross-gender power imbalance such as exists between male guards and female inmates, sexual misconduct has been rampant. Here is a summary of the report's findings:

> The custodial sexual misconduct documented in this report takes many
> forms. We found that male correctional employees have vaginally, anally,

and orally raped female prisoners and sexually assaulted and abused them. We found that in the course of committing such gross misconduct, male officers have not only used actual or threatened physical force, but have also used their near total authority to provide or deny goods and privileges to female prisoners to compel them to have sex or, in other cases, to reward them for having done so. In other cases, male officers have violated their most basic professional duty and engaged in sexual contact with female prisoners absent the use of threat of force or any material exchange. In addition to engaging in sexual relations with prisoners, male officers have used mandatory pat-frisks or room searches to grope women's breasts, buttocks, and vaginal areas and to view them inappropriately while in a state of undress in the housing or bathroom areas. Male correctional officers and staff have also engaged in regular verbal degradation and harassment of female prisoners, thus contributing to a custodial environment in the state prisons for women which is often highly sexualized and excessively hostile. (p. 1)

Human Rights Watch (1996) takes the U.S. government to task for failing to protect the women who are subjected to institutionalized rape by prison authorities. The placing of male officers in contact positions over female prisoners is in violation of the United Nations Standard Minimum Rules for the Treatment of Prisoners.

The persons who are most vulnerable to sexual abuse are first-time offenders, the young or mentally ill, and lesbian and transgendered persons. The gripping prison Hollywood drama *Love Child,* produced in 1982, tells the true story of an inmate who became pregnant by a guard in Florida and fought for her right to keep the baby. Many times female inmates willingly trade sex for favors; male guards who have been involved in sexual relations with inmates are transferred to men's prisons rather than being fired. Prisoners, such as those in Georgia who are not given a stipend for their work, have no means of purchasing the many supplies they need or the cigarettes they so badly crave. This dependency enhances their vulnerability to sexual exploitation (Human Rights Watch, 1996). In many instances, women have been impregnated as a result of sexual misconduct, placed in segregation if they filed a complaint, and sometimes pressured to get an abortion (Human Rights Watch, 1996).

According to psychologist Louis Rothenstein, who worked for six years in the federal prison in Dublin, California, it was not uncommon for guards to go into women's cells and have sex (cited in Stein, 1996). Complaints by women inmates and their advocates were ignored. "You would be blackballed if you were thought of as an advocate for the inmates," he said (p. 24). A code of silence within the prison industry shields it from public scrutiny, he added. In 1998, at the U.S. District Court in San Francisco, a settlement was reached providing $500,000 for three female inmates who filed a grievance after being raped by male inmates while housed at the male facility at Dublin, California (*Prison Legal News,* 1998a). The inmates reportedly had been given access to women after bribing a male officer.

INMATE LITIGATION

We begin by summarizing litigative events at the notorious women's prison in Georgia. These events have special meaning for van Wormer; she was personally escorted out of the Milledgeville facility in 1973 by a correctional officer speaking on behalf of the warden (this prison had gone through five wardens in that one year), who said, "It has been decided that you cannot consider your [dissertation] study here; you might see some things you don't understand."

The *New York Times* (1992) described some of the things that might, in truth, have been understood by the investigator only too well: Although women in Georgia's prison sued the prison for sexual abuse in 1984, they had to wait eight years to win their case in November 1992. In the end, fourteen former employees—ten men, including the deputy warden, and four women—were indicted on sexual abuse charges, including rape, sexual assault, and sodomy in "one of the worst episodes of its kind in the history of the nation's women's prisons" (p. 1). The incidents took place in the warden's house, in a prison rest room, and in other areas.

These indictments at the Georgia Penitentiary were only the tip of the iceberg at the penitentiary. Whether brought about through trade-offs or coerced through violence between male guards and female inmates, sexual involvement was not deviant behavior in that setting; it was the norm. Even female staff members were implicated in sexual abusive behavior, according to court records cited in the Human Rights Watch (1996) report. There is no way to begin to estimate the number of inmates involved before the lawsuit was filed in 1992. Between 1992 and 1996 (Human Rights Watch, 1996), when better records were kept owing to the investigations taking place, attorney Bob Cullen told Human Rights Watch that he had learned of approximately 370 reported incidents during this period. Some of the cases have been publicized in the media.

Recent legislation in the form of the Prison Litigation Reform Act was passed by the U.S. Congress and signed into law in 1996 (Human Rights Watch, 1996). The intent was to stifle the spate of frivolous lawsuits coming from prisons and mainly from men's prisons. Unfortunately, the ability of women inmates and their legal advocates to sue over human rights violations is now drastically curtailed, according to the Human Rights Watch.

Not surprisingly, extensive litigation concerns the sexual mistreatment of female inmates. According to Chesney-Lind (1997), scandals have erupted in California, Georgia, Hawaii, Ohio, Louisiana, Michigan, Tennessee, New York, and New Mexico. Most of these scandals have come to light only because of publicity surrounding legal suits. The past decades, as Feinman (1994) suggests, may portend a new trend in the nature of legal action taken against the criminal justice system. In addition to sexual abuse, female prisoners are raising issues of clemency for battered women who killed in self-defense, drug treatment, prison nurseries, decent dental care, and health care for the aged and for those with AIDS/HIV.

Much of the litigation concerns the lack of employment and vocational training opportunities for women, compared to men, in prison. Correctional policy makers often justify the poor training options in light of the numbers of women in prison being too small to provide many options, few of the female inmates have marketable skills, and interest in men's prison programs such as auto mechanics is minimal (Feinman, 1994). Accordingly, most work in prison relates to the everyday running of the prison—washing, cleaning, and cooking.

A major problem with the litigation to equalize employment training opportunities for men and women is that male prisoners are heavily exploited as a source of cheap labor, making only a few dollars per hour, at the most. The extent of this exploitation is revealed in an article in the 1997 summer issue of *Iowa Commerce Magazine:* "Employers pay an hourly wage only. No workers' compensation. No unemployment. No health insurance. No benefits" (cited in Basu, 1998, p. 6). Instead of going to Mexico, many private companies, as Basu (1998) contends, are relying on this state-subsidized program to get inmates to work. The issues are the same as with the exploitation of cheap labor overseas: wages for regular labor can be driven down and work opportunities are provided for persons in no position to bargain. Controversial convict-for-hire agreements have been reached across the United States. The risk of displacement of free-world labor is a real fear in some quarters (Lomax, 1998).

Historically, almost all the legal action for prisoner rights was pursued on behalf of men. Suggested reasons for gender differences in filing litigation are women's general passivity, their prisons' locations far from urban centers and legal aid attorneys, and the scarcity of jailhouse lawyers among them (Feinman, 1994). A unique explanation is that the female inmate tendency to form play-families and to pair off as "married couples" serves inadvertently to suppress troublemakers and absorb women's energies, while having a subduing effect on their activism (see Giallambardo, 1966; van Wormer, 1987).

Knight (1992) states that women prisoners recently have had some success as litigants in areas in which the courts have recognized a constitutional basis for men's rights in prison. For example, women have by definition the same judicial protection as men concerning Eighth Amendment and Fourteenth Amendment due process. Significantly, "the protection against cruel and unusual punishment has been interpreted to require adequate medical care during pregnancy and delivery and the right to be released in a timely manner to obtain an abortion" (p. 112). When claims do not involve constitutional status, she adds, but rest on administratively or legislatively created privileges, women prisoners have had some success in using the equal protection clause. But even when equal protection claims are successful, courts have not required identical treatment for men and women in prison. Thus, separate can be equal.

In other countries, although there has been litigation, corrections reform for women has come more often from highly publicized efforts on their account and a concerned public enlightened by sympathetic press accounts. In Canada, for example, a 1990 task force report on federally sentenced women led to construction of model prisons designed for the offenders' well-being. In 1994, a Canadian federal inquiry into strip searches by a male riot squad at the women's federal prison resulted in a castigating report written by Madam Justice Louise Arbour (Duffy, 1997). A human rights issue desperately in need of litigation, but that seems unlikely to benefit from court action, is the extremely brutal treatment of detained political refugees who, because they are not U.S. citizens, are considered to be outside the jurisdiction of the Constitution. Kassindja's harrowing memoir, *Do They Hear You When You Cry?* (1998), graphically recounts the horrors of her oppression during confinement by the Immigration and Naturalization Service. Kassindja, who arrived in the United States as a refugee from forced genital mutilation in Togo, Africa, was successful only because her story received rare national press coverage.

WOMEN ON DEATH ROW

In Europe, in early February 1998, editorial writers called the execution of Karla Fay Tucker a "barbaric act." The *Irish Times,* in contrast to the major papers in the United States, featured the story on page 1 for two consecutive days (Carroll 1998; *Irish Times* 1998). Entreaties from all over the world and from the Pope failed to gain clemency for Tucker, the first woman executed in Texas since 1863. Tucker, despite being an admitted axe murderer who had killed strangers in a drug-induced rage, galvanized the sympathy of the world. Like Velma Barfield before her, Tucker was a born-again Christian whose femininity and good works in prison endeared her to people. Following Tucker's execution, but this time without much fanfare, Judias Buenoano, an unrepentant woman prisoner known as the Black Widow, was executed in Florida's electric chair in March 1998.

The deaths of these women, like all executions, were highly political. The message sent to the public by the state execution of these women is that justice is without mercy and, as for women, that if they want equality of opportunity they can also have equality of punishment. Laster's (1994) astute analysis of women executed in Australia between 1842 and 1967 demonstrates that politics rather than law influences the sentencing outcome for women. Women were hanged in Victoria not for what they did but for what they were. They were not hardened criminals or a threat to society; their crimes were different from those of their male counterparts. Overwhelmingly, their victims were intimates. Execution of women, as Laster argues, is a kind of social control in a society stressing traditional family values. In a twisted irony, in today's world, the insistence of feminists for equal treatment is used as a way of advancing antifeminist political agendas.

Today, significantly, the United States has the largest number of condemned women on death row in its history. As of February 1998 a total of sixty-eight women were on death row; this is 2 percent of the total of death row inmates. The breakdown by race as given in the most recent U.S. Department of Justice study (Bureau of Justice Statistics, 1997a) is one-third African American and two-thirds white. Death row conditions vary from state to state (Thompson, 1997). Some states allow the women to mingle for visits and yard time, but most allow no contact visits (only visits behind glass, by means of a telephone), no work, and solitary confinement for 23 hours per day. Death row inmates have some limited contact with correctional officers, prison chaplains, and treatment staff (Feinman, 1994).

The literature on women on death row has been sparse until recently. Velma Barfield's (1985) autobiography, *Women on Death Row,* mainly concerns her religious conversion and her work in spreading the word to other women to whom she talked through the walls. Thus we learn of her routine at the Raleigh, North Carolina, penitentiary:

> I was put in an end cell that, like all the others, contained four bunks. "No one else," the officer said, "will ever occupy the cell with you."
>
> I didn't realize it then, but for the next four and a half years, my world would consist of a room ten feet by ten feet, with bars for two sides and concrete walls for the other two. Little natural light penetrated the cell. . . . A guard led me out of my cell every day for one hour of exercise. Aside from that daily hour and occasional trips to the administrative building or to the mental health unit or when I was taken to court, I never moved outside my cell. (p. 106)

Cathy Thompson (1997), an inmate confined on death row in Chowchilla, California, writes to the Irish anti–death penalty organization, Lifelines, "It is known factually that women sentenced to death are usually first-time offenders. The vast majority of these women come from abusive families and easily fall prey to abusive relationships. Other than when their crimes occur or when an execution date is scheduled for one of us, we remain totally invisible to society" (p. 3).

Kathleen O'Shea, a former nun, has made it her life's work to publicize conditions for women sentenced to die. In her absorbing newsletter, *Women on the Row* (1998), O'Shea describes the grim circumstances facing one of these women: "[She] told me they had changed from cuffing her hands to go to the shower from the front to the back, so that it is extremely difficult to carry anything on the way. They have to literally sit down on a filthy floor to pick it up and the male guards just watch, and according to this woman, enjoy it quite a bit" (p. 7). In her book, *Women and the Death Penalty in the United States, 1900–1998,* O'Shea (1999) describes the utter secrecy surrounding how women on death row are treated by the men who supervise them. The prisons, according to this author, try their best to keep conditions in these "prisons within prisons" from coming to light.

It is impossible to discuss the death penalty as the ultimate cruelty without revealing its curious attraction to suicidal inmates. Elsewhere, van Wormer (1995) has documented twenty cases (nineteen men, one woman) of persons who committed murder as a form of wished-for state-assisted suicide. Some of them were serving life sentences in prison. In personal correspondence with the author, Beverly Seymour (1998) describes her legal suit in Ohio in which she requests the death penalty as a form of euthanasia. "If I don't get it," she writes, "I'm outa here."

Chaplain Kopatich (1998) describes the scene for women inmates in Iowa, a state without the death penalty:

> *I have heard that over and over again, they wish that they could end this agony. And they would like to have the death penalty. But that is probably cyclical too because the urge for life is very strong. So when they first come in I hear that a lot, "I wish that I would have gotten the death penalty." But they haven't faced death row so I'm not sure about that. But I just know it's very harsh to face life in prison. (p. 3)*

INNOVATIVE PROGRAMS

To move from the grimmest aspect of penal policy—executions—to the brightest, we now briefly review some laudable innovations within the context of women's imprisonment. Some of the innovations are holistic and structural and woman-centered from top to bottom. The others discussed in this section are piecemeal, positive programs operating against a backdrop of punitiveness and antifeminism. We could refer to these as beacons of light. These types of programs are family centered, cultural, specific, and educational.

We start with two international approaches. First, Denmark, a country with a strong social welfare state and a nonpunitive philosophy toward offenders, maintains a state prison at Ringe that is the prototype of progressivism. As described by Feinman (1994), Denmark's prison accommodates sixty-five young men and twenty-five young women in totally integrated housing. A man and woman are permitted to be alone in each other's rooms until 10:30 at night; they also may entertain spouses or lovers from the outside in their rooms. All prison activities are completely integrated. The Denmark example typifies Scandinavian cultural values, values that promote sexual equality and fewer restrictions on sexuality. For our second example, we look north to Canada.

Feminist Empowering Programs

Canadian culture, although having much in common with that in the United States, is generally regarded as having a more humane social welfare system (see Turner and Turner, 1995). Canada's prison system is less harsh, but the

Canadian Correctional Service has recently gone to great lengths to improve the negative status of women prisoners. Placing female offenders in regional, woman-centered facilities has reduced the pains of imprisonment for these women considerably. Although treatment for female offenders in Canada was not always this good, Shaw (1996) attributes the change to extensive lobbying by feminist and Aborigine (Native Canadian) organizations. A task force, comprising voluntary and governmental members, spelled out five feminist principles on which all future developments should be based. These principles are: empowerment of women; the offering of meaningful choices; respect and dignity; a supportive, healthy living environment; and shared responsibility.

The Canadian approach follows a "special-needs" model as opposed to a gender-neutral one. The special-needs approach for women prisoners caters to women's special needs, such as privacy, self-esteem work, and maintenance of family ties. The gender-neutral model, on the other hand, is exemplified in Denmark's prison programming, which emphasizes gender equality. An outgrowth in the United States of feminist-inspired court cases demanding equality of opportunity (in jobs and vocational training) for female inmates, enforcement of the gender-neutral has led to solutions that, in turn, have created new problems. For example, co-correctional (often called coeducational) establishments have subjected women, who are in the minority, to exploitation by male inmates and guards and to special restrictions on their freedom of movement to prevent sexual activity among inmates.

Hannah-Moffat (1994) argues forcefully against the placing of women in male-oriented facilities. For empowerment of women to occur, she suggests, male and female inmates need programs especially geared toward their needs. Ignoring women's reality is not the way to sexual equality, and the whole notion of incarceration for women needs to be carefully evaluated.

At the Amerswiel women's prison in the Netherlands, the authorities attempt to follow the U.N. Standard Minimum Rules for the Treatment of Prisoners. Davis and Martinez (1996) describe the Dutch model honoring the right to life and integrity of the person as well as respect for one's dignity and family life. In the Netherlands, female inmates have private rooms with a bath and a desk; they can rent luxuries such as a CD player with money they earn working 20 hours a week. The importance of alternatives to incarceration is also stressed by the Dutch government (Ortmann, 1998).

Family Programs

There are a few exemplary prison programs for mothers of small children. Bedford Hills in New York State is the one most written about. (For a recent report, see Boudin, 1998.) The Bedford Hills program provides a nursery where babies up to 18 months old can live with their mothers. A playroom is available for older children, who are encouraged to come and visit with their moms. The mother-child bonding has been excellent in this program; mothers learn child-care skills from child development experts. Political opposition to the program, however, has been constant (Smith, 1997).

The Nebraska Correctional Center for Women, similarly, has a prison nursery and allows overnight visits for older children to maintain the bonds between mother and child. Children can stay up to five days a month. According to the male warden, the presence of children has a harmonizing effect on the whole population (Dowling, 1997).

In Australia, inmate mothers can usually care for their children until they reach the age of 2 or 3. In western Europe, except for Norway (a country that makes extensive use of long-term foster care), children are kept at the prison for up to several years. Germany has, perhaps, the most outstanding prison nursery system. In this program, described by Harris (1988), teachers and social workers help mothers learn how to be good mothers. A California state program allows female prisoners with small children a chance to move to one of seven homes in the state where they can live with their children and take parenting classes. Several hundred women, only a fraction of the mothers in California's prison system, have graduated from the program.

Other family programs involve conjugal rights for prisoners and their spouses. Russian women are entitled to a couple of three-day visits a year with their husbands. In the United States, only eight states allow conjugal visits (Dowling, 1997). At Bedford Hills, families can spend 48-hour periods together in trailers on the campus.

Ethnic-Specific Programs

The Correctional Service of Canada has now endorsed Native Canadians' right to practice Native ceremonies and healing circles. With help from spiritual teachers, Native women have formed healing circles and have revived such practices as fasting; having potlatches; burning sweetgrass, sage, and cedar; and holding medicine bundles (Faith, 1993).

Increasingly, Spanish radio and television programming is available for the influx of Hispanic women entering prison for drug-related offenses. A great deal more needs to be done for Latina inmates with culturally specific programming. For African Americans, also, Afrocentric consciousness-raising is helpful in engendering pride. Many of the newly developed substance abuse programs, imported from the outside by substance counselors, offer cultural-sensitive group counseling sessions for inmates.

SUMMARY

Today, women make up 6 percent of the prison population, and 10 percent of those are confined in jail cells. Although their percentage of the total is small, the increase in the numbers of female inmates has well exceeded the increase for male prisoners, as a study of the latest U.S. government statistics shows.

Race, gender, and class, as we have seen in this chapter, intersect in the reality, indeed, the tragedy, of women's prisons. Viewed another way, one could easily make the argument that the antifeminist and antiwelfare movements are being played out in the courtrooms and prisons of the United States. The War on Drugs has taken its toll on poor minority women and on their children, who are destined to grow up in foster homes while their mothers serve their time.

The euphemisms known as "sentencing reform" and "welfare reform" are not a threat to rich, white women. The few rich, white women one finds behind prison walls are generally there for murder.

The new antidrug laws bring their effects to bear disproportionately on persons without political and legal leverage in U.S. society.

In this chapter, we have seen the circumstances for women in prison come full circle—from confinement in overcrowded, male-run prisons, to removal into maternal reformatories focusing on inmates' moral development, to confinement once again in overcrowded, punitive prisons run by a predominantly male staff. We have turned our attention to two developments in the administration of women's institutions since the 1970s: the rise of prisoner litigation, and the replacement of matrons with male officers.

Today's scandals, which center around sexual abuse and exploitation of female inmates, echo those days gone by when females were originally placed under male authority. Surprisingly, the media, which in the United States have concentrated on the drug war and harsher sentencing laws, seem to have largely overlooked the shocking developments as revealed in the international investigations conducted by Human Rights Watch. In Canada, in contrast, there has been considerable local media coverage of rough treatment of women by male prison officers. In any case, in both countries current litigation has offered prisoners some protection they might not otherwise have had.

In the 1980s, equality for women was the word. In the field of corrections, the focus was on equality of opportunity for female correctional officers in men's prisons and equality of educational and vocational opportunity for male and female offenders. In light of some unintended consequences of the bid for equality, namely, the widespread sexual harassment of female prisoners by male correctional officers (the counterpart of female officers who work without restriction in men's prisons) and the mandatory harsh minimum sentences for drug possession and dealing, women's advocates today are arguing for an empowering feminist approach geared toward women's special needs.

REFERENCES

Aamot, G. (1998, May 24). Pregnant in S.D.? Don't try drinking. *Daily News, Bowling Green, KY,* p. 13A.

Albor, B. J. (1997, July 18). The women behind bars who could go free. *The Independent* (London), p. 10.

Allen, H. E., & Simonsen, C. E. (1995). *Corrections in America: An introduction.* Englewood Cliffs, N.J.: Prentice-Hall.

American Friends Service Committee. (1971). *Struggle for justice: A report on crime and punishment in America.* New York: Hill & Wang.

Barfield, V. (1985). *Woman on death row.* Minneapolis, Minn.: World Wide Publications.

Basu, R. (1998, March 15). What's at work in Iowa prisons? *Des Moines Register,* p. A6.

Bennetto, J. (1997, July 18). The women behind bars who could go free. *The Independent* (London), p. 10.

Boudin, K. (1998). Lessons from a mother's program in prison: A psychosocial approach supports women and their children. *Women and Therapy, 21*(1):103–125.

Brownmiller, S. (1975), *Against our will: Men, women, and rape.* New York: Bantam Books.

Bureau of Justice Statistics. (1997a). Capital punishment 1996. Washington, D.C.: U.S. Department of Justice.

Bureau of Justice Statistics. (1998a). Prison and jail inmates at midyear 1997. Washington, D.C.: U.S. Department of Justice.

Bureau of Justice Statistics. (1998b). *Prisoners in 1997.* Washington, D.C.: U.S. Department of Justice.

Bureau of Justice Statistics. (1994). Women in prison. Washington, D.C.: U.S. Department of Justice.

Carlen, P., and Tchaikovsky, C. (1996). Women's imprisonment in England at the end of the twentieth century: Legitimacy, realities, and utopias. In R. Matthews and P. Francis (eds.), *Prisons 2000* (pp. 179–200). New York: St. Martin's Press.

Carroll, J. (1998, February 4). Tucker executed by lethal injection. *The Irish Times,* p. 1.

Chesney-Lind, M. (1997). *The female offender: Girls, women, and crime.* Thousand Oaks, Calif.: Sage.

Chesney-Lind, M. (1995). Rethinking women's imprisonment: A critical examination of trends in female incarceration. In B. R. Price and N. J. Sokoloff (eds.), *The criminal justice system and women: Offenders, victims, and workers* (pp. 105–117), 2nd ed. New York: McGraw-Hill.

Crites, L. (1976). *The female offender.* Lexington, Mass.: Lexington Books.

Davis, A., and Martinez, E. (1996, May 9). *A conversation on women, culture, and politics.* (Cassette Recording No. 1). San Francisco: Herbst Theater.

Diaz-Cotto, J. (1996). *Gender, ethnicity, and the state: Latina and Latino prison politics.* Albany, N.Y.: New York State University Press.

Donaldson, S. (1995, May). Can we put an end to inmate rape? *USA Today, 123:* 41–42.

Dostoevsky, F. (1969) [1864]. *Notes from the underground.* Washington, D.C.: University Press of America.

Dowling, C. G. (1997, October). Women behind bars. *Life:* 77–90.

Driedger, S. D. (1997, January 27). Showdown of P4W; women are being moved into men's prisons. *Maclean's, 110:* 4.

Duffy, A. (1997, January 24). "Gentle prisons" marked by violence, escape, crowding. *Montreal Gazette,* p. A10.

Erez, E. (1988). The myth of the new female offender: Some evidence from attitudes toward law and justice. *Journal of Criminal Justice, 16:* 499–509.

Faith, K. (1993). *Unruly women: The politics of confinement and resistance.* Vancouver, British Columbia: Press Gang Publishing.

Feinman, C. (1994). *Women in the criminal justice system,* 3rd ed. Westport, Conn.: Praeger.

Fox, J. G. (1984, March). Women's prison policy, prisoner activism, and the impact of the contemporary feminist movement: A case study. *The Prison Journal 64:* 25.

Gable, K., and Johnson, D. (1995). Female criminal offenders. In *Encyclopedia of social work* (pp. 1013–1027), 19th ed. Washington, D.C.: NASW Press.

Gaouette, N. (1997, May 19). Prisons grapple with rapid infux of women—and mothers. *Christian Science Monitor:* 1ff.

Giallombardo, R. (1966). *Society of women: A study of a woman's prison.* New York: Wiley.

Goffman, E. (1961). *Asylums: Essays on the social situation of mental patients and other inmates.* Garden City, N.Y.: Doubleday.

Hairston, C. (1995). Family views in correctional programs. In *Encyclopedia of social work,* 19th ed. (pp. 991–996). Washington D.C.: NASW Press.

Hannah-Moffat, K. (1994, January). Unintended consequences of feminism and prison reform. *Forum in Corrections Research, 6*(1): 1–4.

Harris, J. (1988). *They always call us ladies: Stories from prison.* New York: Zebra Books.

Hart, C. B. (1995). Gender differences in social support among inmates. *Women and Criminal Justice 6:* 67–68.

Hughes, R. (1987). *The fatal shore: The epic of Australia's founding.* New York: Alfred A. Knopf.

Hugill, B. (1997, August 3). Nightmare of teenage girls held. *The Observer,* p. 1.

Human Rights Watch Women's Rights Project (1996). *All too familiar: Sexual abuse of women in U.S. state prisons.* New York: Human Rights Watch.

Irish Times. (1998, February 5). Robinson critical of U.S. execution of double killer.

Irwin, J. (1980). *Prisons in turmoil.* Boston: Little, Brown.

Jones, A. (1980). *Women who kill.* New York: Holt, Rinehart & Winston.

Kassindja, F. (1998). *Do they hear you when you cry?* New York: Delacorte Press.

Knight, B. B. (1992). Women in prison as litigants: Prospects for post-prison futures. *Women and Criminal Justice 4:* 91–116.

Kopatich, K. (1998, May 8). Interviewed by social work student Lynette Keefe at the women's prison in Mitchellville, Iowa.

Kurshan, N. (1996). Behind the walls: The history and current reality of women's imprisonment. In E. Rosenblatt (ed.), *Criminal injustice: Confronting the prison crisis* (pp. 116–164). Boston: South End Press.

Laster, K. (1994). Arbitrary chivalry: Women and capital punishment in Victoria, Australia 1842–1967. *Women and Criminal Justice, 6*(1): 67–95.

LeBlanc, A. N. (1996, June 2). A woman behind bars is not a dangerous man. *New York Times Magazine,* 34–40.

Lewis, W. D. (1965). *From Newgate to Dannemora.* Ithaca, N.Y.: Cornell University Press.

Lomax, A. (1998, May). Prison jobs and free world unemployment. *Prison Legal News,* 14.

Martin, M. (1997). Connected mothers: A follow-up study of incarcerated women and their children. *Women and Criminal Justice 8:* 1–23.

Moir, A., and Jessel, D. (1991). *Brain sex: The real difference between men and women.* New York: Delta.

National Crime Prevention Council Canada (1995, September). Offender profiles: Prevention and Children Committee.

New York Times. (1992, November 14), pp. 1, 7.

O'Mahony, P. (1994). The Irish psyche imprisoned. *The Irish Journal of Psychology 15*(2/3): 456–468.

Ortmann, D. (1998). Mothers behind the walls. *Social Work Perspectives, 8*(1): 58–62.

O'Shea, K. (1998, May 25). *Women on the Row* (Special issue based on an online discussion): 1–18.

O'Shea, K. (1999). *Women and the death penalty in the United States, 1900–1998.* Westport, Conn.: Greenwood Press.

Owen, B. (1998). *In the mix: Struggle and survival in a women's prison.* Albany, N.Y.: State University of New York Press.

Pate, K. (1998, August 20). E-mail correspondence with Katherine van Wormer, p. 1.

Pollock, J. M. (1998). *Counseling women in prison.* Thousand Oaks, Calif.: Sage.

Prison Legal News. (1998a, May). Bureau of prisons sexual abuse suit settled for $500,000. *Prison Legal News,* p. 9.

Prison Legal News. (1995). New stateside data show prison rape a widespread problem. *Prison Legal News 6*(11), 17.

Seymour, B. (1998, June 4). Personal correspondence from Franklin Pre-Release, Columbus, Ohio.

Shaw, M. (1994). Women in prison: A literature review. *Forum in Corrections Research 6*(1): 1–7.

Siegal, N. (1998). Women in prison: The number of women serving time behind bars has increased dramatically. *Ms Magazine 9*(2): 64–73.

Smith, T. (1997, October). *Sunday Edition.* National Public Radio.

Stein, B. (1996, July). Life in prison: Sexual abuse. *The Progressive:* 23–24.

Thompson, C. (1997, autumn). The invisibility of women on death row: A personal view. *Lifelines Ireland, 3*(3): 3.

Tracy, Smith, and Steurer, S. J. (1998, April). Standing up for education. *Corrections Today:* 144–145, 156.

Turner, J. C., and Turner, F. J. (eds.). (1995). *Canadian social welfare,* 3rd ed. Scarborough, Ontario: Allyn and Bacon Canada.

Tyler, K. (1998, June 10). Personal correspondence from Iowa Correctional Institute for Women.

van Wormer, K. (1995). Execution-inspired murder: A form of suicide. *Journal of Offender Rehabilitation, 23*(3/4): 1–10.

van Wormer, K. (1987). Female prison families: How are they dysfunctional? *International Journal of Comparative and Applied Criminal Justice, 11*(2): 263–271.

Walker, S. (1980). *Popular justice: A history of American criminal justice.* New York: Oxford University Press.

Watterson, K. (1996). *Women in prison: Inside the concrete womb.* Boston: Northeastern University Press.

Weisheit, R., and Mahan, S. (1988). *Women, crime, and criminal justice.* Cincinnati, Ohio: Anderson.

PART III

WOMEN AS VICTIMS AND SURVIVORS

Whether a woman is subjected to one-time rape by a stranger or to a pattern of brutality by a family member, the emotional scars will be with her always. Although women have more social and legal rights now than at any other time in history, vestiges of the old attitudes still prevail. Given the natural tendency to blame the victim, combined with a backlash against women's advancement, these antiwoman, antivictim attitudes continue to rear their ugly heads.

The victimization of women at the personal level is matched by the oppression of women in the wider society. Chapter 5 focuses on the crime of rape. The very existence of this crime has unique ramifications for all girls and women everywhere. The amount of compassion and respect accorded the victims of this crime is a barometer of a society's regard for women in general. Woman hating is at the heart of both rape and battering; rape can be construed as assault that is sexualized, and partner violence often includes sexual abuse.

Chapter 6 examines victimization closer to home and more enduring—battering or wife (partner) abuse. Both forms of victimization—rape and battering—are about power and humiliation; they are both about male dominance and female subordination. The essence of the male power structure is further reflected in paternalistic courtroom practices concerning these crimes. The criminal justice system itself can be seen as an instrument of control and one that reflects women's economic and political station in society. It is through the great awakening that took place among women of the 1970s, women who had been seasoned through protests for peace and social justice of that era, that we recognize rape and battering

83

for what they are. Before that time women were consistently blamed for causing their own victimization. Many are still blamed and blame themselves for their mistreatment. An empowerment approach is crucial to helping such women find their own voices, in the first instance to articulate their pain, and in the second, to share their insights with others. Consistent with feminist tradition, the word *victim* is used to denote a person who has sustained an injury and *survivor* for one who has lived through and is attempting to heal from an assault. Survivorship is a state of empowerment; victimhood is not. Together, these chapters offer a framework for empowerment therapy, a framework for helping people move from a position of "I am a victim" to "I am a survivor" or, better yet, "We are survivors."

4

RAPE

In Chapter 3 we learned of the tremendous overlap between early childhood sexual abuse and the later development of addiction in women. Women under the influence of intoxication are especially vulnerable to sexual exploitation and rape. Chapter 3 also explored the link between women's victimization in society—sexually, economically, and personally—and their criminality. Then we saw how once in prison many women become retraumatized by the invasive strip searches sometimes performed by male guards that are a part of the prison regime. Direct incidents of guard-inmate violations were described. Now we come to a look at rape in the community, a crime that is always anti-woman, even when it is practiced by men against men.

Martha Ramsey (1995) was raped at age 13. There was one brief moment of openness between her mother and herself, then nothing. Now after two decades, she has decided to "speak about this hurt that people do not want to hear about" (p. 105). Returning to the police station after all these years, she thanks the detective whose kindness meant so much to her. "I remember you as being very sensitive and gentle," she says (p. 105). They both cry.

Raped thirty-four years ago, Gerry Cummins, a white woman, reluctantly gave the mixed-race baby up. And now, her grown daughter comes looking for her roots, only to discover that she was a child of rape. Still the reunion of mother and daughter is wonderful. "My life is now complete," the mother says (O'Neill, 1996, p. 98).

Gang raped at a northern New York State bar by five men, Krista Absalom, a single mother, was too drunk at the time of the rape to remember events clearly. Although the case was clear-cut, the jury let the men off because of the victim's drinking. Feminists are outraged. Today a civil case is pending against the men (Jensen, 1996).

These incidents, drawn from popular literature, offer just a glimpse of the many ramifications of the crime of rape. In addition to the ones we have mentioned, there are also the risk of AIDS, the intrusive fears and nightmares, and the enduring sexual problems.

The word *rape* comes by way of the Anglo-Norman *raper* from the Latin *rapere,* to seize by force (Ayto, 1990, p. 431). Legally, the definition of rape varies by state. The National Crime Victimization Survey (Bureau of Justice Statistics, 1997), the most reliable source of data on this highly unreported crime, defines *forcible rape* as "forced sexual intercourse where the victim may be either male or female and offender may be of the same sex or a different sex from the victim" (p. 5). Some states continue to restrict the definition of rape to crimes against a female. *Sexual assault* includes a wide range of victimizations involving attacks in which unwanted sexual contact occurs between the victim and the offender.

To the victim, rape is a painful violation of the self. The humiliation of the act leads to a secrecy that, in itself, can further maximize a sense of shame in the person violated. To be raped is to enter unwittingly the bizarre sisterhood of the victimized, a sisterhood in which the membership is secret, often even among individual victims. The reality of having been unable to fight the attacker off is haunting. The reality of being physically defiled and sexually scarred may stay with a woman forever. The trial, if there is one, instead of bringing catharsis or even closure, reopens the old wounds and subjects the victim to new wounds of public accusation and labeling. To offset the trauma and promote healing, intensive counseling should be provided to all rape victims, especially in the early period of the aftermath of the crime. Because victims of this type of crime often find the circumstances unmentionable—no one wants to hear about it—survivor self-help groups can be a godsend. Fortunately today, through the work of rape crisis lines and victim assistance programs, the help that is needed, at least for adults, is widely available.

To glimpse how rape victims were treated yesterday versus the way they are treated today, we begin this chapter with a historical overview. Then, the prevalence of rape and the impact of the mass media are discussed. From the victim's standpoint, we look at types of rape, including acquaintance rape, mass rape, and child sexual abuse. The chapter concludes by revealing the criminal justice response and with a discussion of an empowerment approach for work with survivors of this type of crime.

HISTORICAL OVERVIEW

In terms of official treatment, there has never been a time of greater sensitivity to the needs of rape victims than today. Campaigns by women's groups and rape crisis centers worldwide have resulted in significant changes in the law and legal procedures in relation to sexual offenses against women. To know how much better the climate is now, let us look at how things were before the mid 1970s, when feminist voices began to make themselves heard. After that time, victims of rape still had it rough, but never again would they be so alone.

We begin with the law. The law always reflects social values. In our recent past, a rape victim's behavior before the claim of rape, her behavior during the sexual encounter, and her relationship to the perpetrator were often all taken into consideration by legal officials in deciding whether a "real" rape occurred. Until the 1970s, the law in most states recognized that a rape occurred only when a man forced a woman to have sex under the threat of injury, when she had resisted strenuously, and when there was outside corroboration (Maschke, 1997).

To understand these traditions we need to go back centuries to a time when a man who wanted a woman simply raped her and brought her into his tribe (Flowers, 1987). Later, the status of women as property was embodied in custom and law. Rape entered the law as a property crime of man against man; women were the property (Brownmiller, 1975). Indeed, rape has been a part of war in most societies throughout history. Rape within marriage, of course, was considered an oxymoron. Only in recent years, in fact, has marital rape come to be recognized in some places as a crime.

In the decades before Brownmiller (1975), Burgess and Holmstrom (1974), and Griffin (1971) revolutionized the concept of rape by desexualizing it, virtually no research was done on this form of female victimization. In the 1960s, for example, there were a few studies on sexual deviance that focused exclusively on the stranger-rapist. The rapist was characterized as a sexual psychopath who was unable to control his urges (Donat and D'Emilio, 1992). The word *rape* was rarely spoken in polite circles. From the earliest age, girls were merely warned in hushed tones against strangers who might try to lure them away with candy to "do terrible things to them." At the same time, virginity in the unmarried female was a requirement for successful marriage; women who were sexually violated were said to be "ruined" and "damaged goods." Compounding the problem, psychoanalytical theory maintained that girls and women unconsciously desired to be raped (Brownmiller, 1975).

African American Women and Rape

Whether they were raped by white men as a legacy of slavery (there was no way a slave could resist a master's advances) or by their black brothers, African American women have learned to be silent about sexual assault. Stereotypes of hypersexual African Americans grew out of the slavery era ethos (Robinson, 1997). The protection of the white woman's virtue became the rationalization for brutalizing black men and women. The rape of African American women has been given little or no attention by the larger society. For a black woman to accuse a black man of raping or sexually harassing her (as Anita Hill did Clarence Thomas) is to risk attack within her own community for speaking out against one of her own kind. As a survivor wanting to end this legacy of silence in the black community, Lori Robinson courageously tells us:

> *I guess more than anything, what I carry with me and walk out of this valley in my life is a commitment to help end the silence. A close male mentor of my family could not bring himself to speak to me about my rape for an*

*entire year. The last time we were both together was at Spelman on my grad-
uation day.*

*I have learned that he cried when told about my rape. I wonder how it
would have been if we had cried—and healed—together. (p. 53)*

In a recent survey of readers of an African American news magazine, 89
percent of respondents perceived that African American females report acts of
sexual violence less frequently than do white females (*Emerge,* 1997). The primary reason given is the fear of not being believed. Distrust of the authorities
compounds the reluctance to tell (McNair and Neville, 1996).

Reconceptualization of Rape

Until recent times, a woman who engaged in sex outside marriage, even
against her will, was considered a "fallen" woman and often was blamed for
her own victimization (Donat and D'Emilio, 1992). An unmarried woman
who wished to prosecute her rapist had to have a good reputation without
any previous sexual experience to get a conviction for the rapist. The victim,
not the defendant, was on trial; the typical caution to the jury was that the
charge of rape was easy to make and hard to disprove. Few cases were prosecuted, and for those that were, the conviction rate was very low. In 1972, in
Chicago, for example, of more than 3,000 reported rapes fewer than 1 percent
resulted in jail terms (Deckard, 1983).

Some of the early research on rape, even after 1970, played into victim-
blaming. The publication of Menachem Amir's *Patterns in Forcible Rape* (1971)
marked the first sociological study of its kind. This investigation of *victim-
precipitated* crime was very influential in criminological circles and much studied throughout the next decade.

About the same time, the feminist movement offered a framework for
viewing male-on-female violence that was to turn the conceptualization of
rape upside-down and to be a complete eye-opener to men and women both.
For the first time, sexual assault was redefined from the victim's and society's
perspective. Rape was seen as the violence that it is. Through the efforts of the
antirape movement, it would soon become clear that such violence against
women is one more mechanism for male social control (Schechter, 1982). In
a landmark article entitled "Rape—The All American Crime," Susan Griffin
(1971) articulated for the movement how rape and the fear of rape work to
keep women dependent on men. Rape was recognized in this article, among
others, as an act about domination and control, not sex.

The work of such feminists such as Brownmiller and Griffin has further
helped us to conceive of rape not in either-or terms but as a series of acts along
a continuum. Far from being an isolated event that could be rooted out from
the society at large, the crime of rape was now seen as only the logical extension of what was there already. Walker and Brodsky (1976), for example, spoke

of the forms of sexual harassment that were commonplace, the "little rapes" that ranged from teasing and innuendos to making unwelcome sexual advances. Considered fair game, women were targeted as legitimate objects of sexual aggression. Unless protected by a man, a woman's personal territory could be violated by suggestion and intimation.

According to the feminist school, the violation to the self caused by everyday whistles and unsolicited greetings on the street is but one aspect of the cultural perspective that defines women as objects and men as possessors. And in the spectrum of male behavior, rape violence is the penultimate violent act (Griffin, 1971).

PREVALENCE

Thanks to recent incentives to gather extensive data about sex offenders, the U.S. Department of Justice has prepared a special report analyzing data on rape and sexual assault (Bureau of Justice Statistics, 1997). This report draws on crimes known to the police as well as reports from national corrections and victimization surveys. Among the survey's most significant findings:

- In a high percentage of cases, the victims are children; teenagers report the highest exposure to rape and sexual assault according to self-reports. Police reports revealed that 44 percent of rape victims were under age 18. Convicts report similar rates with nearly 4 in 10 saying their victims were age 12 or younger.
- In child rapes, 90 percent knew the offender.
- Offenders tended to be white and over age 30.
- In 1995 about half of all reported rapes were cleared by an arrest. Yet only 32 percent of rapes were reported to the police.
- Nearly 6 out of 10 self-reported incidents occurred in the home or at the home of a friend.
- Three out of four rape/sexual assault victimizations involved offenders with whom the victims had a prior relationship as a family member, intimate, or acquaintance.
- Strangers were involved in 76 percent of victimizations involving multiple offenders. This was about 7 percent of all victimizations.
- Law enforcement agencies indicated that 8 percent of reported rapes were unfounded.
- About half of those arrested for rape were convicted, and most of those convicted entered a guilty plea.
- Victims of rape were about evenly divided between whites and African Americans; about 88 percent of rapes were intraracial.
- About 12 percent of rapes involved use of a weapon.

- About 19 percent of rapists were rearrested for a new felony within 3 years.
- Since the 1980s, the percentage of rape-murders (for which rape was the predominant circumstance) declined from 2 percent of murders to less than 1 percent.

Byington (1995) offers insight into the high number of rape cases plea-bargained to lesser charges: Rape victims understandably are anxious to avoid the humiliation of a public trial, including vigorous cross-examination by the defense attorney, and therefore often do not press for a trial. The relatively low conviction rate for sexual crimes against adult women is a further factor in the prosecutor's willingness to settle such a case through negotiations with the accused's attorney. A figure not given in the BJS report is the percentage of women victimized by rape in their lifetimes. Victimization rates for Latinas, Asian Americans, and Native Americans are also lacking. Until now, empirical data on the relationship between certain types of violence against women, such as childhood victimization, and subsequent adult victimization have been limited.

To further our understanding of violence against women, the National Violence Against Women Survey, under the sponsorship of the federal government, conducted a national survey of 8,000 men and 8,000 women. Among the key findings: 1 out of 7 women and 1 out of 48 men has been raped over his or her lifetime; twice as many girls raped before age 18 were raped after the age of 18 as women who were not raped in childhood; and the typical female rape victim is a child (Tjaden and Thoennes, 1998, pp. 3, 6).

The National Violence Against Women Survey also clarified racial and ethnic differences. American Indians disclosed a higher rate of rape and physical assault than women of other racial/ethnic backgrounds, while Asian/Pacific Islander women were significantly less likely to report rape and physical assault. However, among Asian Americans sexual assault may be underreported because of the sense of shame this crime brings to the victims and their families (Tseuneyoshi, 1996).

Hispanic women in the national survey reported a lower rate of rape victimization than did non-Hispanic women. Previous studies have produced contradictory findings on this score. A survey of Mexican Americans in Los Angeles found that Anglos had two and one-half times the rate of sexual assault as Mexican Americans (Sorenson and Siegel, 1992). Reasons given for the lower rate were the greater sense of community as well as the protective restrictions on Mexican American females.

A review of literature reveals that, not surprisingly, more men than women (Crowell and Burgess, 1996) and boys than girls (Cowan and Campbell, 1995) subscribe to rape myths. A number of studies have found a significant association between acceptance of rape myths in men and self-reported sexually aggressive behavior (Koss, Leonard, Beezley, and Oros, 1985; Reilly, Lott, Caldwell, and Deluca, 1992). For a number of rape myths, see Box 4.1.

BOX 4.1 Rape Myths

What are rape myths? Basically they are false beliefs that are refuted by the statistics provided in this chapter. Typical rape myths are:

- Most rape claims are false; women feel guilty about sex and redefine the situation later.
- Rape happens only to bad women such as prostitutes.
- Unconsciously, women want to be raped.

- Most rape is committed by a stranger in a dark alley.
- When women say no, they mean yes.
- Women's wearing of seductive clothes causes rape.
- Rapes are impulsive acts committed by men unable to control their passions.
- Rapes are black-on-white crimes.
- Rape is caused by male deviance and pathology.

IMPACT OF THE MASS MEDIA

The impact of the television drama *Something about Amelia,* first shown on MTV in 1984, is hard to describe. The subject was incest in a middle-class family. Extensive coverage was given to this production in the general mass media and in specialized newletters for the counseling professions. The interest of professionals was heightened, no doubt because of the central role given to family therapy in the film. In the drama, when the incest is discovered, the father, not the daughter, is removed from the home. Then intensive professional attention is devoted to this family in crisis. Following the broadcast there was a flurry of phone calls to hotlines and children protective services. A few years later when Israeli television aired this startling and well-acted program, the impact was similarly sensational (Oppenheimer, 1998).

When the movie *The Accused* hit the screens in 1988, it was another first of sorts: at last, a portrayal of the difficulty of prosecuting a gang-rape case from the point of view of the victim! Portrayed convincingly by Jodie Foster, the victim meets her fate while she is drinking at a bar. *The Accused* is based on a true story of a working-class Portuguese woman from New Bedford, Massachusetts, who brought criminal charges against Portuguese onlookers who cheered as she was raped. In her heroic fight for justice, the survivor emerges as victor, and the prosecutor learns something about courage and determination. It is a sad commentary that when the movie was first shown, some young men in the audience hooted and cheered at the rape scene (Faludi, 1991). The real victim on which *The Accused* was based was condemned by her community for the negative attention brought on them by the crime. She died of alcoholism several years later.

As Faludi suggests in her book *Backlash* (1991), it is a sad day when a sympathetic portrait of a rape victim is hailed as a daring feminist statement. Yet this portrayal is certainly an improvement over the way Hollywood dealt with rape in the past. In *Gone With the Wind,* which was released in 1939, Rhett Butler forces his attentions on Scarlett, who has been "getting out of hand." Although frightened at the time, the next day she wakes up in her luxurious bed humming. Mammy comments that she looks extra cheerful this morning, and Scarlett grins ear to ear. Contrast this with *A Streetcar Named Desire,* the Tennessee Williams masterpiece that was produced as a movie in 1951. The class and sexual tensions between Stanley (played by Marlon Brando) and Blanche (Vivien Leigh) result in a climactic rape scene. (This scene was watered down for the movie.) Sinking into the chasm of mental illness, the violated sister-in-law is taken away. Perhaps because of his sexual orientation or artistry, Tennessee Williams handled the rape with a rare sensitivity.

Newspaper coverage of rape cases has tended to be sensationalized when they involve celebrities, fraternity members, or athletic teams. In recent years, some women courageously have identified themselves publicly and spoken out, an event practically unheard of before the 1980s. Rape victims, in fact, have been "in the closet" far more than gays and lesbians have been, and male victims remain the most hidden of all. Rape is a crime unlike any other; the sordidness of the crime somehow attaches to the unwilling party as much as to the instigator and sometimes even more so.

Racism is evident not only in the reduced prosecution of cases of African American victimization but also in mass media accounts. Media attention rarely focuses on African American victims of crime (Rollins, 1996). Outrage seems to be reserved for white victims, especially those of high socioeconomic status. Rollins cites the case of a white jogger who was raped and set on fire by a group of black youths. This case was the talk of the media for months. Meanwhile, comparable cases of inner-city victimization were largely ignored.

Paralleling the growth of two revolutionary developments from the late 1970s—feminism and the self-help movement—reports of childhood sexual abuse rose to prominence. A deluge of newspaper articles, books, and television movies appeared in North America and western Europe. Political progress in child welfare has historically been linked to the success of feminism, and the fact that women are disproportionately victims of sexual abuse has cemented the linkage in the modern period (Finkelhor, 1994). When feminists joined forces with child welfare professionals, who tend for the most part to be trained in social work, child protection advocacy got off the ground. Despite a formidable backlash against false accusations in recent years, there is a public and professional awareness of the exploitation of children that did not exist in previous decades. The Canadian press is inundated with reports of court cases involving child molesters who were in positions of authority, such as priests and teachers.

Blaming the Victim

A counterforce to feminist awareness of the personal as political, one related to society's antifeminist backlash, is the age-old blame-the-victim phenomenon. Writing a *Time* cover story on the new feminism, Bellafonte (1998) chides the new feminism which "has come to seem divorced from matters of public purpose" and obsessed with celebrity, the body, and image (p. 60). The postfeminists seek to get beyond an ideology of victimhood into an awareness of their sexual power over men; men are simply untamable according to this view. Feminism today, claims Bellafonte, is "wed to the culture of celebrity and self-obsession" (p. 57).

Denial of the suffering of victims can be understood not only in terms of current trends, but also because the natural social-psychological tendency has been always to belittle the load that others carry and to look away from others' pain. We do not want to see the homeless, hear the complaints of those on welfare, and certainly not hear of bad things happening to good people. A concept derived from social psychology, victim-blaming refers to a fundamental tendency in American culture to hold the downtrodden or underdogs of society responsible for creating their own distress (Zastrow, 1996). Because of the reciprocity involved, the victim tends to internalize the blame attached to his or her condition ("I have failed"), and the negativity may become a self-fulfilling prophecy ("I am a tainted person").

In an article aptly titled "All the World Loathes a Loser," Lerner (1971) indicates our vulnerability to the suffering of other people: We are vulnerable though only to the suffering of a hero. Condemning the victim (of crime, of disease, of a bad relationship) is a process that takes its place in a long series of American ideologies that have rationalized cruelty and injustice (Ryan, 1971).

The fact is that the closer we try to identify ourselves with victims, the more vulnerable we are to their suffering. Although we have a tendency to put ourselves in the place of someone who is suffering, there is also the counter-tendency to believe that the unfortunate victim in some sense merited his or her fate. In the case of crimes of personal violation, we attach a stigma to the victim almost out of fear of contamination. Accordingly, we may develop an unfavorable perception of a rape victim and are apt to reject her.

In a survey of 200 undergraduate students at Kent State University in the early 1980s, van Wormer found that although the majority of respondents did not blame the rape victim, some students attributed blame to the victims of rape far more than they did victims of non–person-oriented crimes. More negative reaction was expressed by males than females toward sexual offense victims. Male students reacted intensely to two possibilities: their own victimization by a fellow male and knowledge that their mothers had once been raped or were victims of incest. They often had no response to the former possibility (two students wrote in that they'd kill the guy). Regarding knowledge that their mother was sexually abused, over half did not wish to know that this happened. A replication of this study in 1998 with another 200 students at the University of Northern Iowa revealed few gender differences and less victim-blaming, but a strong male reluctance to reveal their own victimization persisted.

Because of the myth that the typical rapist looks like a rapist—rough and disheveled in appearance—blame is transferred to the victim if the accused rapist defies the stereotype. This is what happened in the crime documentary *Our Guys* (Lefkowitz, 1997), a work that has stirred up much talk in criminology circles. *Our Guys* stands as an indictment of suburbia where when the high school jocks are charged with sexual crimes; the entire community turns the other way. As Lefkowitz writes:

> *What kind of place was Glen Ridge anyway? A large group of charismatic athletes. A retarded young woman. The silence of the students and adults. The inclination to blame the woman and exonerate the men. These elements seemed to be linked by a familiar theme in my life in journalism. I began to frame Glen Ridge as a story of power and powerlessness: The power of young males and the community that venerated them, and the powerlessness of one marginalized young woman. (pp. 2–3)*

Lefkowitz found in Glen Ridge a microcosm of the affluent small town, a town where girls were labeled in distinct categories and treated accordingly. "Little mothers" provided tea and sympathy; other girls served as party decorations, and still others were targeted for a blend of sexual release and abuse. Girls who were targeted received vulgar nicknames by the boys; such girls were used sexually, then passed on to the boys' friends. The surprising aspect of the rape of the brain-injured girl was that arrests were made and convictions followed. What is not surprising, given our knowledge of victim-blaming, is that the town rallied around the accused jocks, "our guys." Following the arrests, the townspeople spoke of the tragedy that had befallen these boys, a tragedy that would scar them forever: "In the bosom of their hometown, they were greeted like returning warriors who had prevailed in a noble crusade. Or, if you prefer, martyred heroes" (p. 5).

Some have argued that the tremendous effort we put into teaching aggression to athletes leads to an increase in aggressive behavior off the field (Schwartz and DeKeseredy, 1997). In an age of sports hero idolatry, star athletes get the message that they can break the law with impunity and that a certain amount of violence against women will be tolerated. This message protects star athletes from taking responsibility. It sets girls and women up for abuse and denigration.

Compounding the victim-blaming ethos is the social-psychological phenomenon called *erotophobia,* or fear and ambivalence concerning sex. Erotophobia is unconsciously conveyed to children so that they will have the socially acceptable inhibitions to keep them from being a source of embarrassment to their parents in polite company. Foremost among the challenging tasks of growing up is to unlearn some of the inhibitions that one so conscientiously has been taught. Even learning the language of sexuality presents difficulties; one must employ a different vocabulary in different circles. In adulthood, a vague feeling that sex is dirty may persist (see van Wormer,

Wells, and Boes, 1999). If problems exist in dealing with sex as a part of making love, the problems of dealing with sex under forced and frightening circumstances, sometimes with multiple violators, are insurmountable.

Erotophobia combined with victim-blaming even affects our handling of cases involving children. Our revulsion against sexual contact with children causes us to distance ourselves from child molesters in treatment, those who provide the treatment, and even children who claim to have been sexually abused. The result, according to Baartman (1998), is that almost all who hear of these situations feel an automatic inclination to look for arguments that contradict the accusations.

TYPES OF RAPE

The types of rape that occur most frequently are acquaintance rape, mass rape, and child abuse or sexual abuse. (Marital rape is discussed in connection with wife abuse in Chapter 5).

Acquaintance Rape

Acquaintance rape is any rape in which the parties know one another. Included in this definition are date rape, campus rape, and partner or marital rape. Stranger rape was thought at one time to be the most common form of sexual violence. Yet, thanks to self-report surveys of both men and women, we now know that most victims know their rapists. Acquaintance rape is extremely common on college campuses.

In one midwestern survey, 100 percent of all rapists knew their victims (Meyer, 1990). *Rape in America,* a report issued by the National Victims Center (1992), found that only 22 percent of all women in the national sample who had been raped were assaulted by strangers. Friends, neighbors, boyfriends, husbands, ex-husbands, and relatives headed the list of perpetrators. In-depth interviews with a random sample of 420 women in Toronto revealed that of those who had been sexually assaulted after age 16, 58 percent were assaulted by husbands, boyfriends, or dates (Randall and Haskell, 1995).

When rape occurs in a dating relationship, it does not necessarily lead to the breakup of the relationship. The likelihood of multiple experiences of forced sex increases substantially if the rapist is a woman's husband or lover (Kelly, 1988). In many women's minds, the boundaries between rape and strong pressure to have sex are unclear. For this reason, rape surveys often ask if respondents were "forced to have sex" instead of "raped" for greater accuracy in results (Koss et al., 1985).

Kelly conducted in-depth interviews with sixty English women volunteers who had experienced sexual violence. Her book, *Surviving Sexual Violence* (1988), is a study of how women cope and survive very bitter experiences with men. Her illustrations of women's reactions to bad experiences across the spectrum of sexual violence are gripping. For instance:

> *"I didn't say no, I didn't dare to . . . you know you don't want to, but you are still doing it. That's why in my eyes now it's rape with consent. It's rape because it's pressurized, but you do it because you don't feel you can say no."*
>
> *"I remember an occasion where he wouldn't let me get up, and he was very strong. He pulled my arms over my head. I didn't put up much of a struggle. I mean I wouldn't have seen that as rape because I associated rape with strangers, night and struggle. I didn't put up much of a struggle, but I didn't want to, so in a sense that was rape, yes." (p. 113)*

Although sexual aggression in dating relationships has been studied for more than thirty years, most U.S. citizens still have problems accepting that rape can occur among friends and especially among intimates (Wallace, 1998). Cases of forced sex when there have previously been sexual relations are rarely reported and, if they are reported, they are rarely prosecuted. Many campus rapes are handled internally through student conduct board hearings. One advantage of this process is that the perpetrator is forced to admit his bad behavior under threat of otherwise having the matter turned over to the police. This may spare victims the agony of the adversarial process and allow the perpetrator to "come clean." Typical in-house punishments are probation, suspension, and substance abuse counseling.

Date rape is commonly viewed as less serious and less traumatic than rape by a stranger. Whether or not this is the case, date rape has significant consequences for women. Shapiro and Schwartz (1997) determined, in a study of forty-one college women who had been date raped, that when compared to those who had not been victimized, the former showed more trauma symptoms and lower sexual self-esteem than the latter. Similarly, Kowalski (1995) found that the emotional effects of acquaintance rape are profound and that appropriate intervention is crucial.

Who is vulnerable to rape, and how can rape be avoided? In fact, all women are vulnerable to rape. Factors associated with avoiding stranger rape, according to Rollins (1996), are being tall, having been the oldest daughter, and having had major household responsibilities, all factors associated with assertiveness. Based on a survey of studies of women who escaped their attackers, Rollins recommends physical resistance, screaming, and reasoning with the rapist, but not pleading or arguing with him. African American women, she notes, are most likely to avoid rape by having "street smarts" in dangerous situations. Surveys of convicted rapists indicate they stalk potential victims first, noting how women carry themselves as they walk. Those who seem weak and fearful are singled out as likely targets.

One area of much public concern has been the growing use of the drug Rohypnol ("roofies") to sedate women to take sexual advantage of them on dates. Mixed with alcohol, the drug makes the victim easy prey. Prosecution is difficult because the victim typically suffers from drug-induced amnesia. Actually, alcohol has been used successfully by men for years to achieve the same results. "Candy is dandy, but liquor is quicker" goes the saying.

The fact that acquaintance rape is rampant on college campuses and that stereotypical stranger rape is relatively rare outside so-called high-crime areas has important implications for prevention. College rape prevention efforts are devoted to blue lights all over the campus, student escort services, and warnings to women about how to avoid rape. Zero attention is paid to date rape (Schwartz and DeKeseredy, 1997). Efforts would be better spent on education and on men educating men about the risks of aggressive masculinity and objectification of women. Because of the alcohol abuse typically present on college campuses, stepped-up substance abuse prevention efforts could be immensely helpful as well.

Mass Rape

Susan Brownmiller's landmark study, *Against Our Will: Men, Women, and Rape* (1975) put the crime in an international and cultural perspective. She defined rape as "a conscious process of intimidation by which all men keep all women in a state of fear" (p. 5). As a collective act, rape can promote male bonding. Among adolescent boys and gangs of bikers, rape is a ritual of manhood. In an anthropological study of fraternity gang rape, Sanday (1990) argues that the sexual and drinking practices of fraternities on American university campuses encourage gang rape. Sorority women therefore are at heightened risk for attack. Gang rape and rape of the enemy's women in war are documented extensively in this study.

In their book, *Sexual Assault on the College Campus* (1997), Schwartz and DeKeseredy probe what they term the "hypererotic subculture" that permeates the college scene. Men socialized into this subculture regard sex in terms of gaining possession of a woman. The more "girls you can have sex with," in fact, the better (p. 35). "Frat" house conformity combined with strong peer-group pressure to "score" leads some to experience a sense of relative deprivation. As Schwartz and DeKeseredy thoughtfully suggest, "the frustration caused by a reference group–anchored sex drive often results in predatory sexual conduct" (p. 35). All-male alliances can reduce sexual intercourse to a violent power game, one that says more about relationships between men and their brothers than between men and women.

Where there is hostility between enemies, women are particularly subject to predatory attack. Although rare, interracial sexual assault can take on political overtones. Such attacks against women can serve to "get at" an entire racial or ethnic group. Writing in his autobiography, *Soul on Ice*, Eldridge Cleaver (1968) showed little respect for his black sisters as he declared:

> *I became a rapist. To refine my technique and* modus operandi, *I started out by practicing on black girls in the ghetto. . . and when I considered myself smooth enough, I crossed the tracks and sought out white prey. (p. 26)*

The dynamics of wartime rape are similar. General George Patton is quoted by Brownmiller (1975) as follows, "I then told them that, in spite of my most diligent efforts, there would unquestionably be some raping" (p. 23). General Patton was speaking from experience and from his knowledge of history. Rape is more than an accident of war. Its widespread use under military occupation reflects the special terror it holds for the enemy's women. It also reflects the inequalities and discrimination women face in their everyday lives in peacetime (Amnesty International, 1995).

Mass rape of women by conquering warriors is so much a part of conquest that it is more remarkable in its absence than in its presence. In the battles of ancient Greece, the Crusades, the U.S. Civil War, World Wars I and II, and the Vietnam War, rape was used as a physical and psychological weapon of war (Wing and Merchan, 1993). In the Civil War, Union soldiers were said to have raped former slave women as they plundered towns and plantations (Wyatt, 1997). The rape that accompanies war is both a tremendous act of aggression and humiliation against a conquered people and a reward to soldiers who are encouraged by their officers to loot villages and rape the women at will. Rape is the act of patriotism, misogyny, and lust rolled into one (van Wormer, 1997). In the name of victory and the power of the gun, war provides men with a tacit license to rape (Brownmiller, 1975). In her analysis of rape in warfare, Brownmiller does not mince words:

> *Sexual sadism arises with astonishing rapidity in ground warfare, when the penis becomes justified as a weapon in a logistical reality of unarmed non-combatants, encircled and trapped. Rape of a doubly dehumanized object— as woman, as enemy—carries its own terrible logic. In one act of aggression, the collective spirit of women and of the nation is broken, leaving a reminder long after the troops depart. And if she survives the assault, what does the victim of wartime rape become to her people? Evidence of the enemy's bestiality. Symbol of her nation's defeat. A pariah. Damaged property. A pawn in the subtle wars of international propaganda. (p. 37)*

This is happening now in Haiti, Bosnia, and Rwanda. Today, 70 percent of Rwanda's population is female, and the vast majority have lived through rape. "We are the living dead," said one survivor (Flanders, 1998, p. 30). Compounding the injury to the victims, the husbands often transfer their feelings of revulsion from the enemy to the victimized wives. Such rejection of women as defiled beings is consistent with traditional patriarchal ideology that universally demands that women should not allow more than one man to have access to their bodies (Wetzel, 1993).

A descendant of Confederate General Beauregard and one of his slave-mistresses, law professor Adrien Wing draws a gripping parallel between the ethnic cleansing and forced impregnation in Bosnia and the history of rape and miscegenation in the American South (Wing and Merchan, 1993). The early American South and Bosnia share common ground in terms of six key attributes that are all related to "spirit injury" of a people. These traits are:

1. rape as defilement not only of the individual woman but of a whole culture;
2. rape as silence as the women internalize their experience of oppression, rendering them more vulnerable to males within their own group;
3. rape as sexuality in which raped women are seen as promiscuous and impure;
4. rape as emasculation of men due to their sense of helplessness to protect their wives and daughters;
5. rape as trespass on the "property" rights of men, which was most pronounced under slavery in which the women were the property of their white masters, as were the racially mixed offspring; and
6. rape as pollution of the victim and of her children born as the result of nonconsensual sex.

Rape as an instrument of war is clearly a violation of international law and its proscriptions against war crimes, taking of hostages, torture, and violation of human dignity (Wing and Merchan, 1993). Deplorably, although torture has been prosecuted as a war crime, only recently was war rape considered anything more than an inevitable by-product of war (Goodman, 1993; Mahoney, 1995). Now, at last, women's rights are seen as human rights.

Changes in the conceptualization of rape have been reflected in significant changes in the treatment of victims. Women's group counseling centers and rape crisis centers were developed by grassroots organizations in local communities, at medical centers, and on college campuses. Numerous magazine and newspaper articles appeared, chronicling the reality of rape and its aftermath and especially the courtroom denigration of the victim's character and insinuations about her sexual history. Federal funding for a time poured into rape crisis centers and other crisis intervention programs for victims. Perhaps the most noteworthy outcome of the rape reform movement was the progress made on the legal front. Law enforcement officers gradually became more sensitized to the feelings of women who had been sexually abused. We consider the criminal justice response to rape later in this chapter.

Child Sexual Abuse

Child sexual abuse was rediscovered in the late 1970s and early 1980s when a deluge of newspaper articles, books, and television movies about this subject appeared in North America and western Europe. The percentage of women in the general population who report having been sexually abused as children varies from study to study. Reports range from a low of 6 percent of all females to a high of 62 percent (Kadushin and Martin, 1988) and 3 to 31 percent of males (Conte, 1995). In 1991, researchers concluded that as many as 10–15 percent of boys and 20–25 percent of girls had experienced at least one instance of sexual abuse (Briere, 1992; Finkelhor, 1986). Because the overwhelming majority of cases are not known to authorities and national crime statistics do not include crimes against children, the only measures available are small-sample retrospective surveys.

Incest, usually differentiated from other forms of sexual assault, is defined as sexual acts performed within a family by an adult or an older family member against a child (Byington, 1995). Incest is the ultimate violation of a child's trust and love. Because of the child welfare issues involved, these cases are often handled by departments of human services, and prosecution is waived in lieu of treatment and reform. In both clinical and nonclinical American samples, perpetrators are predominantly male. In general population samples, which reflect reality more accurately than samples of persons in treatment, sexual abuse by parent figures constitutes 6 to 16 percent of the cases, abuse by other relatives constitutes 25 percent, abuse by strangers equals 5 to 15 percent, and the rest of the cases involve acquaintances (Berliner, 1995). Boys are more likely than girls to be abused by nonfamily members. All types of sexual acts occur, and attempted or completed intercourse is reported in 20 to 40 percent of the cases. Because of the secrecy and shame attached to incest, its prevalence is hard to determine. Diane Russell's (1986) estimate that one out of six American women had been molested by a relative is the most widely cited in the literature. The rates for all ethnic groups were comparable, except for Asian and Filipino women, who had a rate of only 8 percent. Incest was more prevalent in higher-income families.

From research we learn that father-daughter incest is associated with social isolation, religiosity, illness in the mother, and a daughter who assumes homemaker roles (Storer, 1992). The presence of a stepfather in the household may be a further precipitating factor (Finkelhor, 1984).

The classic pattern of incest is a progression from fondling of breasts, buttocks, and genitals to mutual masturbation to full intercourse. The ongoing need for secrecy is handled through a combination of threats and bribery. Typically, the pattern continues until the child runs away or otherwise escapes the situation. If the family discovers what is going on, often through a teacher or doctor, there may be disbelief and strong pressure on the child to keep her mouth shut. "It didn't happen and don't tell anyone" is the typical twisted message given. Years later the adult is left to try to pick up the pieces from a stolen childhood.

To survive psychologically, children in a continuing incest situation may dissociate their moods from their bodies during sex. Such altered consciousness can result in clouded memories of the abuse. The unconscious, unresolved trauma may result in symptoms both in childhood and much later, such as phobias, which appear to be meaningless in themselves (Meiselman, 1990).

The words of Maya Angelou (1969), who, at the age of eight, was raped by her mother's boyfriend, resonate:

Then there was the pain. A breaking and entering when even the senses are torn apart. The act of rape is a matter of the needle giving because the camel can't. The child gives, because the body can, and the mind of the violator cannot.

I thought I had died—I woke up in a white-walled world, and it had to be heaven. But Mr. Freeman was there and he was washing me. His hands shook, but he held me upright in the tub and washed my legs. "I didn't mean to hurt you, Ritie. I didn't mean it. But don't you tell. . . . Remember, don't tell a soul." (p. 76)

CRIMINAL JUSTICE RESPONSE

Because of the work of the women's movement, the contemporary understanding of rape and the legal response to this crime have undergone significant revision. Most police officers today view rape as a serious crime. A nationwide survey revealed that law enforcement officers who had received training to demolish the myths about rape credited the training with changing their attitudes (Horne, 1993). The entry of increasing numbers of women into this field has further promoted change from within the system. Yet, considering the long cultural tradition of women bearing the guilt for sexual victimization, it is not surprising that the legacy of the past is with us still.

The legacy of antiquated concepts that have been translated into law and custom and an innate distaste for this type of crime by all parties often cause the victim of sexual assault to feel victimized a second time. The woman's problem in confronting the law stems from three sources: attitudes of the police, the difficulty of answering questions of an intensely personal nature, and treatment by the courts. In some prosecutors' offices, rape victims are routinely asked to take lie detector tests.

Rape is a unique crime both in the low rate at which it is reported to the police and in the low conviction rate if it is prosecuted. It is the only crime in which the victim, at least in part, is considered guilty until proven innocent. From the first police encounter, the victim is gauged in terms of respectability and believability, and these attributes may be judged on a racial and class basis. Abused hitchhikers or women who went alone to a bar can expect to have marks against them from the start.

Why is rape so rarely reported? More to the point, why is it *ever* reported? In light of the feared mistreatment by justice officials of sexual assault victims and the ordeal of continually reliving the crime, it is remarkable that it is reported at all. Perhaps persons who have experienced crime go to the law for protection as a matter of course. Perhaps a vague sense of responsibility or a determination to get justice guides them. Caring and sensitive treatment by law enforcement officers can instill in the survivor a sense of not wanting to let them down by failing to follow through with prosecution. Sometimes the aim is to expiate the shame by publicly declaring it to have been a crime, the desire of the victim for some sort of vindication. Because what the victim really wants is for someone, an expert in these matters, to tell her, "You handled it well; you were fighting for your life. There was no other way."

Immediately after the attack, the victim approaches the authorities in an extreme state of emotional vulnerability. Because of her heightened awareness, words spoken to her at this time may stay with her forever. Rough treatment during the medical exam can cause physical pain and retraumatize the victim. A recent article in the popular press takes us through the process from the viewpoint of the good and the bad in criminal justice treatment. From *Glamour,* Karen Houppert (1996), a reporter with *Village Voice,* tells the story of Jeannie Dampf.

It is four months after the rape when the reporter travels to Tulsa to interview Jeannie. As the reporter describes the timing, "The rape has not yet become a manageable part of her personal history; it intrudes on her present, raw and relentless, and talking about it still brings on tears" (p. 274).

Jeannie describes the rape not as an isolated trauma, but as a catalyst—an event that sparked a series of traumas for which she was unprepared. Once the act was over, the repercussions began. Nevertheless, the treatment Jeannie received combined the thoroughness of the legal requirements with the support afforded by a rape crisis volunteer and later treatment at the rape crisis center.

One week later, Jeannie was receiving sensitive and skilled counseling at the rape crisis center. She needed to work through her unarticulated feeling of being dirty and wanting to hide, and the counselor helped her express and normalize her feelings. The preliminary hearing was difficult, but Jeannie got through it by keeping herself angry. In the trial, the rapist was convicted. Today, Jeannie reports, the flashbacks have mostly gone away, and she has tried to resume a normal sex life with her boyfriend. She has been tested twice for AIDS, but this is still a constant worry for both her and her partner.

Because new technologies such as the use of DNA evidence can clearly reveal that the defendant made contact with the accused, defense attorneys are hard put to find a way around the facts. Rather than try to counter this evidence, defense attorneys attempt to frighten witnesses away with threats to reveal personal information drawn from medical and counseling records. Among the personal details presented by O'Malley that served to scare witnesses away was testimony about drinking habits, a prior eating disorder, and revealing clothing worn while jogging (1997).

Victims' Rights

In the United States, the jury selection process, whereby each opposing side can eliminate a certain number of prospective jurors, is unique. Whole trials can be won or lost on the basis of who occupies the jury seats. In rape trials, in which victim-blaming is a common component, a key question is whether men or women are the most likely to vote to convict an accused rapist. In the past, it was commonly believed that women would be harsher on other women. Three studies, however, indicate that men are more likely than women to excuse the perpetrator in jury trials (Johnson and Jackson, 1988; Kleinke and Meyer, 1990; Clark and Nightingale, 1997). New York Assistant District Attorney Linda Fairstein (1993) contends that getting a conviction in a date rape case is especially difficult. According to Fairstein, people have a fixed image of how a rapist should look. "But he doesn't look like a rapist" is the typical comment of jurors in date rape cases, which Fairstein has tried (p. 155).

Justice F. B. Kelly's Canadian study from the International Centre for Criminal Law Reform and Criminal Justice Policy (1998) compares victims' rights cross-nationally. In the past two or three decades, Kelly observes, an unprecedented international movement has evolved, devoted to the plight of victims of crime. In the United States and Canada one heralded change is the introduction in court proceedings of victim impact statements. In the United States, uniquely, victims play an active role in the plea-bargaining process. In both countries, evidence about the sex life of victims is excluded from sexual offense cases where it could be used to imply consent by the victim. In North America and Britain, more protection is being granted to children in sexual abuse cases by allowing them to testify on videotape or behind a screen away from the accused molester.

A favorable development is the allotment of financial compensation by the government for pain and suffering as a result of crime. Some Canadian provinces cover the maintenance of a child born as a result of rape. In the United States, victims may receive financial assistance from state victims' compensation programs. Victims must, however, demonstrate financial need.

Canadian laws are very strict concerning protection of the assault victim's right to privacy. The witness, if she so desires, can apply for a ban, and her identity will be protected. In the United States, half of the states restrict the publication of victims' names. In the other states, the newspapers usually do not publish the names out of custom. In Britain, the anonymity of rape victims is strictly maintained.

Despite all the obstacles described in North America and Europe, participation in the criminal justice process can be cathartic for the survivor, a way of getting beyond the pain. As Fairstein (1993) describes one woman's experience, "She had courageously faced her attacker and accused him with confidence and dignity. No one had humiliated or debased her, and none of the 'myths' of a complaining witness's ordeal had befallen her" (p. 261).

In Box 4.2 on page 104, the themes of gender, race, and class are examined in terms of the criminal justice system's response to the crime of rape.

**BOX 4.2   Gender, Rape, and Class and the
Justice System's Response to Rape**

LaFree's *Rape and Criminal Justice: The Social Construction of Sexual Assault* contends that it is not enough to look at decisions at one point of the criminal justice system to determine if sexism and racism are present. It is also necessary to look at various points in the decision-making process as well to examine the cumulative effect. He also notes the importance of examining racial composition (the race of both the victim and the offender). LaFree's comprehensive analysis comprises two data sets on sexual assault cases processed in Indianapolis, Indiana. The first study examines police, prosecution, and court records of the 881 officially reported cases in 1970, 1973, and 1975, and the second study comes from data collected from sexual assault cases tried in Indianapolis from July 1978 to September 1980.

In applying conflict theory to his data sets, LaFree concludes that "the law is applied to control the behavior of individuals who threaten the power of dominant groups," whether they are African American men accused of raping white women or nontraditional women who are rape victims. Conflict theory was also supported to the extent that

African American offender–white victim cases were treated the most seriously; white intraracial cases were in the middle; and African American intraracial rapes were treated least seriously in the cumulative scope of processing and sanctioning of offenders. Moreover, LaFree found that racial composition appreciably improved predictions of outcomes (from arrest to sentence length) "with the greatest increases occurring for later sentencing outcomes." Accordingly, even when controlling for legal characteristics, African American offender–white victim rapes incur significantly more severe penalties than other rapes, and African American intraracial rapes resulted in the least severe penalties. In addition, LaFree links conflict theory and the feminist approach in that both argue that "women in our society who behave nontraditionally are less likely to receive justice from the criminal justice system." He adds that criminal sanctions are based at least to some degree "on definitions constructed through social interaction and the corollary argument that these definitions are closely linked to the characteristics of the people involved."

Source: Gary D. LaFree, *Rape and Criminal Justice: The Social Construction of Sexual Assault* (Belmont, Calif.: Wadsworth Publishing, 1989).

PSYCHOLOGICAL TRAUMA

In an extensive review of international studies that looked at long-term effects, Finkelhor (1994) found an association between early sexual abuse and adult mental health impairments. Symptoms of anxiety and fear that are consistent with posttraumatic stress disorder (PTSD) are found in approximately one-third to one-half of sexually abused children (Berliner, 1995). PTSD includes intrusive, unpleasant recollections of the event and avoidance and numbing symptoms. Guilt feelings and a generalized sense of feeling dirty and damaged are common. Long-term sexual dysfunction is a corollary of childhood abuse. Repressed memories may be associated with phobias of a disabling sort. In short, the destruction of childhoods and the wreckage of adult lives in the wake of child abuse is monumental (Steed, 1995).

Increasing evidence shows that childhood trauma significantly alters the biochemistry of the brain (Dziegielewski and Resnick, 1997; Gabbard, 1999). Adaptation to trauma, such as hypervigilence, prepares the victim for fight-or-flight responses and may become biochemically ingrained when triggered again and again (Waits, 1993). We have a great deal to learn about how childhood trauma affects brain chemistry and how the tendency toward depression and addiction figure into the equation.

For women who suffer with addictive problems and with the law, a history of early childhood sexual abuse is almost a given. Ironically, a history of abuse seems to predispose women to adult victimization such as rape or battering. Even the early teenage pregnancy phenomenon so derided by the media and politicians is associated with a history of childhood sexual abuse (*NASW News,* 1995).

Maya Angelou shares with us—in her moving autobiography *I Know Why the Caged Bird Sings* (1969), in speeches, and in interviews—the trauma that rape produced in her life. In the years following the rape, she did not speak. The fact that her family killed the perpetrator made a bad situation worse. Maya was a victim with blood on her hands. Only the efforts of a lovely English teacher who introduced her to the world of literature brought out her gifts of self-expression. Today she is one of America's foremost poets.

In a book on sexual offenders, Tony Parker (1969) captures the sense of a survivor's early pain:

> *Afterwards I was suffering from shock: I had been physically hurt, I was numb, but then the first feelings which began were those of self-questioning—whether I shouldn't have struggled harder, whether in some way I might even at the last have prevented it. (p. 303)*

On top of the normal reaction to what may have been a near-death assault, the person who has been victimized suffers from her involvement in a hideously sordid sexual activity, an involvement that may be known by the entire community. For this reason the victim may have to not only change jobs but leave town as well. Even marriages do not always survive such an attack, because long after the wife is ready to forget (and she *will* want to go on to other things) her husband may not be able to.

Approximately 5 percent of rape victims become pregnant as a result of the rape. Today, some emergency rooms dispense morning-after pills to prevent pregnancy. If the rapist is of a different race from the victim, child-rearing problems and difficulties in explanation abound. A recent award-winning British film, *Secrets and Lies,* portrays the stirring reunion between a white working-class woman and the mixed-race daughter she gave up for adoption years earlier in the aftermath of interracial rape. In this film, a young woman who gave birth to a son as a result of rape describes her feelings, which were exacerbated by thoughtless initial reactions by her family.

The concept of "the rape trauma syndrome" was first identified by Burgess and Holmstrom (1979). This syndrome is now considered a part of PTSD. Based on their emergency room work with rape victims, Burgess and Holmstrom identified two stages of adjustment to rape. The initial or acute stage, lasting approximately two weeks, involves shock and disbelief and some seeming acceptance of what has taken place. A common coping mechanism at this stage is forgetting. In her in-depth interviews with sixty British survivors of rape, Kelly (1988) discovered that forgetting or repression can help in the short term but causes serious problems in the long run. The need to suppress horrible events derives from the threat they represent to the person, as Kelly explains. Typically, part of the experience is remembered and part shut out of the mind. These acute reactions are a normative response. According to a comparison study of 215 assault and sexual assault victims, Valentiner, Riggs, Foa, and Gershung (1996) found that symptom severity decreased significantly after three months.

In the second phase of adjustment to the rape, the survivor may begin to experience physical and emotional turmoil—insomnia, unexpected crying fits, and extreme fear related to the violence of the attack. Kelly's (1988) interviewees spoke of intrusive flashbacks that harked back to the scene of the crime. The fear was compounded if the attacker was an ex-boyfriend or ex-spouse. Such a man, who used rape to punish a woman for the breakup of their relationship, would occasionally strike again. Sometimes the harassment was so bad that the woman, feeling utterly helpless, would return to her abuser.

Many women feel anger during this second stage, anger at the police, the courts, their families, and the offender. Over 90 percent of the women Kelly interviewed felt that their attitudes toward men had been affected by the encounter. Others, with a less healthy reaction, internalize their anger and sense of shame and become suicidal. Valentiner and colleagues (1996), in their large sample of victims, found that women who had severe trauma reactions earlier were likely to develop chronic PTSD later. This was especially true of rape victims. Since one-third of the victims developed enduring problems, it is clear that early intervention is vital, according to these research findings.

Kelly (1988) provides a list of the losses women may experience as a result of sexual violence. Among them are sense of safety, independence, control, self-esteem, memories, trust, positive feelings about sex, support networks, and health. Sexually inexperienced victims experience loss of virginity and a linking in their minds of sex and violence. As research indicates, younger women are more deeply traumatized than are more mature women who have had a positive experience of sex. Those who were sexually assaulted as children were the most likely to develop anxiety and other emotional disorders (Burnam et al., 1988).

TREATMENT AND EMPOWERMENT

Recovery from trauma occurs when the child or woman who has been victimized is transformed into a survivor who is able to integrate the catastrophe into her life history and see it as a source of strength. Recovery takes place when the world seems a beautiful and trusting place again and your body feels whole and like yours alone.

Research shows that the initial meeting and relationship between a rape victim and the first person-friend or authority figure who responds has more impact on the victim's eventual recovery than anything else. The initial response by a trusted individual also determines the extent to which the survivor will blame herself and even whether or not she will acknowledge that what happened to her was a crime. A study of college rape victims, cited by Schwartz and DeKeseredy (1997), revealed that if the victims got the message that they were loved no matter what they had undergone, they tended to blame themselves. But if survivors got the message that it was not their fault, they tended to shift the blame to the perpetrator. Society's reaction to a woman's victimization, therefore, has long-term consequences.

The need for expert help is crucial following victimization. To prevent life-long problems, the sooner one gets professional counseling, the better. One study showed that completed rape led to PTSD symptoms in as many as 90 percent of women at four weeks following the assault and remained as high as 47 percent three months later (Rothbaum, Foa, Riggs, Murdock, and Walsh, 1992). In a random sample of 1,007 young members of a large health maintenance organization, a higher prevalence of PTSD was found in women than in men; of the sixteen women who experienced rape, thirteen developed PTSD (reported in *Science News,* 1991).

From van Wormer's experience counseling adult survivors of rape and incest and from the literature, we have filtered out four phases of adjustment to the shock and horror of forced sexual contact. In reality, the stages overlap and many survivors get stuck at one stage or bypass it altogether. This model represents an ideal type, in short, for the purpose of constructing a working intervention scheme. We must always recognize, however, that each survivor experiences a unique crime under unique circumstances and that her constitutional and environmental contingencies will have a strong bearing on her resolution of the crisis. The duration of the abuse, the degree of violence and terror experienced, the age of the victim, and the initial reactions of the authorities and significant others all fall into play in determining the course of the recovery process. These are the four phases: denial-avoidance, guilt and sexualization, reexperience and rage, and finally, healing.

Denial-Avoidance

In denying the gravity of the event and minimizing the difficulties ahead— "I'm alive; I'm all right"—the recent victim enables herself to handle as much as she can at that time. Repression of some of the most disturbing aspects, coupled with dissociation of the self from the act, allows victims to cope with experiences they are not yet ready to absorb into their reality. Feelings of detachment and emotional withdrawal from others are common.

To enhance long-term recovery, referral to crisis counseling services should be made at the earliest possible moment. Much personal tragedy and self-destructiveness can be avoided if the survivor can receive support during the critical early period of trauma. Brief crisis intervention early on may offset the need for intensive in-depth psychotherapy at a later stage. The worst thing that can happen to a child who has been abused is to leave her or him to sort out these experiences alone (Wyatt, 1997). Key elements of counseling during this initial period are psychological support—listening, caring, nurturing the strengths in the survivor as they manifest themselves—and education. Education includes providing information about the criminal justice process if the client chooses to get involved in this system and health care information if the client has not yet received medical care for the attack.

Victim/witness assistance programs, usually situated in local county prosecutors' offices or nearby court buildings, are designed to boost witness cooperation and to provide advocacy for their needs. For victims of rape and domestic violence, however, more specialized treatment is needed. The ideal arrangement is the provision of crisis intervention programs, which may be lodged in police departments, hospitals, or nonprofit agencies and are prepared to act within the first 24 hours after the victimization (Roberts, 1995). Help is given in filling out victim compensation forms, and crisis counseling and referral to extended counseling and psychotherapy are provided. Treatment in both short- and long-term counseling consists of a great deal of reassurance that the victim did not precipitate or deserve the assault. Because, according to a government video on crime victimization (U.S. Department of Justice, 1997), 13 percent of victims develop a plan for suicide, survivors need to be informed about actions to take to save their lives, such as hot-line numbers to call. Above all, as this training video further indicates, it is vital for criminal justice personnel to communicate that they believe the victim and that they are sorry about what has happened. This simple acknowledgment can mean a great deal to a recently traumatized person; it can bring tears of relief. One helpful approach is to ask the victim about her fears and concerns and always to validate and not disregard or dispute her feelings.

Guilt and Sexualization

The greatest irony is that the sexual offender often feels no remorse at all, while the victim is left with a sense of uncleanness and even guilt. The guilt feelings that are internalized by the child victim and that may remain with her until adulthood seem to make little sense on the surface. Sexual trauma survivors, however, feel guilty because they have engaged in forbidden sex often under sordid and horrible circumstances.

In adults, *traumatic sexualization* can occur also (see Patten, Gatz, Jones, and Thomas, 1995). Problems can range from negatively charged sexuality or association of all aspects of sex with self-loathing and disgust to inappropriately compulsive eroticism. Often the problems do not emerge until the survivor enters or tries to enter a committed relationship; only then does the seriousness of the trauma become apparent. *Stigmatization,* according to the same source, is associated with shame and guilt feelings that are internalized by the abused individual, especially if this individual is a child. The child may believe she is tainted forever by a bad experience, as we have seen.

The survivor therapy approach utilizes the strengths perspective to help reempower the client. Reestablishing trust in herself and the world and rediscovering her sense of personal control are primary goals in recovery from victimization. Group therapy is an invaluable technique for helping survivors let go of their self-blaming thoughts and regain their self-confidence. As group members, each of whom may unconsciously blame herself for her own suffering, come to share each other's stories of brutalization, a revelation may take place. In conjunction with an emerging sense of *we* instead of *I*, the revelation "We did not deserve this to happen to us" may come to light.

Reexperience and Rage

Adult survivors can benefit from intensive thinking and feeling work at any stage in the recovery process. Implicit in the philosophy of feeling work is the belief that feeling and thinking are in constant interaction with each other, that it is not the *event* itself that is significant but one's view of the event that shapes its impact. Whether a person is a victim or a survivor may be shaped more by the *definition* of the situation than by the situation itself.

The primary goal of treatment for sex trauma survivors is to help them reprocess their trauma and integrate it into their lives so as to resolve symptoms and related issues. A Canadian report of intervention with female survivors of childhood sexual abuse showed excellent results in raising self-esteem and reducing depression among members of thirteen closed-process groups (Richter, Snider, and Gorey, 1997). Group exercises ranged from reading relevant poetry, prose, or a chapter in *The Courage to Heal* (Bass and Davis, 1994). As for the women's sexual abuse experiences, the social workers gently and in a noncoercive way encouraged each woman to talk about what happened to her as a way of relieving the burden of the "secret."

An effective approach toward empowerment is to affirm the resourcefulness and competence of women who managed to use all the wiles at their disposal to survive and who have continued to survive ever since. In recovery, the survivor reviews a situation in which she seemed to have been completely overtaken yet, in fact, used many creative maneuvers for her own protection. In this way, a new meaning can be given to the trauma of rape or childhood sexual abuse. Some individuals, as they discard their sense of a damaged self, embrace instead the belief that the misfortune they endured made them stronger and more compassionate (Harvey and Harney, 1995). Only when safety and self-care are reliably established, as Harvey and Harney indicate, will the survivor be ready for this process of reviewing, reliving, and integrating the traumatic past.

Healing

Healing is simply the inner change, the sense of peace that may result from therapy work on labeling feelings and controlling them through cognitive techniques, reframing troubling events in one's life, and recognizing how past events influence present feelings, thoughts, and behavior. Reclaiming lost and damaged childhood selves may occur through the joint effort of treatment and support group relationships.

The aim of such memory retrieval work, as Harvey and Harney (1995) indicate, is to place the past in the past and to realize the role that past events play in shaping one's present life. Through sharing a painful and conflict-ridden episode in her life with a concerned professional, the survivor begins to perceive events increasingly through the eyes of the listener-observer. bell hooks (1993) speaks eloquently of the joy of reconciliation, the gift of healing. Referring to Alice Walker's (1982) novel, *The Color Purple,* hooks recalls how Celie, the black heroine, begins to recover from her traumatic experiences of incest/rape, domestic violence, and marital rape only when she is able to tell her story, to be open and honest. Telling one's story in any form, giving voice to the unmentionable, is the first step, according to hooks, in releasing the bitterness and in healing the inner wounds that makes reconciliation possible.

SUMMARY

Childhood sexual abuse, incest, and rape are predatory acts that constitute serious problems for society and have long-lasting consequences for victims. In this chapter, we viewed this problem from a feminist/strengths approach; the emphasis was structural, on the power dynamics of a male-dominated society in which the threat of rape can serve, as Brownmiller (1975) suggests, to keep all women in a state of fear. Rape is thus at once both a personal and a political phenomenon. At the personal level, as we have seen, women are not only susceptible to being raped but also to being blamed for their own vulnerability.

To understand the political dimensions of rape, we looked to history, to the European-American heritage. Considered the property of men, of their fathers and husbands, women who were attacked were considered ruined and contaminated; the attack itself was conceived as an attack on their menfolk. In wartime, the victor has access to his enemy's women. Under the institution of slavery, access to slave women was a given.

Today, although rape in war and sexual slavery persist, there is growing international recognition, through the United Nations, of the human rights of women. The right to exercise control over one's sexuality is an important basic right. Without protection from physical and sexual violation in the home or elsewhere, previous guarantees of political and economic equality remain hollow.

The theoretical approach presented in this chapter, consistent with contemporary feminist theory, conceives of sexual aggression and abuse as a continuum or series of behaviors ranging from ordinary harassment to full-blown violent, life-threatening attacks. The common thread of dehumanization is the unifying element. Surveys show that although stranger rape is the prototype of rape, date rape and marital rape are far more common. Self-reports of college males and of women in national victim surveys reveal that sexual aggression by peers on the college campus is commonplace.

Rape victims suffer psychological as well as physical trauma. Because of the stigma attached to this crime, survivors often feel torn between the desire to talk about it, even years later, and a reluctance to tell people what they probably don't want to hear. Society's tendency to blame the victim, especially the victim of a sexual crime, effectively silences the survivor of rape. In cases of stranger rape, the omission of the victim's name from newspaper accounts, although advisable, prevents people from reaching out to the woman who has survived a life-threatening experience. Such an individual may forever wonder who knows and who doesn't know about this unmentionable crime. Shrouded in silence and internalizing society's blame, the survivor desperately needs someone to talk to. The importance of a rape crisis telephone line, rape advocates, and victim assistance programs cannot be underestimated. The choices and problems facing a recently victimized woman will seem insurmountable: whether to report the crime, how to endure the medical procedures, whom to tell, and how to go forward are just a few of the immediate concerns. Victimized children and their families need help most of all. Participation in group counseling sessions can reinforce girls' and women's self-worth and keep any self-destructive tendency that may arise in check.

Personal empowerment of women has its counterpart in political empowerment. We have the feminist movement to thank for both the recognition that violence against women is a public issue and the funding for prevention and intervention efforts to curb the impact of this type of crime. Women's interests and the state's political interests coinciding at this time of heightened attention to victims of crime provides an opportunity that should not be overlooked. To end the widespread rape and sexual harassment of women, we must continue our work toward legislative reform, educational initiatives, improved child-rearing practices, and better-funded advocacy/counseling services.

REFERENCES

Allison, D. (1993). *Bastard out of Carolina.* New York: Plume.

Amir, M. (1971). *Patterns in forcible rape.* Chicago: University of Chicago Press.

Amnesty International. (1995). *Amnesty international report.* New York: Amnesty International U.S.A.

Angelou, M. (1969). *I know why the caged bird sings.* New York: Random House.

Ayto, J. (1990). *Dictionary of word origins.* New York: Arcade.

Baartman, H. E. (1998). Compassion and scepticism in child sexual abuse: Some historical aspects and explanations. *International Reviews of Victimology 5*(2): 189–202.

Bass, E., and Davis, L. (1994). *The courage to heal: A guide for women survivors of child sexual abuse,* 3rd ed. New York: Harper Perennial.

Bellafonte, G. (1998, June 29). Feminism: It's all about me! *Time:* 54–62.

Berliner, L. (1995). Child sexual abuse: Direct practice. *Encyclopedia of Social Work,* 19th ed. (pp. 408–417). Washington, D.C.: NASW Press.

Briere, J. N. (1992). *Child abuse trauma: Theory and treatment of lasting effects.* Newbury Park, Calif.: Sage.

Brownmiller, S. (1975). *Against our will: Men, women and rape.* New York: Bantam.

Bureau of Justice Statistics (1998). *Alcohol and crime.* Washington, D.C.: U.S. Department of Justice.

Bureau of Justice Statistics (1997, February). Sex offenses and offenders: An analysis of data on rape and sexual assault. Washington, D.C.: U.S. Department of Justice.

Burgess, A. W., and Holmstrom, L. L. (1979). Rape trauma syndrome. *American Journal of Psychiatry 131:* 981–986.

Burnham, M. S., Stein, J. A., Golding, J. M., Siegel, J. A., Sorenson, S. B., Forsythe, A. B., and Telles, C. A. (1988). Sexual assault and mental disorders in a community population. *Journal of Consulting and Clinical Psychology 56:* 843–850.

Byington, D. B. (1995). Sexual assault. *The encyclopedia of social work,* 19th ed. (2136–2141). Washington, D.C.: NASW Press.

Clark, H. L., and Nightingale, N. N. (1997). When jurors consider recovered memory cases: Effects of victim and juror gender. *Journal of Offender Rehabilitation 25*(3/4): 87–104.

Cleaver, E. (1968). *Soul on ice.* New York: Dell Publishing.

Conte, J. (1995). Child sexual abuse overview. In *Encyclopedia of social work,* 19th ed. (pp. 402–408). Washington, D.C.: NASW Press.

Cowan, G., and Campbell, R. R. (1995). Rape and causal attitudes among adolescents. The *Journal of Sex Research 32*(2): 145–153.

Crowell, N. A., and Burgess, A. W. (eds.). (1996). *Understanding violence against women.* Washington, D.C.: National Academy Press.

Deckard, B. S. (1983). *The woman's movement: Political, socioeconomic, and psychological issues,* 3rd ed. New York: Harper and Row.

Donat, P., and D'Emilio, J. (1992). A feminist redefinition of rape and sexual assault: Historical foundations and change. *Journal of Social Issues 48:* 9–2.

Dziegielewski, S. F., and Resnick, C. (1997). Assessment and intervention: Abused women in the shelter setting. In A. Roberts (ed.), *Crisis management and brief treatment.* Chicago: Burnham.

Emerge (1997). Sexual assault survey results. *Emerge 8*(9): 512.

Fairstein, L. (1993). *Sexual violence: Our war against rape.* New York: Morrow.

Faludi, S. (1991). *Backlash: The undeclared war on American women.* New York: Doubleday.

Finkelhor, D. (1984). *Child sexual abuse.* New York: Free Press.

Finkelhor, D. (1994). The international epidemiology of child sexual abuse. *Child Abuse and Neglect 18:* 409–417.

Finkelhor, D. (1986). *A sourcebook on child sexual abuse.* Beverly Hills, Calif.: Sage.

Flanders, L. (1998, March/April). Rwanda's living casualties. *Ms:* 27–30.

Flowers, R. B. (1987). Women and criminality: *The woman as victim, offender, and practitioner.* New York: Greenwood Press.

Gabbard, G. O. (1999, January). Psychodynamic theory in an age of neuroscience. *The Harvard Mental Health Letter:* 4–5.

Goodman, E. (1993, March 6). Women activists in a hundred countries. *The Washington Post,* p. 1.

Goodwin, J. (1994). *Price of honor.* Boston: Little, Brown.

Griffin, S. (1971). Rape: The all-American crime. *Ramparts 10*(3): 26–35.

Harvey, M. R., and Harney, P. A. (1995). Individual psychotherapy. In C. Classen (ed.), *Treating women molested in childhood* (pp. 63–93). San Francisco: Jossey-Bass.

hooks, b. (1993). *Sisters of the yam: Black women and self-recovery.* Boston: South End Press.

Horne, F. (1993). The issue is rape. In R. Muraskin and T. Alleman (eds.), *It's a crime: women and justice.* Englewood Cliffs, N.J.: Prentice-Hall.

Houppert, K. (1996, April). After the rape. *Glamour 94*(4): 274–277, 298.

Jensen, R. H. (1996, July/August). A surprising verdict. *Ms:* 26–27.

Johnson, J. D., and Jackson, L. A. (1988). Assessing effects of factors that might underlie the differential perception of acquaintance and stranger rape. *Sex Roles 19:* 37–45.

Kelly, F. B. (1998). *The unfinished triangle: The criminal justice system, the victim, and the offender.* Ottawa, Canada: International Centre for Criminal Law Reform and Criminal Justice Policy.

Kelly, L. (1988). *Surviving sexual violence.* Minneapolis: University of Minnesota Press.

Kleinke, C. L., and Meyer, C. (1990). Evaluation of rape victims by men and women with high and low belief in a just world. *Psychology of Women Quarterly 14:* 373–353.

Koss, M. P., Leonard, K. D., Beezley, D. A., and Oros, C. J. (1985). Nonstranger sexual aggression: A discriminant analysis of the psychological characteristics of undetected offenders. *Sex Roles 12:* 981–992.

Kowalski, L. B. (1995) *School Social Work Journal 20*(1): 1–12.

Lefkowitz, B. (1997). *Our guys.* Berkeley: University of California Press.

Lerner, M. J. (1971). All the world loathes a loser. *Psychology Today 5:* 51–66.

Maclean's. (1997, March 31). Hanging for rape? *Maclean's 110*(13): 41.

Mahoney, K. (1995, July 29–August 1). Theoretical and practical suggestions to implement equality rights and overcome gender bias in the courts. Paper presented at the International Social Welfare in a Changing World Conference, Calgary, Alberta.

Maschke, K. (ed.) (1997). *The legal response to violence against women* (pp. vi–xi). New York: Garland Publishing.

McNair, L. D., and Neville, H. A. (1996). African American women survivors of sexual assault: The interaction of race and class. *Women and Therapy 18*(3/4): 107–118.

Meiselman, K. C. (1990). *Resolving the trauma of incest: Reintegration therapy with survivors.* San Francisco: Jossey-Bass.

Meyer, T. (1990, December 5). Date rape: A serious campus problem that few talk about. *Chronicle of Higher Education,* p. A15.

NASW News. (1995, October). Teens and age differences. *NASW News:* 13.

National Victims Center (1992). *Rape in America: A report to the nation.* Arlington, Va: author.

O'Carroll, A. (1997, August 21–23). Defense counsels' response to women who have been raped. Paper presented at the World Congress on Violence, Dublin, Ireland.

O'Malley, S. (1997, August). The new reason rapists are going free. *Redbook:* 16–80, 108.

O'Neill, A. M. (1996, September 2). *People:* 94–98.

Oppenheimer, J. (1998). Politicizing survivors of incest and sexual abuse: Another facet of healing. *Women and Therapy 21*(2): 79–87.

Parker, Tony. (1969). *The twisting lane: The hidden world of sex offenders.* New York: Harrow Books.

Patten, S. B., Gatz, Y. K., Jones, B., and Thomas, D. L. (1995). Posttraumatic stress disorder and the treatment of sexual abuse. In F. Turner (ed.), *Differential diagnosis and treatment in social work* (pp. 456–487). New York: Free Press.

Progressive. (1995). Refuge for women. *Progressive 59*(7): 9.

Ramsey, M. (1995, November). Remembering rape. *Harper's Bazaar:* 104–105.

Rand, M. R. (1997). Violence-related injuries treated in hospital emergency departments. Unpublished report.

Randall, M., and Haskell, L. (1995). Sexual violence in women's lives. *Violence against Women 1*(1): 6–31.

Reilly, M. E., Lott, B., Caldwell, D., and Deluca, L. (1992). Tolerance for sexual harassment related to self-reported sexual victimization. *Gender and Society 6:* 122–138.

Richter, N., Snider, E., and Gorey, K. M. (1997). Group work intervention with female survivors of childhood sexual abuse. *Research on Social Work Practice 7*(1), 53–69.

Roberts, A. R. (1995). Victim services and victim/witness assistance programs. *In Encyclopedia of Social Work* (pp. 2440–2444), 19th ed. Washington D.C.: NASW Press.

Robinson, L. (1997). "I was raped." *Emerge 8*(7): 42–53.

Rollins, J. H. (1996). *Women's minds, women's bodies: The psychology of women in a biosocial context.* Upper Saddle River, N.J.: Prentice-Hall.

Rothbaum, B. O., Foa, E. B., Riggs, D. S., Murdock, T., and Walsh, W. (1992). A prospective examination of post-traumatic stress disorder in rape victims. *Journal of Traumatic Stress 5:* 455–475.

Russell, D. E. (1986). *The secret trauma: Incest in the lives of girls and women.* New York: Basic Books.

Ryan, W. (1971). *Blaming the victim.* New York: Random House.

Sanday, P. R. (1990) *Fraternity gang rape: Sex, brotherhood, and privilege on campus.* New York: New York University Press.

Schechter, S. (1982). *Women and male violence.* Boston: South End Press.

Schwartz, M. D., and DeKeseredy, W. S. (1997). *Sexual assault on the college campus: The role of male peer support.* Thousand Oaks, Calif.: Sage.

Science News. (1991). Trauma disorder strikes many young adults. *Science News:* 139, 198.

Shapiro, B. L., and Schwarz, J. C. (1997, June). Date rape: Its relationship to trauma symptoms and sexual self-esteem. *Journal of Interpersonal Violence 12*(3): 407–419.

Sorenson, S. B., and Siegel, J. M. (1992). Gender, ethnicity, and sexual assault: Findings from a Los Angeles study. *Journal of Social Issues 48:* 93–104.

Steed, J. (1995). *Our little secret: Confronting child sexual abuse in Canada.* Toronto: Vintage Canada.

Storer, J. H. (1992). Gender and kin role transposition as an accommodation to father-daughter incest. In T. L. Whitehead and B. Y. Reid (eds.), *Gender constructs and social issues* (pp. 70–102). Urbana: University of Illinois Press.

Tjaden, P., and Thoennes, N. (1998). *Prevalence, incidence, and consequences of violence against women: Findings from the national violence against women survey.* Washington, D.C.: U.S. Department of Justice.

Tseuneyoshi, S. (1996). Rape trauma syndrome: Case illustration of Elizabeth. In F. H. McClure, E. Teyber et al. (eds.), *Child and adolescent therapy: A multicultural-relational approach* (pp. 287–320). Fort Worth, Tex.: Harcourt Brace.

U.S. Department of Justice (1997). Meeting the mental health needs of crime victims. Video produced by the Office for Victims of Crime. Washington, D.C.: U.S. Department of Justice.

Valentiner, D. P., Riggs, D. S., Foa, E. B., and Gershung, B. S. (1996). Coping strategies and posttraumatic stress disorder in female victims of sexual and nonsexual assault. *Journal of Abnormal Psychology 105*(3): 455–458.

van Wormer, K. (1997). *Social welfare: A world view.* Chicago: Nelson-Hall.

van Wormer, K., Wells, J., and Boes, M. (2000). *Social work with lesbians, gays, and bisexuals: A strengths perspective.* Chicago: Nelson-Hall.

Waits, E. A. (1993). *Trauma and survival.* New York: Norton.

Walker, A. (1982). *The color purple.* New York: Harcourt Brace Jovanovich.

Walker, M., and Brodsky, S. (1976). *Sexual assault: The victim and the rapist.* Lexington, Mass.: Lexington Books.

Wallace, H. (1998). *Victimology: Legal, psychological, and social perspectives.* Boston: Allyn and Bacon.

Wetzel, J. (1993). *The world of women.* London: Macmillan.

Wing, A., and Merchan, S. (1993). Rape, ethnicity, and culture: Spirit injury from Bosnia to black America. *Columbia Human Rights Law Review 25*(1): 1–46.

Wyatt, G. E. (1997). *Stolen women: Reclaiming our sexuality, taking back our lives.* New York: John Wiley and Sons.

Zastrow, C. (1996). *Introduction to social work and social welfare,* 6th ed. Pacific Grove, Calif.: Brooks/Cole.

5

WIFE AND PARTNER ABUSE

Where is the single most dangerous place for women? The family home. What is the leading cause of death for women at work? Homicide by a spouse or partner. When is the battered woman most likely to get killed? When she leaves the relationship.

This chapter concerns female partner abuse or battering. Such abuse occurs in a marriage or other close relationship and consists of intentional acts to cause injury. *Battering* is physical aggression with a purpose to control, intimidate, and subjugate another human being. It is always accompanied by emotional abuse and normally always causes fear in the battered woman (Jacobson and Gottman, 1998a). *Domestic abuse* is the term that came into common usage in the 1970s; this term is gender neutral and encompasses a wide range of abuse within families.

Stordeur and Stille (1989) state that "there is a continuum of violence against women in our society that includes sexist and degrading language, pornography, wife assault, child sexual assault, rape, sexual mutilation, resource deprivation, and murder" (p. 34). From this perspective, one that is consistent with the perspective found in this chapter, "wife assault is seen as one behavior on a continuum of behaviors that serve the purpose of maintaining the domination and power of a patriarchal society" (pp. 34–35).

Research on partner violence has enjoyed explosive growth in recent years, and the mass media have continued to focus attention on this serious problem. In Iowa, for example, a spate of male-on-female murder-suicides has been featured in the regional news, and in Canada the media attention has focused on sexual abuse against women and controversial cutbacks in funding for women's shelters. Meanwhile, throughout North America, the death toll of women at the hands of their partners continues to mount. A relatively new phenomenon in some schools is the mass shootings by boys of girls that have arisen out of rejected courtships.

Our emphasis in this second chapter on female victimization is on the kind of violence that takes place in intimate relationships. The issues of authority and control by men over women, both physically and emotionally, are explored first, with an historical overview and later by an examination of theories of partner abuse. To dispel the myths about partner violence, we consider statistical data from both national police reports and crime victimization surveys. Special attention is devoted to several areas often neglected in the literature: the substance abuse connection, marital rape, suicide-murder, and the relationship between battering and child abuse. In the final sections of these pages we consider the criminal justice response and successful treatment interventions for both the batterer and the battered. Throughout this discussion, variables of race, ethnicity, and class are considered.

See Box 5.1 to learn about an annual ritual performed by women who care.

BOX 5.1   The Tombstone Project

The stories of fifty-two women killed by domestic violence since 1990 are etched on tombstones in front of the lawn at Valley View Baptist Church, Cedar Falls, Iowa. It is a blustery night in late October 1996. Twenty to thirty of us, all women, are holding candles to commemorate those who did not survive partner violence. Each of us, in turn, reads the story of one victim, then places the lit candle before the wooden tombstone. In the eerie quiet, one woman reads:

"Laura Garrison, 30, of Waterloo, died July 7, 1990. She was shot to death in front of her small children by a man she had dated. The man then shot himself and later died."

She places the candle before the tombstone. Now it is my turn: I read: "Loretta Ellen Foster, 29, of Waterloo, died November 21, 1991. Foster was shot to death by the man she lived with and the father of her children in front of their 5-year-old daughter and 7-year-old son. He then killed himself."

After all fifty-two of the slain women are remembered in this fashion, we all stand in a circle and read in unison a closing poem composed by women's shelter advocates Sharon Spring, Mary Langholz, Mary Roche, and Nicole Rowan:

Oh Connectedness of Life
Of that we cannot see
As air we breathe
and wind we feel
Embrace us in this moment
As we stand here to
Remember
Honor
And give name to all women
Whose voices have been silenced.
May we know they are us
And we are them.
In this month of remembering
Affirm us as we
Remember their names
Remember our own
And give voice to both.

Source: Katherine van Wormer. Poem printed with permission of Mary Langholz, Sharon Spring, Mary Roche, and Nicole Rowan.

HISTORICAL OVERVIEW

In the United States today men who beat their wives are going against cultural norms and the law. Historically a man's right to chastise his wife was affirmed in church doctrine as well as in early Roman law and English common law. Under English common law, which influenced law on this side of the Atlantic, to be a wife meant becoming the property of one's husband. There was some effort, however, to prevent excessive violence. Men could beat their wives as long as the diameter of the rod they used was "no bigger than their thumb" (Blackstone, 1979). (This phrase is the origin of the expression "rule of thumb.") All through the years, even after physical punishment of one's wife was outlawed (in the late 1800s), domestic violence was considered a private matter, not one for intervention by the state. One may recall testimony in the O. J. Simpson trial that when Nicole Simpson called the police for help, her husband persuaded the authorities that the problem was "a family matter" (see Ingrassia and Beck, 1994). So the legacy of the past is with us still.

Nevertheless, in the 1970s, when the women's liberation movement took hold, attention was drawn to rape as a crime of power, the very threat of which frightened all women and restricted their movements. Exposing victim-blaming not only produced new theoretical understandings but also laid the groundwork for pushing institutions to change the treatment of victims (Schechter, 1982). It laid the groundwork as well for collective political action and social support. The efforts of this movement culminated in the landmark Violence against Women Act of 1994, federal legislation providing for improved prevention and prosecution of violent crimes against women and children and for the care of victims (Kurz, 1998). The law also provides funding for prevention, shelter services, and legal advocacy. Unfortunately, however, as Kurz indicates, the new welfare "reform" legislation puts poor women who are trying to escape abuse at grave risk. Forcing them to seek child support from violent men puts them in jeopardy; the scarcity of affordable housing means that large numbers of them will end up homeless; restrictions on welfare recipients crossing state lines to receive benefits makes escape from the batterer more difficult.

NATURE AND SCOPE OF THE PROBLEM

Women often experience their greatest risk of violence from their intimate male partners and spouses. Although one of the most underestimated and underreported crimes in the United States and the single most significant cause of injury to women, intimate partner violence has received increased national attention in recent years. Research informs us that "one woman in four will be physically assaulted by a partner or ex-partner in her lifetime" (Ingrassia and Beck, 1994). Another study suggests that "as many as 37 percent of obstetrics patients are physically abused during pregnancy" (Council on Scientific Affairs, 1992). The Bureau of Justice Statistics special reports (1996, 1998) entitled *Female Victims of Violent Crime* and *Violence by Intimates,* provide the most comprehensive data on reported victimization. From *Violence by Intimates,* we learn the following:

- Although less likely than males to experience violent crime overall, females are five to eight times more likely than males to be victimized by an intimate (defined as a spouse, ex-spouse, partner, or close relative).
- Women aged 16–24 experience the highest per-capita rates of intimate violence; the rates are highest among African American women, urban and poor women.
- In 1996 just over 1,800 murders were attributable to intimates; nearly three out of four victims were female.
- The percentage of female murder victims killed by intimates has remained at about 30 percent since 1976; this compares to 5.9 percent for male murder victims.
- Although the per-capita number of female victims of murder by intimates has remained about the same, the rate of intimate murders of men, especially of African American men, has sharply decreased. Still, in 1996, the African American male rate was eight times that of white males, and the African American female rate three times the white female rate.
- More than half of both prison and jail inmates serving time for violence against an intimate had been using drugs and/or alcohol at the time of the crime.
- Nearly one-third of female victims were victimized at least twice during the previous 6 months.
- Only half the women victimized by an intimate reported the violence to the police or a victim assistance agency.
- Ultimately about one in three offenders identified by the victim was arrested. (pp. v, vi, 13, 15, 19, 20)

In one of the largest studies of its kind, a survey of 3,455 women interviewed at rural and urban emergency rooms in California and Pennsylvania found that nearly 14 percent of the women reported sexual and physical abuse at the hands of an intimate partner (Dearwater, Cohen, Campbell et al., 1998). Only 2.2 percent of the patients, however, over the preceding year were treated at that time for acute trauma for the abuse. Women who had ended a relationship within the previous year were seven times more likely to report abuse than women who had not. Reports of domestic abuse were more frequent in California than in Pennsylvania; those most at risk were young women with children who had extremely low incomes.

Although reports indicate women initiate domestic violence as often as men (Straus and Gelles, 1990), reports of injuries received tell a very different story. Data from the National Victimization Survey reveal that women make up 85 percent of all intimate assault victims (Bureau of Justice Statistics, 1998).

Lesbian partner battering, according to what limited research is available, is at least as common as heterosexual partner battering, although the use of small sample sizes in most such studies casts doubt on the findings. The National Coalition on Domestic Violence estimates that almost one in three same-sex relationships are abusive (Ingrassia and Beck, 1994). The breakdown for gender—gay men versus lesbian—is not given. This same-sex violence is linked to violence in the family of origin, homophobia in the society, and alcohol abuse (West, 1998a). Lesbian batterers tend, like their heterosexual counterparts, to be overly emotionally dependent on their partners (Rollins, 1996).

Rates of Violence among Ethnic Minorities

Women living in cultures that value community over individuality, as well as those that hold women responsible for holding the community together, face enormous barriers when it comes to reporting abuse. This reluctance to bring shame on the community is strongest among Asian Americans. African American and American Indian women also may want to protect their men from law enforcement contact due to a history of discrimination. For these defensive reasons, comprehensive data on ethnic and racial minorities are hard to come by.

Rates of wife abuse are higher among African Americans than for their white counterparts. On average each year between 1992 and 1996 about 12 per 1,000 African American women experienced violence by an intimate compared to about 8 per 1,000 white women (Bureau of Justice Statistics, 1998). Hispanic rates were slightly below the white rates, about 7 in 1,000. These figures are drawn from the National Crime Victimization Survey.

Henriques (1995) charges that African American women continue to be victims of racial oppression, sex discrimination, and class stratification. Victims of a trilogy of oppression, "she is the only woman in America, who is almost unknown, a woman for whom nothing is done, a woman without sufficient defenders when assailed, a woman who is still outside of that world of chivalry that in all the ages has apotheosized womankind" (p. 68). It is not surprising, then, that "African American women appear to endure unnecessary abusive relationships" (p. 69).

Concerning Latino/Latina Americans, West (1998b) notes that when face-to-face bilingual interviews are conducted, a more complete picture of the violence among ethnic groups can be discovered. Kaufman-Kantor, Jasinski, and Aldarondo (1994), for example, found that Puerto Rican husbands are approximately two times more likely than Anglo husbands to beat their wives. Cuban Americans were found to have a low rate of wife abuse, only 2.5 percent.

Studies of Mexican-born immigrants indicate that they have significantly lower rates of partner violence than either Anglos or U.S.-born Mexican Americans (Sorenson and Telles, 1991). A strong possibility exists, however, that immigrant women fear reporting incidents of violence because they are insecure. Data from a household survey in Mexico City show that 38 percent of women had experienced some form of marital violence (Natera, Tiburcio, and Villatoro, 1997). Partners' drinking and jealousy were found to be significantly associated with violent acts and threats.

A rare study of Chinese battered women in North America conducted by Lee and Au (1998) indicates the tremendous pressures foreign-born battered women experience in trying to break through the abusive cycle within their cultural milieu. Because the family name has to be protected at all costs and because individual well-being should be subordinated to the common good, Chinese women do not admit to the occurrence of abuse. In a survey of directors of women's shelters in cities in the United States and Canada with large Chinese populations, Lee and Au discovered that women of Chinese origin endured much abuse in silence, that they perceived marriage as a license for the man to have sex with his wife whenever or however he desired, and that they did not consider divorce an option to escape physical abuse. Unique to the Chinese culture, gambling, rather than alcohol or drugs, was associated with violence. A second culturally specific aspect of Chinese North American wife abuse is the conjoint physical and emotional abuse by the husband's parents along with the husband.

West (1998b) summarized partner violence research on American Indian groups by indicating that all the studies cited show a very high rate of battering in American Indian couples. He also indicated that the relatively small nonrandom sample sizes make it difficult to reach definitive conclusions. Given that Native Americans have the highest alcoholism rate of all ethnic groups, a high rate of family violence would not be unexpected.

International Research

Following the Beijing Women's Conference in 1995, Japan is one of the nations that has demanded accountability in response to antifemale violence. Despite a slow start due to its legacy of traditionalism, increasing public awareness today is being devoted to violence against women in general and to that by male intimate partners. In her review of research on domestic violence in Japan, Yoshihama (1998) concludes that although some services are available, a high degree of tolerance for domestic violence against women still exists. Japanese college students surveyed, for example, tend to minimize such violence. Similarly, in other research surveys, many believed that the wife abuse was a private matter and that the wife likely had provoked the abuse.

An earlier nationwide survey of domestic violence in Japan in 1992, in which Yoshihama participated, revealed a shockingly high rate of male-on-female violence. In dating, marriage, and separation, 77 percent of the 796 women surveyed revealed that they had experienced some type of violence from their partners. It is not uncommon in Japan, according to this writer, for the man to demand, through threats of violence, that the woman quit her job. Unlike in the United States, where domestic violence is recognized as a serious public health problem, the awareness among health care workers in Japan is extremely low. There is a need, as Yoshihama argues, for reform in the criminal justice system and in civil and family law as well.

In Britain, as elsewhere, a woman is more vulnerable to violence in her home than in public. Diane Dwyer (1995), in a comparative study of the United States and Britain, highlights the prevalence of domestic assault and the role of the British criminal justice system in processing domestic violence cases. Despite a much lower overall level of violence in British society and despite a much stronger feminist movement, Dwyer found that the prevalence of domestic violence was similar to that in the United States, that the British criminal justice response had been relatively less progressive, and that victims' assistance units were absent from prosecutorial services. Based on her cross-cultural study, Dwyer concludes that woman abuse is gender-based rather than just a reflection of violence in the wider culture.

Statistics Canada (1998) provides a thorough portrait of violence against women in the report, "Family Violence in Canada." In 1993, a national telephone survey conducted by Statistics Canada found that the rate of physical or sexual assault was 29 percent of ever-married women. Somewhat lower rates were found in comparable U.S. and Australian studies. Yet New Zealand reported higher rates. In Canada, over 89 percent of spousal assault reported to the police was attacks on women. More than half of these assaults resulted in serious injuries. Similar to studies in Mexico, the strongest predictors of wife assault are the young age of the couple, chronic unemployment by male partners, women and men who witnessed parental abuse as children, and the presence of emotional abuse in the relationship. Just over half the violent partners usually drank at the time of the assaults.

Sparked by a series of articles on domestic violence in the *Toronto Star,* an inquest was held to examine the widespread problem. The inquest was held after the death of a woman in a murder-suicide case. Testimony by experts at the inquest revealed that the murderer's behavior was typical—stalking his previous wives and using his children as pawns, a breakup with his present wife followed by a series of death threats. Many Canadian women are safer on the streets than in their own homes, a clinical psychologist told the inquest (Darroch, 1998).

Another Canadian newspaper report (Loomis, 1998) reveals problems for women within Canadian ethnic groups. In the East Indian community, an incident of a woman who was thrown off a balcony by her husband spurred plans for a new women's shelter in the neighborhood. Many of the abused women in this community were part of arranged marriages and cut all family ties when they left India, according to the article. In India if a man hurts a woman, the community will go after the man. But in Canada, such abuse of immigrant women who are culturally isolated and unable to speak the language of the country often goes undetected. Abusive men in all immigrant groups, in fact, can isolate their women by keeping them from learning the language of the adopted country. To enhance services to the East Indian women, several volunteers at the new shelter will speak Punjabi.

An analysis of Statistics Canada data reveals that in 1996 the rate of male spouses killed by their wives had declined, but the number of women killed by their husbands had stayed about the same. Comparable data from the United States shows a similar trend. One could speculate that the growth in women's shelters is saving *men's* lives more than women's lives by providing a way out for battered women besides murder. The fact that women's professional opportunities and economic independence have increased may give women more confidence to escape domestic violence as well.

To summarize, we can say of ethnic/cultural variations in domestic abuse that essentially, the universal, underlying dynamic in battering is control and dominance, but that violence also is correlated with stress factors in the environment. Thus, the manifestation of violence in a relationship is influenced by cultural and contextual factors.

DYNAMICS OF INTIMATE ABUSE

Since physical abuse of a woman is about power and control, it is accompanied emotionally by psychological abuse. Psychological or emotional abuse, in other words, is the context within which the slaps, hits, kicks, and so forth occur. Emotional abuse can include verbal assaults, ridicule, isolation from family and friends, unwarranted accusations about infidelity, control of finances, damage to property, stealing, torture or killing of pets, and threats to harm children and others. The effect of these acts is to attack the woman's sense of self-worth. A kind of brainwashing occurs as the victim internalizes the insinuations and accusations of her attacker, gradually coming to believe them. Psychological abuse among lesbians may include the threat of "outing" a partner to her boss or family.

In any country, when psychological abuse moves on to physical abuse, the added element is terror. Women who are beaten know that they are at high risk of being killed if they try to leave. As the director of crime-victim assistance of the Iowa attorney general's office, Marti Anderson suggests that victims of such domestic terror live in perpetual fear of the next attack, of losing their children and their home, of being stalked, of losing their lives. "And yet people ask," she writes, "Why doesn't she leave?" (Anderson, 1997, p. 4AA). Protection orders, safety plans, and divorces do not stop an attack, a bullet, or a knife. These attempts at self-protection, in fact, often precipitate an attack by paranoid individuals with a history of out-of-control violence.

Instead of asking the question so resented by battered women, "Why don't you leave?" we will consider the practical and psychological barriers to escape. Angela Browne (1995) summarizes the barriers in terms of practical realities, fear of retaliation, and the shock reactions of victims to constant danger. The practical barriers include such issues as finding a place to live, fear of losing one's children, and difficulty in receiving public assistance while married. The woman who works cannot hide, nor can she protect her children who are in school and day care from being taken for ransom. The woman who does not work has no means of support. Moving into a shelter is only for a brief period of time. If the woman gets a legal separation, her spouse will have visitation rights with the children.

Fear of reprisal is made more compelling by death threats. Browne compared forty-two battered women who killed their abusers with 205 women who did not kill their abusers. In the homicide group, many of the women stayed out of terror of further victimization or because they had tried to escape and were beaten for it. Expecting to get killed, they saw no way out of the danger. In fact, violent men do search out the women after they leave. And as their husbands, they know all the hiding places.

Research on victims of trauma helps explain how women cope in the height of danger by denying the threat, by being extremely suggestible, or by withdrawing emotionally so that they can survive. Chronic fatigue and tension coupled with sleep disturbances keep the victim in a state of confusion. Typically, little anger is shown toward the victimizers who are seen as all-powerful and even admired. Browne's theories are reminiscent of social psychological studies of brainwashed prisoners of war who, over time, submit to their captors and even come to admire them. Referred to as the *Stockholm Syndrome,* this phenomenon is named for an incident in Stockholm, Sweden, where four bank employees were held hostage in the bank's vault for four days. Following the ordeal, the women's expressions of gratitude toward the offenders was disturbing to many people (Wallace, 1998).

Dutton and Painter (1993) developed the *traumatic bonding* theory to explain why battered women stay in abusive relationships. Power imbalance in combination with intermittent good–bad treatment was predicted to increase the emotional attachment in an abusive situation, a prediction based on classical social psychological theory (see, for example, Bettelheim, 1943, and Zimbardo, Haney, and Banks, 1972). The authors tested this theory empirically with in-depth assessments conducted on seventy-five women who had recently left abusive situations; emotional involvement was strong. Follow-up measures six months later revealed some decrease in the level of attachment but showed that prolonged effects of the abuse were still evident.

An understanding of the dynamics of social psychology is crucial if we are to make sense of situations and reactions that may seem irrational on the surface, especially for victim service counselors who have not experienced such long-term abuse firsthand. Much criminal behavior by accomplices who are forced into it by their abusers, moreover, can be understood in the context of traumatic bonding. The story of Patty Hearst, kidnap victim, a woman locked in a closet and periodically raped over a period of many long months is well known. Hearst inevitably fell in love with one of her captors and joined their gang—the Symbionese Liberation Front—to commit robberies (Castiglia, 1996). Unfortunately, at her trial the jury was not informed of the phenomenon of psychological traumatizing that can occur in such cases, and Hearst was sentenced to a lengthy prison term for her crimes. There are many women in prison today whose abuse impaired their judgment in a similar vein.

Ulrich (1998) perceives leaving as a process that may involve many attempts to be successful. Stages in the process of breaking loose involve changes in one's level of self-awareness combined with a reevaluation of the relationship as dangerous. During this gradual process of awareness survivors build up their courage to retreat from the danger. In her study of women who have managed to leave, Ulrich found that women with adequate self-esteem to make the break attributed social support as helping them start a new life.

MARITAL RAPE

The laws regarding marital rape offer a clear picture of how society has viewed this phenomenon. Historically, following British law, it was decreed that husbands were exempt from any rape laws (Jerin and Moriarty, 1998). After all, the marriage contract stipulated that a wife willingly must submit to her husband. Accordingly, she could not legally refuse him. In the United States, it was not until 1977 that Oregon became the first state to repeal the marital rape exemption. The controversy that arose in Oregon over its first marital rape case prompted a great deal of mass media coverage and public ridicule of the young woman who had the audacity to charge her husband with this crime. Yet by 1990, forty-eight states had marital rape laws. Today, this is a crime in all states, although some states exempt husbands when no force is used (Jerin and Moriarty, 1998).

In 1983 a Canadian law recognized that any sexual contact without consent within a marriage is sexual assault. But in most other countries, such as Mexico which recently declared rape in marriage legal, wife rape is viewed as an oxymoron.

Because marital rape is rarely differentiated from rape in general in victimization surveys and because victim/survivors of this kind of rape are reluctant to acknowledge its existence even to themselves, the prevalence of marital rape is hard to determine. Resnick, Kilpatrick, Walsh, and Vernonen (1991) estimate that 14 to 25 percent of women are forced by their husbands to have sexual intercourse against their will during the course of their marriage. Approximately one-third to one-half of women who are physically abused by their partners are raped by them (Bergen, 1998; Pagelow, 1992).

Statistics Canada (1998) reports that 8 percent of ever-married women in their 1993 national telephone survey were forced into sexual activity against their will. The National Survey of Wives in Great Britain used a quota sample from ten regions in that country (Painter and Farrington, 1998). Interview results showed that 28 percent of wives had been hit by their husbands. Working-class wives and separated or divorced wives were particularly likely to have been assaulted and also raped. Disproportionately high numbers of raped wives were also raped outside the marriage. Marital rape was more common in Scotland than elsewhere.

Whereas a woman raped by a stranger has to live with the bad memory, a women raped by her husband has to live with the rapist. Bergen (1998) conducted in-depth interviews with a sample of forty survivors of wife rape who had contacted a rape crisis center or women's shelter for help. Based on her findings she divided the causes of wife rape into four categories: entitlement to sex attitudes, sexual jealousy, rape as punishment, and rape as a form of control. The majority of rapes were battering rapes in which the woman was beaten and then raped. Nine of the men performed sadistic rapes on the women, often in connection with porno films. Unlike stranger-rape experiences, marital rape occurs frequently to women who are attacked in this way by their husbands. Like battered women, marital rape victims develop strategies of resistance—going to bed late, spending the night out, getting the husband too drunk for sex, physically resisting, and saving enough money to leave. Above all, when rape seemed inevitable, the women tried to manage the violence by giving in to avoid serious injury. Emotionally, many of the women "tuned out" during the rape. Afterward they would bathe and act as if nothing had happened. Yet only one-third of the women in Bergen's sample defined their experience as rape. Emotionally, the word *disgust* came up over and over in the interviews. In the end, all but three of the women were traumatized; over half considered or attempted suicide. Sexual dysfunction and distrust of other men were among the long-term consequences. Although we can't generalize from these findings because the sample was drawn from women who sought help, the interviews do show the seriousness of the crime of marital rape. The numbers of women who go to the police under these circumstances and have their husbands criminally charged is minuscule (Rollins, 1996). The risk of being killed in such situations is real.

MURDER-SUICIDE

Statistically, murder-suicide is a rare form of suicide (only 1.5 percent of all suicides and 57 percent of all homicides according to Marzuk, Tardiff, and Hirsch, 1992) and yet in spousal homicide, estimates are that one-third of these homicides in the United States and Canada end in suicide (Easteal, 1994). In Iowa a spate of murder-suicides has occurred over the past few years (Clayworth and Erb, 1998). The significance of this wave of spousal murder-suicide (representing almost one-quarter of the total homicide rate for the year) is that in every case the man did the killing and that the killings seemed to have emerged in conjunction with marital breakup.

Palermo (1994) analyzes the psyche of the jealous, paranoid perpetrator who kills both his partner and then himself. The twin nature of murder and suicide are recognized in Palermo's concept, *extended suicide*. Palermo argues that it is plausible to assume that the individual who is dangerously violent and also prone to depression will kill his partner and himself when the relationship goes sour.

WOMEN WHO KILL THEIR HUSBANDS/PARTNERS

As we have seen, in 75 percent of intimate murders in 1996, the woman was the victim (Bureau of Justice Statistics, 1998). This still leaves a substantial number of cases, approximately 450, in which the woman killed her spouse or boyfriend. Since 1977, the number of male spouses and other intimates killed was cut almost in half while the number of female victims killed by spouses and intimates has remained about the same during the same period (Bureau of Justice Statistics, 1998). Pollock (1998) has speculated that the increase in the availability of shelters for battered women has helped to reduce the numbers of women who kill their abusers by removing them from an extremely volatile situation. An added consideration is that since most females arrested for murder are involved in substance abuse in some way, we can further speculate that removal from the drug scene in the home into the more sober shelter atmosphere gives women the chance to think more clearly about the consequences of their actions and prevents them from taking the law into their own hands.

In a comparison study, which builds on an earlier study by Browne (1995) described previously, Roberts (1996) analyzed data drawn in a sample of 105 women in prison convicted of killing their husbands with a community sample of 105 battered women. Compared to the battered women who did not kill their partners, the prison sample was far more likely to have received death threats from their partners that were specific as to time and place and method. The majority of the convicts were more likely than the community representatives to have dropped out of high school, had a history of sexual abuse and a poor work history, cohabitated with her partner, had a substance abuse problem, attempted suicide, and had access to the batterer's guns. Noteworthy in these findings was the murderer's desperation to escape, first through chemical abuse, then through suicide, and finally through a direct attack on the source of the problem.

An article in the *Des Moines Register* (Roos, 1997) tells the story of Katherine Sallis, an African American battered woman who, while drunk in a bar, contracted to have her husband killed. Today, on parole, she counsels women at a domestic violence shelter. Often she hears the women say, "I want to kill my husband."

Sallis knows there are far better options at hand. "I'm helping the community by keeping many women from experiencing the same thing that I went through, by showing them the legal way. There are other ways to express these differences with their spouses" (Roos, 1997, p. 1).

Because battering men are, in all probability, active substance abusers who are not getting the help they need (whether in prison or in the community), their homicide rates against their partners have not declined. The paradox could be expressed in the following imaginary promotion ad: "Save men's lives; increase funding for women's shelters."

Despite occasional well-publicized cases of battered women who kill and are acquitted of murder or manslaughter, the law shows greater leniency toward men who kill their wives than toward women who kill their husbands (Bannister, 1993). The difference seems to be explained by the fact that battered women who have killed will cooperate with the police, making no attempt to cover up their crime. Men who kill their wives, on the other hand, can often afford a lawyer, and since they did not confess, they are in a position to enter a plea of guilty to a lesser charge. The plea of self-defense for a battered woman is often not believed, since she may kill her spouse while he is asleep or drunk or otherwise vulnerable. A woman who kills during a fight will be convicted because the man had no weapon. It is hard for the jury in such cases, as Bannister indicates, to appreciate the danger the woman may have been in. The court system fails women, Bannister concludes, because it is based on a male model of how to determine fact such as self-defense.

In a politicized battered woman's murder trial, expert witnesses often rely on a *battered woman syndrome* self-defense argument. According to this argument—derived from Lenore Walker's (1979) theory of "learned helplessness"—repeatedly beaten women lose their faith in themselves and their judgment becomes impaired. They perceive use of force as their only means of escape. Donald Downs (1997) opposes this line of argument in that its success depends on portraying women as passive victims. (Such a defense additionally may be used against battered mothers fighting for custody of their children; such women are often seen as incapable of protecting their children in their helplessness.) Downs's recommendation regarding homicide cases is that the law be changed to help women argue realistically that danger need not be immediate to be present, that a woman beaten in her home has no duty to retreat when this is her home, and that what is seen as extreme force used by the victim may be proportionate to a man's long history of abuse.

Canadian law has recently been revised under a new Supreme Court decision. Judges must instruct jurors in battered women's cases that the woman is not required to leave the home. Formal consultations are being conducted with lawyers and women's groups on how the law can be brought into line with new thinking on abusive relationships (Geddes, 1998). The justices were divided, however, over use of the battered woman syndrome concept. The fear is that the claims of self-defense by women who do not seem passive and helpless will not be fairly decided if the concept of "learned helplessness" is set as a standard for every case. The inherent contradiction between a "learned helplessness" argument and a woman who took the direct action of committing murder is likely to leave the jury unconvinced. We must keep in mind that many victims do not survive; they are murdered by their batterers: These are the true victims of a long period of domestic abuse. For the ones who kill their assaulters, a more relevant and empowering defense than learned helplessness must be found.

THEORIES OF PARTNER ABUSE

Consider a battered woman who is catering to her partner's every demand, preoccupied with her partner's needs and moods, consistently covering up for him after outbursts, and alternately protective of her children and neglectful of their needs. Is she a codependent woman who was bred for a self-sacrificial, self-destructive role, or has her seemingly bizarre response developed out of the abnormal demands of the situation? We will not answer this rhetorical question now but will instead look at several broad-based theories to explain domestic violence.

Societal Stress

Roberts and Burman (1998) consider a variety of stresses that can increase the potential for violence by men of women. Among them are the birth of children, fear of job loss and work-related problems, financial instability, and a pattern of alcohol abuse. The use of alcohol on the part of highly stressed men can magnify negative feelings, which may be redirected onto family members as a form of displaced aggression. Research confirms a correlation between stress factors such as unemployment and wife abuse (Rollins, 1996). Although some critics of the stress theory of violence, such as Kurz (1998), criticize this conclusion for not explaining why women are the primary targets of violence, women's vulnerability would seem to make them more likely to be the recipients than the perpetrators of violence.

Family Violence Framework

Some researchers challenge the sexual differentiation notion altogether. Basing their conclusions on data gathered by Straus and Gelles (1986) from the Conflict Tactics Scales, researchers claim that wives are as violent as their husbands. Results are based on women's responses to the Conflict Tactics Scales survey. A British study on dating habits used the scale to indicate that more men than women experienced assault by their date, usually in the form of slapping (Carrado, George, Loxam, Jones, and Templar, 1996). The survey measures a continuum of tactics used in resolving conflict. The continuum is extremely broad, including very low levels of violence, and it fails to differentiate initiated violence from acts of self-defense. Sexual abuse is not considered (Kurz, 1998). One study of male/female differences in response to violence indicated that when women were hit they were afraid, but when men were hit, they often laughed (Muchkenfuss, 1998).

The National Violence Against Women Survey of 8,000 men and 8,000 women, which gathered detailed data on a random sample of the population, found that

> *women experience significantly more partner violence than men do: 25 percent of surveyed women, compared with 8 percent of surveyed men, said they were raped and/or physically assaulted by a current or former spouse, cohabiting partner, or date in their lifetime; 1.5 percent of surveyed women and .9 percent of surveyed men said they were raped and/or physically assaulted by such a perpetrator in the previous 12 months. It is important to note that differences between women's and men's rates of physical assault by an intimate partner become greater as the seriousness of the assault increases. . . . They [women] were 7 to 14 times more likely to report that an intimate partner beat them up, choked or tried to drown them, threatened them with a gun, or actually used a gun on them. Eight percent of women and 2 percent of men reported that they had been stalked over their lifetime. (Tjaden and Thoennes, 1998, pp. 2, 7, 12)*

These figures, which were gathered with the most advanced state-of-the-art techniques in terms of sampling and preserving anonymity, should put older, misinterpreted findings to rest. Unfortunately, as Kurz indicates, false claims that levels of abuse between men and women are equal and mutual have been used to cut funding for women's shelters. Such an argument of conjoint violence can also be used to reinforce those family systems therapists who perceive family violence as an outgrowth of faulty communication styles between husband and wife.

Systems Theory

Systems theory offers a multidimensional view of reality. The concept of interactionism, which is central to systems theory, describes the influence of people's feedback on each other simultaneously. Cause and effect under this formulation are viewed as in constant and dynamic interaction with each other.

However useful this framework may be in counseling troubled families and in helping family members improve their skills in communication, when applied to a battering situation, therapy from a systems perspective is fraught with risks. Viewing family pathology as the source of the problem is one step removed from asking questions such as, What is the woman's role in perpetrating the violence? In gender-blind systems theory, each partner is held responsible for his or her contribution to the violence dynamic and for changing his or her behavior accordingly. Within this context, systems theory encourages a denial of the reality of victimization. Under conditions of violence, family counseling can be downright dangerous. Following the sessions, the batterer, in his own insecurity, may attack his wife for revelations made to the therapist.

A concept related to classical systems theory is *codependency,* a term popularized by substance abuse practitioners.The prefix "co-" implies shared responsibility for the behavior of another. So-called codependents are said to have gravitated toward a relationship with an abuser because of an unconscious desire to be enmeshed in an unhealthy relationship. Codependency theory suggests that women remain in an unhealthy situation because of some early deficit in the woman herself (Frank and Golden, 1992). Such a conceptualization overlooks the fact that women who are beaten by a violent man are roughly interchangeable: If one woman manages to extricate herself, she likely will be replaced with another vulnerable woman who will also be beaten. The fact that such a woman may be competent and confident at the beginning of the relationship is no insurance against her subsequent victimization. For example, in their in-depth study of battered mothers presenting children at a hospital for abuse and neglect, Stark and Flitcraft (1998) found no evidence that the mothers were predisposed by their history to be battered. Only the mothers of children suffering from child neglect were found to have had a problematic family history, including disorganization and violence.

Feminist Therapy

Are we looking at a codependent woman, feminists will ask, or are we looking at the results of traditional feminine training? Are we seeing poor communication skills among partners, or are we seeing the effect of severe power imbalance in our society? Because the structure of our patriarchal history has supported the concept of male entitlement vis à vis their wives, many men have trampled on their partners for years with relative immunity (Frank and Golden, 1992). Understanding the context of interpersonal violence in women's lives and examining why such violence continues to happen on a massive scale means calling into question the patriarchal structure in our society (Randall and Haskell, 1995). Feminists perceive the violent family as a microcosm of a society that oppresses and keeps women in their place (Davis, 1995). The recent antifeminist backlash in North American society compounds the original tendency to lean over backwards to avoid anything that hints of "male bashing." As they peruse the literature, researchers need to be especially wary of the taboo against defining an issue in gender-specific terms.

The challenge to feminist theorists is how to explain the often irrational attachment of battered women to their abusers. Most writers of the feminist school, such as Frank and Golden, focus on rational aspects (such as economic considerations and death threats) in a battered woman's decision to stay with her man. Dee Graham (1994), in contrast, refers to Stockholm Syndrome as an explanation for why women who are exposed to intermittent kindnesses by the captor—kindnesses that emerge within the context of a life-and-death situation from which there is only limited possibility of escape—may bond with the captor and even testify on his behalf in the eventual court proceedings. Basically, one's identity with powerful individuals who can exact terrible punishments and withhold the necessities of life can be understood as a regression to a dependent, childlike state. Bettelheim (1943) defined this phenomenon in his classic study of concentration camp survivors. Instead of anger, many prisoners identified with the SS troops and tried to emulate them.

McKenzie (1984:219) defines the Stockholm Syndrome as a "normal process of bonding, accelerated by severe conditions, coupled with attitude change resulting from an inability to reject arguments." In her book, *Loving to Survive,* Graham (1994) extends the concept to describe what she calls the Societal Stockholm Syndrome. Because male violence so permeates our society, as Graham and her associates argue, this engenders a societal response whereby women are rendered isolated, powerless, and subject to male domination. The captive bonds to the captor over time and experiences love in the midst of fear. From their situation of helplessness, women try to placate the men who abuse them through femininity, which shows acceptance of their subordinate role. Joan Crowley's 1996 book review criticizes Graham for being a feminist to the exclusion of all else and for her lack of attention to the male psyche, giving rise to the unhealthy dominance in the first place.

THE SUBSTANCE ABUSE CONNECTION

A high risk factor in intrafamily violence as reported by virtually all the experts is alcohol and drug abuse. Persons who are assaultive are likely to abuse drugs—especially alcohol—and those who abuse alcohol are prone to assault. Although recognizing that many alcoholics are never violent and many aggressors are sober, research findings reveal the following:

- Approximately one-half of clinical spouse batterers have significant alcohol problems. (Tolman and Bennet, 1990)
- One-half to two-thirds of married male alcoholics are physically aggressive toward their partners during the year before alcoholism treatment. (Gondolf and Foster, 1991)
- In men, the combination of blue-collar status, drinking, and approval of violence is significantly associated with a high rate of wife abuse. (Associated Press, 1996)
- Binge drinkers, as opposed to daily drinkers, have an inordinately high rate of reported assault. (Gondolf and Foster, 1991; Murphy and O'Farrell, 1997)
- The female victims of abuse often also have substance abuse problems. (Bennett and Lawson, 1994)
- Sixty percent of female substance abusers have been victims of partner assault, according to estimates by treatment providers. (Bennett and Lawson, 1994; Miller, Downs, and Gondoli, 1989)

- Over one-third of substance abuse patients in a Veterans Administration program survey reported assaulting their wives in the previous year. (Gondolf and Foster, 1991)
- Cocaine, methamphetamine, and alcohol in high doses are all associated with hyperactivity and violence. Marijuana and heroin have not been proved to be associated with violence. (van Wormer, 1998)

The close correlation between substance abuse and relationship violence appears to be unquestionable. The only doubt is over the interpretation of this relationship. What all researchers and treatment personnel agree on is the crying need to put a stop to the violence and the high-risk substance abuse. Unfortunately, the relationship between the treatment providers at substance abuse and domestic violence programs is problematic (Bennett and Lawson, 1994). At the core of the problem is the tendency to dichotomize problems and to treat various components of antisocial behavior as separate entities. The differences arise not only from differing world views—disease model versus feminist approach—but also from a parallel tendency to view reality in terms of linear causation.

In the addictions treatment field, where many of the male clients have been enrolled for treatment for domestic violence offenses, the family is viewed as a system. This viewpoint tends to regard the violence as well as the substance abuse as closely linked and the victim in the family playing as a role in enabling these bad behaviors to continue. Moreover, substance abuse counselors see addiction as the primary problem. The focus is therefore on sobriety: Get the chemicals out of the system and many of the other problems will subside.

The addictions focus in the substance abuse treatment field is matched by the male culture determinism of the domestic violence field. Workers in domestic violence programs have no less firm and sincere a commitment to their clients than do substance abuse counselors to theirs. And just as their counterparts in addictions work tend to be recovering addicts/alcoholics, many of those who counsel battered women have themselves been abused. Women's shelter counselors tend to stress individual/cultural responsibility for antisocial behavior. Drug usage is viewed by these workers as merely an excuse for deliberate acts of aggression. The tendency toward antisocial, risk-taking, and impulsive behavior may play a role in the development of both substance abuse and violence. Studies link low serotonin in the brain to both aggression and addiction as well as to a host of other behaviors.

Social factors link substance abuse and violence against women in regard to cultural expectations. In families in which men are expected to beat their wives when drunk, they will be inclined to do so. Gondolf (1995) argues effectively that the key to the link between alcohol abuse and control is in man's craving for power and control, a craving fostered by distortions of masculinity rooted in social upbringing. The effect of alcohol, in turn, contributes to a misreading of social cues through cognitive impairment, and violence may provide some sense of immediate gratification. A woman's substance abuse often parallels her partner's drug usage. "It takes being drunk to be married to a drunk," as one of van Wormer's clients eloquently put it. Once the man was in recovery, accordingly, his wife's sobriety quickly followed. See Figure 5.1 for a visual representation of the interplay between power and control in an abusive relationship.

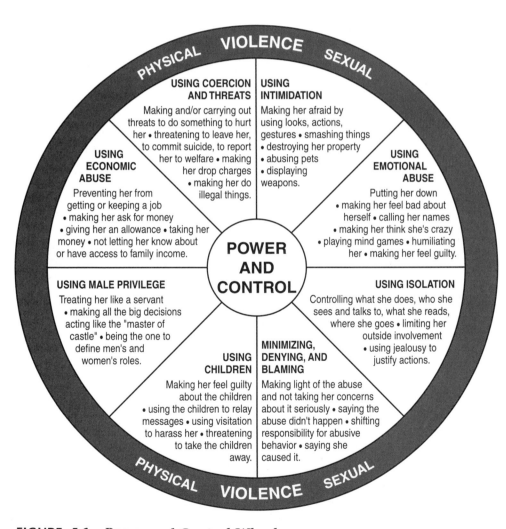

FIGURE 5.1   Power and Control Wheel

Source: Domestic Abuse Violence Project, 202 E. Superior Street, Duluth, MN 55802. Printed with permission of the Domestic Abuse Intervention Project.

THE PSYCHOLOGY OF MALE ABUSE

The question one asks, to a large extent, determines the answer. Instead of asking, Why do they (the women) stay? we should ask, as psychologist Hara Marano (1993), suggests, What makes them (the men) so dependent, so vulnerable? To understand the dynamics of male-on-female violence, we need to consider biological as well as cognitive and social-psychological influences. In his study of battering men, Marano links intrapsychic deficits—a hypersensitivity to abandonment, inability to control negative emotions, and poor impulse control—with biological deficits—low serotonin levels in the brain, high testosterone production, and brain damage from head injury—and with cultural contributions such as traditional gender-role attitudes.

Jacobson and Gottman (1998b) monitored 140 couples with electric sensors while they discussed marital problems. The researchers were surprised to find that the ones they eventually labeled *cobras,* the most violent men who sounded and looked aggressive, were actually internally calm. Those labeled *pit bulls* became internally aroused with heart rates that increased with their anger; they never let up. The wives of pit bulls often took the risk of arguing back. If the women ever left the relationship, such men tended to stalk them. So self-centered were the cobras, that once their women were out of the way, they tended to let go of the relationship. The danger of violence with cobras occurs during the initial separation, whereas pit bulls become more dangerous following separation due to their ambivalent feelings of love. The cobras, about 20 percent of the total of the most violent husbands, are sadistic, prone to death threats, and belong in prison. Because these men have a certain charisma, as Jacobson and Gottman note, their wives tend to find them hard to resist.

A biological proclivity toward rage does not mean control is totally absent in most cases. In analyzing the rationales of eighteen batterers involved in group therapy, Ptacek (1997) found that although most of the men complained of totally losing control, usually in response to their wives' disturbing remarks, their violence was very selective. For example, these men did not attack people outside their family.

Virtually every study of batterers points to their low self-esteem (Stosny, 1997). Afflicted with an inability to compromise with others, they see themselves as powerless victims. Because of their underlying feelings of insecurity, jealousy is an emotion with special meaning for battering men. Marano (1993) summarizes recent research linking wife abuse with difficulty handling jealousy reactions. Violent men were found, in hypothetical jealousy-provoking situations, to consistently misinterpret their wives' motives as intentionally hostile. Nonviolent men in a comparison group did not feel personally threatened by the scenarios presented. Abusive men, according to Marano, may go into a rage when their wives go out with friends. Treatment consists of helping abusers to see that as long as they give their spouses undue power over their emotions and behavior, they will continue to abuse them. Their own overdependence on their spouses causes these men to resent and hate them. This is why murderers may say things like, "I loved my wife so much that I ended up killing her."

CRIMINAL JUSTICE PROCESS

Through the 1970s in most states, the police did not have the authority to make arrests in misdemeanor cases unless they personally had witnessed the offense. In New York State, as in many states, domestic violence cases were heard in family court, a special nonpunitive court, the function of which was to stabilize the family. Married women thus had no legal protection from battery, and unmarried women beaten by their partners had less protection still (Frisch and Caruso, 1996).

Over the next decades, however, drastic changes in the law occurred. The results from a large research study in the Minneapolis Police Department helped change the police perspective regarding the handling of domestic assault calls. In 1981, the Minneapolis Police Department participated in an experiment that assessed the effectiveness of three responses—mediate, separate, or arrest—in preventing future domestic abuse. Sherman and Berk (1984) concluded from this study that "The arrest treatment is clearly an improvement over sending the suspect away, which produced two and a half times as many repeat incidents as arrest (p. 261). This finding held "regardless of the race, employment status, educational level, criminal history of the suspect, or how long the suspect was in jail when arrested" (p. 262).

Even though replication of this experiment has failed to achieve similar results (Dunford, Huizinga, and Elliot, 1990; Hirschel, Hutchison, and Dean, 1992), research indicates that this experiment has significantly changed the policies of police departments nationwide (Sherman and Cohn, 1989). In New York State, for example, the police must provide victims with information about their rights and community services available. Marital rape was criminalized in 1984; then in 1994 new legislation required that the police make arrests where there is probable cause to believe that a felony or misdemeanor was committed or if an order of protection was violated. Because the police are often the first and only contact a victim of domestic violence may have, such improvements in the law are critical. Enforcement of new laws, as Frisch and Caruso indicate, is the greatest challenge to the planned-change process.

Feder (1997) did find from her examination of a large police jurisdiction in south Florida that "officers with more traditional views of women's roles were less likely to self-report an arrest response when answering domestic assault calls" (p. 93). In addition, she found that a belief in the effectiveness of intervention in such calls turned out "to be positively associated with the likelihood of arresting" (p. 93).

Domestic violence among police officers themselves has gained recent recognition as a major problem. As indicated in two studies cited by Fields (1998) as many as 40 percent of the officers had been violent with their spouses or children in the preceding year. Because of such findings, the International Association of Chiefs of Police, headed by Nancy Turner, has introduced new guidelines to address potentially problematic behavior. According to the guidelines, coworkers will be held responsible for withholding information about troubled officers. Supervisors will be trained to look for trouble signs, including increased controlling behavior, greater amount of alcohol or other drug use, and unwarranted verbal abuse.

A major development that sprang out of Duluth, Minnesota ("the Duluth model") is the "no-drop" policy of prosecutors. This policy is now in place in many jurisdictions in the United States and Canada. Instead of dropping charges of assault and battery, which the victim often requests under duress or a change of heart, prosecutors continue the case based on evidence produced by the police. Batterers are viewed as a menace to other potential victims, including their children, and as potential homicide/suicide risks. Victim-support units attached to the prosecutor's office assist with these cases. Requirements for the perpetrators to enter specialized treatment programs are generally a part of any probation plan. Noncompliance, ideally, results in a lengthy prison term. The use of restraining orders to keep offenders away from the survivors offers protection to women in cases of low-level abuse but offers no security in life-threatening situations (Saunders, 1995). A man who is suicidal as well as violent has a high potential to kill his wife or partner.

The entry of women into the legal profession and therefore into the ranks of prosecutors and judges has helped reshape the justice meted out to wife abusers and, more important, the process itself. Raleigh, North Carolina's county courtroom is leading the effort to bring police, prosecutors, and judges under one roof to curb the violence (Nifong, 1997). If a victim refuses to testify, police officers who are specially trained to provide the evidence present the case. A special domestic violence court hears the charges. A standard sentence for first-time offenders is to enter a 26-week social service program for batterers. Judge Joyce Hamilton orders such treatment based on research showing that only 12 percent of offenders involved in a similar program reoffend. In the Raleigh program, a parole officer tracks the offender's progress. Supporters of the new approach say that preventing violence will reduce the murder rate. Judge Hamilton says that's not why she's there; she's there for the kids.

At the national level, the newly created Violence Against Women Office of the U.S. Justice Department has been designed to bolster police and prosecutorial work on domestic and sexual violence cases. Funding is allocated for prevention and victim services programs as well.

HUMAN RIGHTS ISSUES

International law provides for freedom from domestic violence under the 1980 Convention for the Elimination of all Forms of Discrimination Against Women. Former President Jimmy Carter signed the document, which has never been ratified by the U.S. Senate. Every country in Europe has signed. The European Convention for the Protection of Human Rights provides for the same protection against domestic violence. Recently, a complaint was lodged with the European Court on behalf of an Irish woman who sought to separate from her husband due to alleged physical and mental abuse (Barnes, 1998). The complainant was unable to do so because, under the new divorce law in Ireland (divorce was not allowed until 1996), the costs of separation were prohibitive as was the four-year continuous waiting period. The required mediation sessions retraumatize women in forced face-to-face confrontations. Moreover, the nondisclosure stance of the mediation means that if the abused woman is subjected to psychological abuse during mediation, secrecy must prevail. The European Court ruled against the separation fee to make divorce accessible. The extent to which the Irish government will follow this decision is unclear.

This example of reliance on international law to link partner violence with human rights violations has important implications worldwide for women who are subjected to behaviors that could be described as torture, including the element of captivity. Hamby (1998) brings our attention to advocacy efforts to reclassify partner violence as a human rights violation, recognized as such by international organizations such as the United Nations. The significance of such an approach would be in changing societal attitudes and promoting international standards of humanity and equality.

EMPOWERMENT

Sometimes you can learn as much from a negative example as from a positive one. In an ethnographic analysis of services that battered women received, Baker (1996) found that the sixteen Iowa women interviewed encountered varying responses to their situations. On the whole, police encounters were conceived of as negative due to the slowness of response and lack of respect for the woman. Contacts with clergy did more harm than good because ministers tended to focus on the woman's behavior as a cause of the violence. Couples counseling was especially destructive in treating the partners as co-acting equals and leading to assaults immediately afterward for something that was said in therapy. On the positive side, participation in women's support groups led to a heightened awareness and camaraderie that helped group members gain control over their own lives. Baker discovered from her interviews that being stronger, more aware, and knowledgeable about social and political aspects of domestic violence was among the ways battered women felt helped by the group therapy experience.

Crisis Intervention

Immediate care for a woman in a potentially harmful or already abusive situation involves the development of a safety plan (Boes, 1998). Through obtaining crisis intervention services, many women are able to regain control of their lives by identifying current options and goals and by working to attain those goals.

Typically, the battered woman has been subject to psychological and physical abuse for a long period of time before calling for help. She may be mobilized to call a telephone hotline, the police, or a women's shelter or to go to a hospital emergency room. Effective treatment for battered women and their children includes thorough documentation for the possibility of a later legal complaint.

Roberts's (1997) Seven-Stage Crisis Intervention Model offers a framework that can be applied by hospital staff, social workers, or shelter workers. The stages of the crisis intervention model are:

1. Plan and conduct a thorough assessment (including a level-of-danger assessment); inquire about death threats, suicide threats, weapons present, and so forth and immediate psychosocial needs.
2. Establish rapport and rapidly establish a relationship based on genuineness and respect.
3. Identify the precipitating event that led the client to seek treatment; encourage the client to describe the immediate situation.
4. Deal with feelings and emotions. Open-ended questions are recommended. Some examples: *How are you feeling now? What are some of the options you're thinking about? What is the usual situation at home?* Use verbal counseling skills such as reflection of feelings, reassurance, paraphrasing, and attentive silence.
5. Generate and explore alternatives. Helping the client find a safe place is essential.
6. Develop and formulate an action plan. Help the client face her fears and gain control as a self-empowering act. Assistance in a shift from fatalistic thinking toward an attitude of hope and renewal is essential. A cognitive approach will help redirect destructive thought patterns, such as "I can't live without him" or "I must stay for the sake of the kids," and a redirection to empowering affirmations and beliefs, such as, "If other women have made it, so can I."
7. Follow up. Informal and formal agreements should be reached for another meeting to gauge the client's progress and daily functioning. It is hoped that future moves will be toward healing and growth. (p. 43)

Given the enormity and depth of the problems encountered, battered women need a continuity of supportive networks and helping services. Crisis intervention, as Roberts and Burman (1998) indicate, can be the starting point on a longer journey toward safety and renewal. For the majority of battered women, permanently leaving the batterer, regaining self-esteem, and finding safe housing and a job are all necessary.

Shelters for Battered Women

Thanks to feminist activism starting in the 1970s, over 1,250 women's shelters have been established as safe havens for women and their children. Shelters offer more than safety and a way out; living in close quarters with other battered women and participating in group counseling provides an opportunity for consciousness-raising. Unfortunately, due to serious underfunding, most shelters can take in only a minority of the women who need their help. The importance of shelters in preventing further battering, in saving lives, and in revealing options other than returning to an abusive situation is widely acknowledged (Dziegielewski and Resnick, 1996).

Before the establishment of shelters, abused women were whispered about and generally regarded as a source of embarrassment. When shelters were opened to provide safety, they ended up providing a whole lot more. Shelters, as Schechter (1982) observed, offered the supportive framework through which thousands of women turned "personal" problems into political ones, rid themselves of self-blame, and called attention to the sexism that left millions of women violently victimized.

The empowerment philosophy characteristic of women's shelters centers on an awareness of oppression based on race, class, sexual orientation, and gender. Shelter life is woman-centered, chaotic with so much coming and going, emotionally charged, and guided by women who have an agenda and an awareness often different from that of their charges. Threat to life and bodily integrity overwhelms normal adaptive processes. In group sessions, the process of empowerment takes place as women fully acknowledge their vulnerability to male violence. The emphasis on self-protection, on finding one's voice, sharing, and listening to others frees up the mind to contemplate the forbidden and prepares the way for progression from fear to anger to self-expression.

A three-part model of empowerment for women presented by Glen Maye (1998) includes the following:

1. Development of consciousness of self as a woman
2. Reduction of shame and self-blame, and acknowledgment of anger as a catalyst toward change
3. Assumption of personal responsibility for changing self and society. (p. 36)

Overall, about 50 percent of the battered women who get help from shelters or other agencies decide to leave their abusers (Lesser, 1990). The others who return to their abusers have also been frequently changed by their experience. Based on their study of twenty battered Israeli women, Eisikovits, Buchbinder, and Mor (1998) argue that even when a woman decides to stay with the batterer, turning points can still take place. In other words, women may choose to stay in the relationship but never again on the same terms as before. Such a turning point, as these authors indicate, is not sudden but the culmination of a lengthy process in which a woman will actively negotiate, plan, and vow that violence must be stopped. She will confront her partner about her unwillingness to tolerate violence and her involvement with formal organizations specializing in domestic violence.

A woman who decides to stay, nevertheless, needs a safety plan. Such a plan should include acquiring job skills for personal independence, maintaining and reviving friendships; attending a support group on a regular basis; knowing the phone number of the women's shelter by heart; keeping money on hand for emergencies; working out a signal system with a neighbor; getting rid of all weapons and keeping sharp knives in hard-to-reach places; learning how to anticipate violence so as to slip away while it is still safe; preparing older children to call for help; and, finally, preparing to make an escape with the children rather than leaving them behind. See Box 5.2 for a first-hand description of one day's work at a women's shelter.

BOX 5.2 Snapshot—A Social Worker's Daily Reality at a Domestic Violence Shelter

On this beautiful day I'm driving to the local hospital to pick up yet another woman and children affected by the crime of domestic violence. Looking out of my window at everyday people going about their business, I would have little awareness that a woman is assaulted and her children traumatized by this crime that happens every six seconds in this country.

I've been manager of this domestic violence shelter for battered women and children for four years. In that time we have had over a thousand women and children pass through our doors. The stories are all unique and yet all the same. We assist some in relocating out of state to hide and escape the violence; some move in with a mother or sister close to home; and others go back to their homes with promises that the abuser would change.

In my mind I'm making mental notes to prepare to meet the caller and her children. My backseat has three brand-new stuffed animals for the children and a carseat for the baby. There are extra diapers and a blanket in my trunk. I must be alert for anyone suspicious in the parking lot, just in case her abuser has followed her here. That must be her in the waiting room trying to juggle the baby in one arm and two more toddlers in the other. "Hi, I'm Janet from the shelter." She looks scared, but relieved that I'm finally here as I scoop up a toddler. Thus begins another journey that I will take alongside this woman and her babies.

I know that she will have many decisions to make and many obstacles to overcome. Later I find out that this mother is only nineteen years old, uneducated and with few job skills. Her income came totally from her abuser and now is no more. I marvel at her bravery and her desire for a better life.

Another factor complicating this battered woman's life is the fact that she is Caucasian and her children are biracial (African American). I've seen many women come through the shelter under such bicultural circumstances that pose their unique set of problems. In many cases the support systems for these women and, most of all, for the children are lacking. The white world does not embrace biracial children with white mothers. There is a negative stigma in our society attached to a Caucasian woman with biracial children, especially if she has personal problems. Oftentimes her own family has cut her off, disapproving of her choice of partners. The African American community seems more accepting of her and her children, but not when there are accusations of abuse toward one of its members. This leaves her in limbo. Where can she go for help? It is very difficult to find a safe, supportive, nurturing place for her and her children.

Now, we will sit down and begin the process. First come the pain and tears. Then, the harsh reality of figuring out what to do and where to go. I hope we can find some answers.

Source: Janet Wood, LBSW. Printed with permission of Janet Wood.

Treatment for Batterers

Can batterers change their behavior? This is a major consideration because if all the treatment effort is directed toward rescuing the woman, sooner or later the batterer will find another family to victimize. If the partner's behavior can be changed, however, a far more effective form of crime prevention is available.

In intensive group therapy sessions, such as that offered at the Domestic Abuse Project in Minneapolis, offenders confront each other whenever they rationalize and minimize their behavior. Follow-up studies suggest that two out of three clients in the program have not battered their partners 18 months following treatment (Cowley, 1994). Unfortunately, only one-fourth of the court-ordered men who are registered in the program actually complete it.

Because aggression is associated with low serotonin levels in the brain, drug treatment, such as with antidepressant therapy, is becoming increasingly common. "I always tell abusers to try antidepressants," says psychologist Roland Maiuro (1998), who has been conducting a controlled study using the antidepressant Praxil. He adds that "anything that increases serotonin will reduce shame," and shame causes anger and aggression (p. 83). Jacobsen and Gottman (1998a) claim excellent results in their harm reduction program for abusive men, which utilizes feeling-regulation techniques to keep them from getting out of control.

With regard to violence intervention, much more programming is needed, especially at the high school level, to help youths develop healthy relationships. More culturally specific programming is needed as well. Anecdotal evidence from programs designed specifically for African American men suggest that such programs are more successful with African Americans than are other batterers' programs (National Research Council, 1996). For an example of the goals of a healthy relationship, see the equality wheel depicted in Figure 5.2, designed by battered women of Duluth, Minnesota.

Martinez (1996) explains that the abuse victim being subjected to her first assault is a very different person from the one who comes to the attention of the authorities years later. Before the assault, the abuser has spent months or years wearing her down psychologically, using minor acts of aggression to control her. The wife or partner is thus undermined psychologically by the time the physical abuse reaches a dangerous level.

Empowerment can come to a survivor of domestic abuse in working closely with a counselor or other helper as she becomes conscious of inner strengths of which she was unaware, even strengths paradoxically that emerged from her history of abuse. Like many other women who have survived trauma and called for help, she may come to recognize her strength in retrospect. Viewed in the context of the abusive situation and the structural oppression of women, all coping strategies can be recognized as valid resourcefulness and resistance in the face of severe stress.

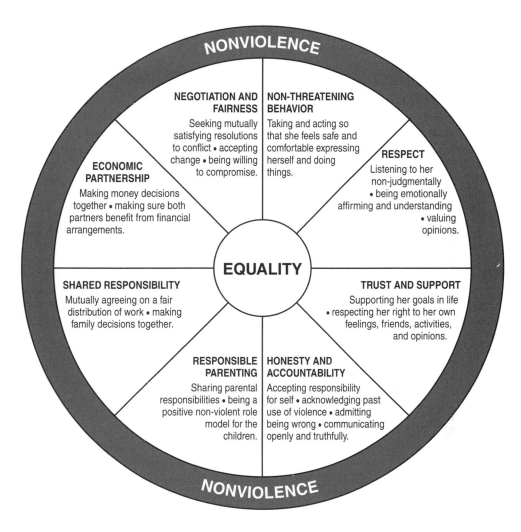

FIGURE 5.2   Equality Wheel

Source: Domestic Abuse Violence Project, 202 E. Superior Street, Duluth, MN 55802. Printed with permission of the Domestic Abuse Intervention Project.

A serious hindrance to adequate long-term treatment for survivors is the unavailability of affordable services. Sadly, mental health providers must compete with other human service agencies for scarce economic resources in a climate that defines non-emergency services as expendable whenever there is a budget crunch. The hope is that, with the current political focus on the needs of crime victims, advocates for prevention of domestic violence and for treatment of its survivors will be heard.

SUMMARY

Learning to believe in oneself as a woman is a lifelong process in a patriarchal society. Learning the functions that violence and the threat of violence serve for the abuser in quelling all criticism and dialogue is a part of that process. Partner abuse is pervasive and an unrecognized cause of chronic psychological and physical health problems. One of the most underreported crimes in the United States, family violence is the single most significant cause of injury to women. About two million women are victimized in this way each year. In whatever capacity we encounter these victim/survivors, whether we are police officers, court officials, child welfare workers, or shelter advocates, we must recognize and challenge the dominant ideology of victim-blaming, welfare "reform," and anti–affirmative action backlash. Moreover, we must do more to educate our children into nonviolent ways of resolving disputes and teach them how to deal with powerful feelings and about the danger signs of psychological abuse.

We began this chapter with a historical overview of domestic woman violence. During Colonial times and even before that, the man was "the lord and master" of the household; he could physically chastise his wife to correct her behavior. In the twentieth century, physical punishment of wives was outlawed. Nevertheless, one form of violence that was retained was marital rape, which is still legal in some states today. Wife beating was not defined as a significant social problem until the 1970s when, in the wake of the civil rights movement, feminists publicized this issue as one that affected all social classes.

Feminist perspectives on wife and partner abuse have encompassed both a challenge to the presumption that domestic violence is rare—demonstrating that on some levels and in some parts of society wife beating is normative—and a call to public action. Incredible strides have been made; the establishment of thousands of women's shelters across the North America is the most obvious example. Despite these advances, much more needs to be done at the societal level to aid women on the road to independence. Welfare reforms are a priority. Public assistance programs need to be responsive to women at risk of being trapped in a situation of abuse and much more flexible regarding workfare requirements. Moreover, allowance must be made for the risks that battered women face in cooperating with child support enforcement efforts. Safe and affordable housing must be provided for families on the run. Finally, to be self-supporting women require access to an array of educational and vocational training opportunities.

Repeated physical and sexual violation are assaults on the integrity and value of the self. Empowerment is critically important so that battered women can recover, heal, and lead lives free from fear and psychological cruelty. Economic and social empowerment are essential to personal survival. Equally essential are institutional and group support to help women subjected to violence to survive and thrive. Substance abuse treatment may be a necessary but not sufficient requirement to end male violence and threatening power plays. What is both necessary and sufficient is to sacrifice a sick relationship for personal wellness, perhaps even embracing a survivor mission as a part of the recovery process. Whichever path is chosen—life within a renewed relationship or apart from it—women released from rigid role stereotypes will be better able to manage their own lives and those of her children.

REFERENCES

Anderson, M. (1997, October 26). The family home is the most dangerous place for women. *Des Moines Register,* p. 4AA.

Associated Press (1996, September 23). Violence research brings startling results. *Waterloo/Cedar Falls Courier,* p. A6.

Baker, P. L. (1996). Doin' what it takes to survive: Battered women and the consequences of compliance to a cultural script. *Studies in Symbolic Interaction 20;* 73–90.

Bannister, S. A. (1993). Battered women who kill their abusers: Their courtroom battles. In R. Muraskin and T. Alleman, *It's a crime: Women and justice* (pp. 316–333). Englewood Cliffs, N.J.: Prentice Hall.

Barnes, A. T. (1998). Ireland's divorce bill: Traditional Irish and international norms of equality in a domestic abuse context. *Vanderbilt Journal of Transnational Law 31*(3): 643–670.

Bennett, L., and Lawson, M. (1994). Barriers to cooperation between domestic-violence and substance-abuse programs. *Families in Society 75:* 277–286.

Bergen, R. K. (1998). The reality of wife rape. In R. K. Beyen (ed.), *Issues in intimate violence.* Thousand Oaks, Calif.: Sage.

Bettleheim, B. (1943). Individual and mass behavior in extreme situations. *Journal of Abnormal and Social Psychology 38:* 417–452.

Blackstone, W. (1979). *Commentaries on the laws of England* (pp. 444–445) facsimile of the first edition of 1765–1769.

Boes, M. (1998). Battered women in the emergency room: Emerging roles for the ER social worker and clinical nurse specialist. In A. Roberts (ed.), *Battered women and their families,* 2nd ed. (pp. 205–229) New York: Springer.

Browne, A. (1995). Fear and the perception of alternatives: Asking "why battered women don't leave" is the wrong question. In B. R. Price and N. Sokoloff (eds.), *The criminal justice system and women: Offenders, victims, and workers* (pp. 228–245). New York: McGraw-Hill.

Bureau of Justice Statistics (1996). Female victims of violent crime. Washington, D.C.: U.S. Department of Justice.

Bureau of Justice Statistics (1998). Violence by intimates. Washington, D.C.: U.S. Department of Justice.

Carrado, M., George, M., Loxam, E., Jones, L., and Templar, D. (1996). Aggression in British heterosexual relationships. *Journal of Aggressive Behavior 22:* 401–415.

Castiglia, C. (1996). *Bound and determined: Captivity, culture-crossing, and white womenhood from Mary Rowlandson to Patty Hearst.* Chicago: University of Chicago Press.

Clayworth, J., and Erb, G. (1998, September 20). Another murder, suicide in Iowa. *Des Moines Register,* p. 1A.

Council on Scientific Affairs, American Medical Association. (1992). Violence against a woman: Relevance for medical practitioners. *Journal of the American Medical Association 267:* 3184–3189.

Cowley, G. (1994, July 4). Stopping abuse: What works. *Newsweek:* 33

Crowley, J. E. (1996). Reinventing the cycle: Two views of the psychology of domestic violence. *Psychology of Women Quarterly 20*(3): 462–464.

Darroch, W. (1998, February 19). Streets safer than home for women, inquest told. *Toronto Star,* p. 1.

Davis, L. V. (1995). Domestic violence. *Encyclopedia of social work,* 19th ed. Washington, D.C: 780–788.

Dearwater, S. R., Coben, J. H., Campbell, J. C., et al. (1998). Prevalence of intimate partner abuse in women treated at community hospital emergency departments. *Journal of the American Medical Association 280*(5): 433–438.

Downs, D. (1997). *More than victims: Battered women, the syndrome society, and the law.* Chicago: University of Chicago Press.

Dunford, F., Huizinga, D., and Elliot, D. (1990). The role of arrest in domestic assault: The Omaha police experiment. *Criminology 28:* 183–206.

Dutton, D. G., and Painter, S. (1993). Emotional attachments in abusive relationships: A test of traumatic bonding theory. *Violence and Victims 8*(2): 105–120.

Dwyer, D. C. (1995). Response to the victims of domestic violence: Analysis and implications of the British experience. *Crime and Delinquency 41*(4): 527–540.

Dziegielewski, S. F., and Resnick, C. (1996). Assessment and intervention: Abused women in the shelter setting. In A. Roberts (ed.), *Crisis management and brief treatment: Theory, technique and application* (pp. 123–141). Belmont, Calif.: Wadsworth.

Easteal, P. (1994). Homicide suicides between adult sexual intimates: An Australian study. *Suicide and Life-Threatening Behavior 24*(2): 140–151.

Eisikovits, Z., Buchbinder, E., and Mor, M. (1998). "What it was won't be anymore": Reaching the turning point in coping with intimate violence. *Affilia 13*(4): 411–434.

Feder, L. (1997). Domestic violence and police response in a pro-arrest jurisdiction. *Women and Criminal Justice 8:* 79–98.

Fields, G. (1998, October 14). Domestic abuse among cops. *USA Today,* p. 5A.

Frank, P. B., and Golden, K. (1992). Blaming by naming: Battered women and the epidemic of codependence. *Social Work 37*(1): 5–6.

Frish, L. A., and Caruso, J. M. (1996). The criminalization of woman battering: Planned change experiences in New York State. In *Helping battered women: New perspectives and remedies* (pp. 102–131). New York: Oxford University Press.

Geddes, J. (1998, February 23). Victims who kill. *Maclean's,* p. 64.

Glen Maye, L. (1998). Empowerment of women. In L. Gutierrez, R. F. Parsons, and E. O. Cox (eds.), *Empowerment in social work practice: A sourcebook* (pp. 29–51). Pacific Grove, Calif.: Brooks/Cole.

Gondolf, E. W. (1995). Alcohol abuse, wife assault, and power needs. *Social Service Review 69:* 274–284.

Gondolf, E. W., and Foster, R. A. (1991). Wife assault among V.A. alcohol rehabilitation patients. *Hospital and Community Psychiatry 42:* 74–79.

Graham, D. L., with Rawlings, E., and Rigsby, R. K. (1994). *Loving to survive: Sexual terror, men's violence, and women's lives.* New York: University Press.

Hamby, S. (1998). Partner violence: Prevention and intervention. In J. L. Jasinski and L. M. Williams (eds.), *Partner violence* (pp. 210–258). Thousand Oaks, Calif.: Sage.

Henriques, Z. W. (1995). African-American women: The oppressive intersection of gender, race, and class. *Women and Criminal Justice 7:* 67–80.

Hirschel, J. D., Hutchison, I., and Dean, C. (1992). The failure of arrest to deter spouse abuse. *Journal of Research in Crime and Delinquency 29:* 7–33.

Ingrassia, M., and Beck, M. (1994, July 4). Patterns of abuse. *Newsweek,* pp. 26–33.

Jacobson, N. S., and Gottman, J. M. (1998a, March). Violent relationship. *Psychology Today,* pp. 60–65, 81–84.

Jacobson, N. S., and Gottman, J. M. (1998b). *When men batter women: New Insights into ending abusive relationships.* New York: Simon and Schuster.

Jerin, R. A., and Moriarty, L. J. (1998). *Victims of crime.* Chicago: Nelson-Hall.

Kaufman-Kantor, G., Jasinski, J., and Aldarondo, E. (1994). Sociocultural status and incidence of marital violence in Hispanic families. *Violence and Victims 9*(3): 207–222.

Kurz, D. (1998). Old problems and new directions in the study of violence against women. In R. K. Bergen (ed.), *Intimate violence* (pp. 197–208). Thousand Oaks, Calif.: Sage.

Lee, M.-Y., and Au, P. (1998). Chinese battered women in North America: Their experiences and treatment. In A. Roberts (ed.), *Battered women and their families* (pp. 448–482) (2nd ed.). New York: Springer.

Lesser, B. (1990). Attachment and situational factors influencing battered women's return to their mate following a shelter program. In K. Pottharst (ed.), *Research explorations in adult attachment* (pp. 81–128). New York: Peter Lang.

Loomis, J. (1998). Balcony incident spurs plans for women's shelter. *Edmonton Sun,* p. 1A.

Maiuro, R. (1998, March/April). Interviewed in "Can they stop?" *Psychology Today:* 83.

Marano, H. (November/December, 1993). Inside the heart of marital violence. *Psychology Today,* pp. 50–53, 76–78, 91.

Martinez, J. (1996). Hostage in the home. In Pennsylvania coalition against rape. *Victim empowerment.* Washington D.C.: U.S. Department of Justice, pp. 58–73.

Marzuk, P., Tardiff, K., and Hirsch, C. (1992). The epidemiology of murder-suicide. *Journal of the American Medical Association 267*(23): 3179–3183.

McKenzie, I. K. (1984). Hostage-captor relationship: Some behavioral and environmental determinants. *Police Studies 9*(4): 219–223.

Miller, B. A., Downs, W. R., and Gondoli, D. M. (1989). Spousal violence among alcoholic women as compared to a random household sample of women. *Journal of Studies on Alcohol 50:* 533–540.

Muchkenfuss, M. (1998, September 13). Battering in teen relationships, too. *Des Moines Register,* p. 6E.

Murphy, C. M., and O'Farrell, T. J. (1997). Couple communication patterns of maritally aggressive and nonaggressive male alcoholics. *Journal of Studies on Alchohol 15,* 83–90.

Natera, G. R., Tiburcio, M. S., and Villatoro, J. V. (1997). *Contemporary Drug Problems 24*(4): 787–804.

National Research Council. (1996). *Understanding violence against women.* Washington D.C.: National Academy Press.

Nifong, C. (1997, October 21). A full-court press on domestic abuse. *Christian Science Monitor,* p. 1.

Pagelow, M. (1992). Adult victims of domestic violence. *Journal of Interpersonal Violence 7:* 87–120.

Painter, K., and Farrington, D. P. (1998). Marital violence in Great Britain and its relationship to marital and non-marital rape. *International Review of Victimology 5:* 257–276.

Palermo, G, B. (1994). Murder-suicide—An extended suicide. *International Journal of Offender Therapy and Comparative Criminology 8*(3): 205–216.

Pollock, J. M. (1998). *Counseling women in prison.* Thousand Oaks, Calif.: Sage.

Ptacek, J. (1997). The tactics and strategies of men who batter: Testimony from women seeking restraining orders. *Violence between intimate partners: Patterns, causes, and effects* (pp. 104–123). Boston: Allyn & Bacon.

Randall, M., and Haskell, L. (1995). Sexual violence in women's lives. *Violence against women* (1): 6–31.

Resnick, H., Kilpatrick, D., Walsh, C., and Vernonen, L. (1991). Marital rape. In R. Ammerman and M. Herson (eds.), *Case studies in family violence.* New York: Plenum.

Roberts, A. R. (1996). Battered women who kill: A comparative study of incarcerated participants with a community sample of battered women. *Journal of Family Violence 11*(3): 291–304.

Roberts, A. R. (1997). Epidemiology and definitions of acute crisis in American society. In A. Roberts (ed.), *Crisis management and brief treatment* (pp. 16–33). Chicago: Nelson-Hall.

Roberts, A. R., and Burman, S. (1998). Crisis intervention and cognitive problem-solving therapy with battered women: A national survey and practice model. In A. Roberts (ed.), *Battered women and their families,* 2nd ed. (pp. 3–28). New York: Springer.

Rollins, J. H. (1996). *Women's minds, women's bodies: The psychology of women in a biosocial context.* Upper Saddle River, N.J.: Prentice-Hall.

Roos, J. (1997, June 30). Abuse victim leads battle cry against violence. *Des Moines Register,* p. 1.

Sakai-shi. (1995). *The report of the 3rd study of attitudes towards human rights.* Osaka: Author.

Saunders, D. G. (1995). Domestic violence: Legal issues. In *Encyclopedia of social work,* 19th ed. (pp. 789–794). Washington D.C.: NASW Press.

Schechter, S. (1982). *Women and male violence.* New York: Macmillan.

Sherman, L. W., and Berk, R. A. (1984). The specific deterrent effects of arrest for domestic assault. *American Sociological Review 49:* 261–272.

Sherman, L. W., and Cohn, E. G. (1989). The impact of research on legal policy: The Minneapolis domestic violence experiment. *Law and Society Review 23:* 117–144.

Sokoloff, N. (1995). In *The criminal justice system and women: Offenders, victims, and workers* (pp. 228–245). New York: McGraw-Hill.

Sorenson, S. B., and Telles, C. A. (1991). Self-reports of spousal violence in a Mexican-American and non-Hispanic white population. *Violence and Victims 6*(1): 3–15.

Stark, E., and Flitcraft, A. (1998). Women and children at risk." In R. K. Bergen (ed.), *Issues in intimate violence* (pp. 25–41). Thousand Oaks, Calif.: Sage.

Statistics Canada (1998). *Family violence in Canada: A statistical profile 1998.* Ottawa: Statistics Canada.

Stordeur, R. A., and Stille, R. (1989). *Ending men's violence against their partners.* Newbury Park, Calif.: Sage Publications.

Stosny, S. (1997). Group treatment of spouse abusers. In G. L. Greif and P. H. Ephrons (eds.), *Group work with populations at risk* (pp. 147–159). New York: Oxford University Press.

Straus, M., and Gelles, R. (1986). Societal change and change in family violence from 1975 to 1985 as revealed by two national surveys. *Journal of Marriage and the Family 48:* 465–479.

Straus, M. A., and Gelles, R. J. (1990). How violent are American families? Estimates from the National Family Violence Resurvey and other studies. In M. A. Straus and R. J. Gelles (eds.), *Physical violence in American families: Risk factors and adaptations to violence in 8,145 families* (pp. 95–112). New Brunswick, N.J.: Transaction.

Tjaden, P., and Thoennes, N. (1998). *Prevalence, incidence, and consequences of violence against women: Findings from the national violence against women survey.* Washington, D.C.: U.S. Department of Justice.

Tolman, R. M., and Bennett, L. W. (1990). A review of quantitative research on men who batter. *Journal of Interpersonal Violence 5:* 87–118.

Ulrich, Y. C. (1998). What helped most in leaving spouse abuse: Implications for interventions. In J. C. Campbell (ed.), *Empowering survivors of abuse: Health care for battered women and their children* (pp. 70–78). Thousand Oaks, Calif.: Sage.

van Wormer, K. (1998). Domestic violence and substance abuse: An integrated approach. In A. Roberts, *Battered women and their families,* 2nd ed. (pp. 345–362). New York: Springer.

Vitanza, S., Vogel, L. C., and Marshall, L. L. (1995). *Violence and Victims 10*(1): 23–34.

Wallace, H. (1998). *Victimology: Legal, psychological, and social perspectives.* Boston: Allyn & Bacon.

Walker, L. (1979). *The battered woman.* New York: Harper and Row.

West, C. M. (1998a). Leaving a second closet: Outing partner violence in same-sex couples. In J. Jasinski and L. Williams (eds.), *Partner violence: A comprehensive review of 20 years of research* (pp. 163–183). Thousand Oaks, Calif.: Sage.

West, C. M. (1998b). Lifting the political gag order: Breaking the silence around partner violence in ethnic minority families. In J. Jasinski and L. Williams (eds.), *Partner violence: A comprehensive review of 20 years of research* (pp. 184–209). Thousand Oaks, Calif.: Sage.

Yoshihama, M. (1998). Domestic violence in Japan: Research program development and emerging movements. In A. Roberts (ed.), *Women and their families* (pp. 405–447). New York: Springer.

Zimbardo, P. G., Haney, C., and Banks, W. C. (1972, April 8). A Pirandellian prison: The mind is a formidable jailer. *New York Times Magazine,* pp. 38–60.

WOMEN AS PROFESSIONALS

The three chapters of this part—on the woman police officer, the woman lawyer, and the woman who works in corrections—have many similarities. They examine the role behavior of women who are attempting to break into a male subculture, one that sees itself as reserved for males. Women lawyers appear to have had the greatest success in breaking into this man's world, but women probation and parole officers have also been widely accepted, both by fellow workers and by clients. Women police officers have had the most difficulty in breaking into the men's club of policing, but women correctional officers in men's prisons are not far behind in encountering barriers and obstacles created by male corrections staff. In addition to the lack of acceptance that women have experienced, sexual harassment, especially in policing and in men's prisons, has posed a real problem for women who are employed in these fields.

Racial discrimination has joined with gender and culture in revealing the oppression that women professionals experience. The African American woman who is a police officer experiences even less acceptance in police agencies than does the white woman who is a police officer. She frequently feels alienated from white male and female officers and often even from African American male officers. In law school, the African American woman may experience discrimination, in areas ranging from acceptance to admittance to student study groups. Subsequent to law school, this pattern of racial discrimination extends to limited opportunities for African American women attorneys to practice in high-status, financially remunerative, and powerful positions.

6

WOMEN IN LAW ENFORCEMENT

Entry into the men's club of policing is difficult for a woman. The resistance to entering this male-dominated world seems to continue throughout a woman's career. The difficulty of finding acceptance may start on the first day in the academy and not end until retirement. The problematic nature of policing as a career for women further expresses itself in the appraisal process of new recruits, in supervisory attitudes and treatment, in attitudes of male line police officers, and in promotional opportunities and career advancement. Reluctance to accept a woman police officer extends also to citizens in the community.

Another expression of the problematic nature of policing for women involves the career adjustments women face to make it as police officers. Even though a number of studies reveal that female police officers are equally as competent as male police officers, policewomen typically feel that they must prove themselves over and over. Women police officers often feel that they must display and identify with a "masculine" role (competency, intelligence, and independence), but the danger is that this may result in their being typecast as pushy, unfeminine, and aggressive (Lord, 1995, p. 631). Women police officers also must decide whether they want to be respected as crime fighters and work with the men or become specialists in community-oriented policing, in juveniles, or in vice. Policewomen must further find ways to establish their own networks and support groups, because they have been excluded from the male-dominated police culture.

In addition, the majority of women acknowledge that they have experienced abuse and sexual harassment and that each woman police officer must decide how much is too much. Susan L. Webb (1994) defines sexual harassment as:

1. The behavior in question is sexual in nature.
2. The behavior is deliberate and/or repeated.
3. The behavior is not welcome or asked for and is not returned.

4. The more severe the behavior is, the fewer times it needs to be repeated before it can be reasonably defined as harassment, and the less responsibility the receiver has to speak up.

5. The less severe the behavior is, the more times it needs to be repeated, and the more responsibility the receiver has to speak up. (pp. 26–29)

Considering this difficulty, why do women want to join this exclusively male club? The first and obvious answer is the freedom to have the same privileges, rights, and responsibilities that men have (Schaper, 1997, p. 32). Pure economics is a second reason. Departments in the 1960s and 1970s could not fill the many vacant positions with qualified male applicants due to the poor image of police, low salaries, and sometimes deplorable working conditions officers faced (Schulz, 1995, p. 135). A third reason, and perhaps even more important, many women enter policing because they have a lot of enthusiasm for and commitment to becoming police officers. They see policing as a career in which they can make a difference, or they may anticipate that policing is an exciting job. Similar to men entering policing, women want to put the uniform on and feel that adrenaline rush when the action goes down. Or they may be attempting to prove something, for example, that they can do this job just as well as men can.

A HISTORY OF WOMEN IN POLICING

The policewomen's movement can be traced to demands of benevolent groups for prison, jail, and police matrons. In the 1820s volunteer Quaker women, along with upper-middle-class women, blamed the poor living conditions of female inmates on "neglect and sexual exploitation by male keepers." For example, "Rachel Welch, one of a small number of women in Auburn Prison in New York, became pregnant while serving a punishment sentence in a solitary cell. As a result of a flogging by a male prison official, Welch died after childbirth" (Schulz, 1995, p. 10).

The pressure for reform that followed this scandalous event resulted in Auburn creating the position of prison matron to oversee women's quarters in 1832 and influenced the passing of the 1928 law requiring the separation of males and females in county prisons. New York City officials followed the Auburn example by responding to pressure from the American Female Moral Reform Society to hire six matrons for its two jails in 1845 (Schulz, 1995, pp. 10–11).

During the post–Civil War period, women again became concerned about the welfare of female prisoners, noting "overcrowding, harsh treatment, and sexual abuse by their male keepers" (Schulz, 1995, p. 11). The Women's Christian Temperance Union and the General Federation of Women's Clubs demanded an increased role for women in caring for women and children in police custody. These organizations helped create and finance the position of police matron in the 1880s, which was women's first entry into police departments, albeit as social workers.

New York was the first city to hire full-time police matrons in 1845 (Berg and Budnick, 1986, p. 314). But in 1887 the Men's Prison Association expressed opposition to placing matrons in each station house in New York City. At this time, the "city detained 14,000 women prisoners and received 42,000 female lodgers for overnight shelter." The association based its objection "on lack of space for a matron, on the violent state of the women, and on their fear of a matron's physical inability to handle the women" (p. 314).

In the late nineteenth and early twentieth centuries, a number of social forces contributed to the appearance of women police officers outside correctional settings. The most significant of these social forces were the expansion of the frontier, the surge toward industrialization, the development of the steam engine, the extension of political democracy, and the development of new economic institutions. This was also an era of religious revivalism, utopian experiments, and increased social consciousness. People joined together to sponsor the temperance movement, to institute public education, and to establish humane management systems for the insane, deviant, and delinquent.

The experience of the female abolitionists, as well as such social problems as widespread poverty, breakdown of the family, child labor, and increases in juvenile delinquency and female-related crime, provided the catalyst for the appearance of a women's movement called the suffragettes. The primary goal of this movement was to eliminate some of the social ills besetting children and women. This movement also gave birth to what is called the "child-saving movement" and the development of the juvenile court and its *parens patriae* philosophy (Platt, 1969, p. 76). The entry of women into law enforcement in a social worker mode during this era was "due to the reformist zeal of the period, an acceptance of a limited and special role for women in law enforcement, and the efforts of a few dedicated progressive reformers" (Lord, 1995, p. 628).

Reformers began to push for the appointment of women with the skills to work in the streets with prostitutes, runaways, and juvenile delinquents (Feinman, 1986, p. 81). In 1905 Lola Baldwin, secretary to the protective group, Travelers' Aid Society, was hired as a "safety worker" as part of the Lewis and Clark Exposition in Portland, Oregon. Hers was the first documented appointment of a woman with police power, and her duties were to protect girls and women from harassment as well as to stop girls and women from pursuing men. The city government decided to retain Baldwin as director of the Department of Public Safety for the Protection of Young Girls and Women after the exhibition ended (Heidensohn, 1992, p. 43).

Neither she nor the police department wanted women to be called "police-women," because neither wished to associate women with the concept or job

*of policemen. The women, called "operatives" or "safety workers," consid-
ered themselves social service workers. (Feinman, 1986, pp. 81–82)*

In 1910, Alice Stebbins Wells was officially classified as a "policewoman"
in Los Angeles, California. Her contributions to women in police were significant. She was hired at the rank of detective after she convinced the city that
a sworn woman police officer could be effective. The publicity about her hiring caused other cities to hire women, and in 1915, she founded the International Association of Policewomen.

Although Alice Wells was pictured in newspapers as "a masculine individual, grasping a revolver, and dressed in unfeminine clothing," policewomen of her era did not consider themselves female versions of policemen,
a concept they derogatorily termed "little men" (Schulz, 1995, p. 4). They
perceived themselves to be superior to policemen in social class, education,
and professionalism. They "embodied the concept of the policewoman-as-
social worker . . . seeking to bring social services and order into the lives of
women and children. . . ." At the same time they avoided "the trappings of
police, opposing uniforms for themselves and choosing not to carry firearms
even if permitted to do so" (p. 4). Despite this limited role, their acceptance
was only marginal, and the demands for policewomen were almost always imposed on police executives from outside sources (pp. 2–5).

Frances Heidensohn's (1992) examination of this period concluded that a
number of factors shaped the development of women policing in both the
United States and Britain. First, this movement had a moral basis: the entrance of women in policing was "vigorously promoted by groups formed for
moral protection, and sometimes feminist causes who did so to attain social
purity, rescue, and welfare goals" (p. 52). Second, volunteers had an important role in the origins of women police officers. A group of women who
sought to be police officers were willing to volunteer their services on patrol.
Third, considerable proselytizing for women took place in policing; supporters of this movement, as well as the pioneers themselves, pursued their cause
with missionary zeal. Fourth, policewomen's strongest opposition came from
both rank-and-file and senior police officers. Fifth, the women movement in
policing advocated specialist work because it sought the right of women to
work with women and children. Finally, women sought gender control, in
that they wanted to protect their own sex and did not seek a mandate to police men (pp. 52–54).

Women's place in policing became more secure after the First World War.
In 1922 there were 500 women officers; by 1932, there were more than 1,500.
Then, partly due to the Great Depression, the number leveled off. In 1950 there
were 2,600 policewomen and in 1960, 5,617 (Heidensohn, 1992, pp. 52–54).
The number of women police officers was to nearly double in the decade of the
1960s due in part to the social experimentation of that period. Both the civil
rights movement and the women's movement benefited from the spirit of the
times, but it was the women's movement that fueled the demands of women

to have equal opportunity and career advancements in police departments (Lord, 1995, p. 628).

The 1950s brought a different type of woman into policing (Schulz, 1993). These "second-generation" policewomen, who were often military veterans, were middle-class careerists. Having more education (most had at least some college) and higher in social-class orientation than their male peers, these women had more similarity with male police officers than did their predecessors. According to Schulz, "they formed a bridge between the upper-middle class, college-educated, feminist, Progressive women who had served as policewomen before them and today's women officers, most of whom are comparable to the overwhelmingly working-class, high school educated men with whom they serve" (p. 7).

The demand for expanded roles in policing for women greatly increased after a 1961 lawsuit that allowed women police officers to compete in promotional examinations. The New York Police Department promoted its first female sergeant in 1964 (Schulz, 1995, pp. 2–5). In 1968 Indianapolis police officers Betty Blankenship and Elizabeth Coffal were the first women to put on a uniform, strap on a gun belt, and drive a marked police vehicle, answering police calls like their male counterparts (pp. 2–5).

The 1964 Civil Rights Act and the 1972 Equal Employment Opportunity Commission (EEOC) expanded the rules of state and civil service bodies and made it illegal to discriminate in employment. The EEOC rules, which pressured police agencies to change hiring practices and show why a woman or minority person is not qualified to become a police officer, had a major impact on the presence of women on the police employment lists.

On September 20, 1974, while attempting to arrest a bank robber, 24-year-old Gail Cobb became the first African American policewoman to die of gunshot wounds (Schulz, 1995, p. 140). Currently, The National Law Enforcement Officers Memorial has 111 female officers' names engraved on its wall, only seven of whom were killed before 1970 (National Law Enforcement Officers Memorial Fund, 1997). Box 6.1 reveals the evolving role of women in policing during the twentieth century.

BOX 6.1   Women in Law Enforcement

Gloria E. Myers's *Municipal Mother: Portland's Lola Greene Baldwin, America's First Policewoman* takes a detailed look at Baldwin's 17-year career. What makes this book so valuable is that Myers analyzes the social and historical factors that led to the appointment of policewomen in a number of cities in the United States and Canada in the early decades of the twentieth century. Baldwin's initial success, as well as her longevity (she

(Continued)

BOX 6.1   *Continued*

remained in her position through the in-
cumbency of six chiefs of police and five
mayors), was not so much a story of police
reform as the story of Progressive Reformers'
concern about morality and sexual activity
among girls and women.

Myers's book describes how issues of
class, crime, and social control merged with
concerns about leisure-time activities to create a climate leading to a new career for
women—that of policewoman. She explains
how Portland's upper-middle-class activist
women used concerns about immorality
among both women and men to forge alliances with social hygiene and temperance
activists to alter societal expectations of police enforcement. It was this combination of
interests in Portland and around the nation
that led to positions for women in police departments.

Gayleen Hays, with Kathleen Moloney's
autobiography *Policewoman One: My Twenty
Years on the LAPD,* offers a candid street-wise
autobiography that explores all aspects of
Hays's professional and personal life. It
traces her career from its beginnings in 1967
as a "policewoman" (not a police officer) to
her retirement in October 1989. In 1972
when the department was forced to sexually
integrate its workforce and eliminate separate and discriminatory job categories, Hays
made the decision not to become a police officer. Thus, she chose to forgo the possibility
of promotion and assignments to regular patrol or traffic duty. She felt that the image of
a policewoman is different from that of a policeman. She comments that there are many
situations "where it's better to have a nurturing female persona than that of a confrontational male."

During her career, Hays worked prostitution as well as rape and child abuse and in
almost every bureau of the Los Angeles Police Department. She even worked in an elite
plainclothes unit whose duty was to pursue
hard-core criminals. Hays frankly discusses
her personal life throughout the book, including her three marriages, her atypical
childhood, being sexually molested, and
how these personal experiences affected her
on the job. Nicknamed as a dinosaur, Hays
was the last of a dying breed. When she left
the force, her badge, "Policewoman #1," was
retired. Today, only police officers are on the
LAPD.

Hosansky and Sparling's *Working Vice*
chronicles the career of Lieutenant Lucie J.
Duvall in the Cleveland Police Department.
In her current position she is head of the department's sex crime and child abuse unit.
She was still working when the book was
published. In the beginning of the book, we
find a confident police lieutenant as she is
put through a yearly firearms qualification
exercise. She is comfortable with her work,
the mechanics of her job, and the decisions
she must make because of the responsible
position she holds. Using "flashback" se-
quences, the reader is taken through her
career. When Lieutenant Duvall began her
career in law enforcement during the early
1970s, she was part of a monumental time in
the history of women in policing, because
women were first hired to do the same job as
male police officers. The book explores fully
her devotion to her life's work. It follows her
personal triumphs as well as hardships; it
reveals other officers' positive and negative
opinions of her police work.

Sources: Gloria E. Myers, *A Municipal Mother: Portland's Lola Greene Baldwin, America's First Police-
woman* (Corvallis, Ore.: Oregon State University Press, 1995); Gayleen Hays with Kathleen
Moloney, *Policewoman One: My Twenty Years on the LAPD* (New York: Vilard Books, 1992); and
Tamar Hosansky and Pat Sparling, *Working Vice: The Gritty True Story of Lt. Lucie J. Duvall* (New
York: HarperCollins, 1992).

COMPARISON OF MALE AND FEMALE OFFICERS' JOB PERFORMANCE

One of the criticisms of women who want to enter policing is that they lack skills to perform well as police officers. In the 1970s, a large amount of research was done to evaluate the performance of women police officers. These studies were conducted for Washington, D.C.; New York City; Denver, Colorado; Newton, Massachusetts; Philadelphia, Pennsylvania; the California State Highway Patrol; and St. Louis County, Missouri (Lord, 1995, p. 632).

In those studies, as well as more recent ones, researchers consistently demonstrated that women can handle the crime-fighting, rescue, combat, peacekeeping, and social service aspects of police work as well as men, regardless of differences in biological constitution and socialization practices (Horne, 1980). A lingering question in the minds of many male officers is whether female officers can handle patrol duties as well as male officers. Although some gender differences were found, all but the second phase of the Philadelphia study found that men and women were equally capable of patrol work (Martin and Jurik, 1995, p. 55). These studies also generally indicate that "men are in no more danger with women as partners than with men as partners" (Feinman, 1986, p. 95).

Differences occurred between male and female police officers in how they performed on the job. Policewomen were typically seen as showing more restraint in using their firearms and in managing family disturbances; as being more sensitive to citizens' needs and using a more community-oriented policing style; and as using less sick time. Policemen generally had better shooting ability, had superior strength and agility, and required less assistance in making arrests (Lord, 1995, p. 632). The findings from the Philadelphia study also reported that women officers were assaulted more often, had more vehicle collisions, and sustained more injuries. Furthermore, some evidence exists that women have higher turnover rates than men in policing (Doerner, 1995, p. 205).

GENDER, RACE, AND CULTURE

The themes of gender, race, and culture are critical to understanding the careers of women in policing. Policing, as the opening section of this chapter suggested, is an extremely biased, gender-oriented occupation. Sexual harassment is a problem that most women police officers confront in some way during their careers. Increased numbers of women police officers have brought this problem to the attention of the courts. Race is also a critical variable in policing. African American women tend to have much different experiences in policing from white women. African American policewomen often feel alienated from white male, white female, and even African American male police officers. Female officers tend to come from higher-class backgrounds than male police officers and to have earned higher educational achievements, but culture is a much more important variable in policing than is class. Police culture has typically excluded the female; it is a club for men, and women are not wanted.

Gender and Culture: Women Are Not Wanted— This Is a Man's Job

Policing has been one of the most resistant occupations to accept women (Belknap and Shelley, 1992, p. 47). Susan E. Martin described the initial resistance as "strong, organized, and sometimes life-threatening" (Martin, 1994, p. 389). Catherine Milton's 1992 study reported that policewomen were being used almost exclusively in clerical or juvenile functions, that they were required to have more education than men, that they were regulated by hiring quotas, and that they were allowed to compete for promotions or openings only in the women's bureau. Donna Schaper (1997) writes about her experience:

> *For me, the myth that women are physically less able than men found a remarkable rebuff one day in San Francisco 20 years ago. The San Francisco police department was in the throes of a lawsuit that would allow women to become police officers. I was taking a group of teenagers on a tour of the police department when the officer guiding us said that the real reason women couldn't be on the force was that they could never pass basic training, which required carrying a 100-pound bag of sand in a straight line for 100 feet. Then, an 18-year-old horsewoman in our group spotted the sandbag in the weight-training room, hoisted it on her shoulders and carried it for the rest of the tour. (p. 32)*

Women have made gains in policing, which Susan Martin (1989) claims are related in large part to the "development of a substantial body of law requiring nondiscrimination on the basis of sex in terms and conditions of employment" (p. 315). As of 1998, women comprised only 13.8 percent of all sworn law enforcement positions in the United States (National Center for Women & Policing, 1998). For other key findings of this report, see Box 6.2 on page 162.

Larger police departments tend to hire more women than smaller departments. The Madison, Wisconsin, police department is an exception. This small university town boasts 29.7 percent women officers, the highest percentage of any department in the nation. For the top ten agencies with the largest percentage of sworn women officers, see Table 6.1.

The resistance toward women in policing must ultimately be viewed in terms of the patriarchal society. For the past three thousand years, society has been based on social, philosophical, and political systems in which men have controlled women. Men have used force, direct pressure, tradition, ritual, customs, law, and language to determine what roles women shall or shall not play. In this male-dominated social role, the female is everywhere subordinated to the male. In policing, women had the "audacity" to desire entrance

TABLE 6.1   Top Ten Agencies with the
Largest Percentage of Sworn
Women Officers, 1998

Madison Police	29.7%
Cook County Sheriff	26.2%
Pittsburgh Police	24.7%
Washington Metro Police	24.6%
Philadelphia Police	23.8%
Detroit Police	23.4%
Caddo Parish Sheriff	22.6%
Bexar County Sheriff	21.7%
Miami-Dade Police	21.5%
Tallahassee Police	20.8%

Source: National Center for Women and Policing, *The
Status of Women in Policing: 1998* (Washington, D.C.:
U.S. Government Printing Office, 1999), p. 8.

to an all-male occupation, one that male officers perceived to demand dominance, aggressiveness, superiority, and power.

In addition to the cultural barrier of the wider society, it is thought that certain aspects of police work are unsuitable for women. First, it is believed that
women are unsuitable for police work because "they cannot cope with danger,
do not command authority, and should not be exposed to degradation." Second, there is the fear that the introduction of women "will undermine male
solidarity, threaten their security, and their self-image" (Heidensohn, 1992,
p. 200). This could be regarded as the "porcelain policeman" argument; that is,
male police officers "are so fragile and delicate that they will feel threatened
and undermined, their solidarity shattered, and their loyalty over-stretched by
the presence of women" (Heidensohn, 1992, p. 216). Third, women officers
must cope with norms that create a disadvantage in interacting with male officers. Swearing and sexual jokes, it is charged, are an inevitable part of police
culture and women should not have to deal with this "seamy" aspect. Finally,
the argument for the exclusion of women is made that their lower status (in
comparison with male officers) creates problems in arrest situations with both
male and female citizens (Martin, 1989, pp. 321–322).

The issue of women as tokenism in policing has received some attention.
Rosabeth Moss Kanter (1976) claims that token women (whose numbers fall
below 15 percent of the total population) perceive themselves to be highly visible, attracting disproportionate attention to themselves. This often results,
asserts Kanter, in dysfunctional performance pressures (pp. 415–430). Joanne
Belknap and Jill Shelley's (1992) research supported Kanter's theory regarding
one aspect of tokenism—visibility—because they found that "the most consistent characteristic significantly related to policewomen's perceptions and
experiences was the percentage of women in the department" (p. 47).

**BOX 6.2   The Percentage of Sworn Women
                  Police Officers, 1998**

- In the last eight years, women have increased their representation in sworn law
enforcement by only 3.2 percentage
points, from 10.6 percent in 1990 to 13.8
percent in 1998.
- The gains for women in policing are so
slow that, at the current rate of growth,
women will never reach equal representation or gender balance in law enforcement agencies.
- Women currently hold only 7.5 percent of
Top Command law enforcement positions,
9.6 percent of Supervisory positions, and
14.7 percent of Line Operation positions.
Women of color hold 1.9 percent of Top
Command law enforcement positions, 3.1
percent of Supervisory positions, and 6.7
percent of Line Operations positions. . . .
- More than 30 percent of agencies report
no women in Top Command law enforcement positions, and over 70 percent of

agencies have no women of color in the
highest ranks.
- Women continue to hold a majority (62.9
percent) of lower-paid civilian law enforcement positions. Women of color hold 28.9
percent of the lower-paid civilian positions
- State agencies trail by a wide margin municipal and county agencies in hiring
and promoting women. Specifically, state
agencies report 6.5 sworn women law enforcement officers, less than half that of
municipal agencies reporting 15.5 percent
and county agencies at 14.8 percent. . . .
- 61.4 percent of agencies surveyed reported that they give preference to candidates
who are veterans or have previous military experience. Such policies reinforce
barriers to women in policing by favoring
a background disproportionately represented by men. . . .

Source: National Center for Women and Policing, *The Status of Women in Policing: 1998* (Washington, D.C.: U.S. Government Printing Office, 1999), pp. 1–2.

Martin's examination of women in policing (1979) found that women are
considered only tokens for male police officers and "they face performance
pressure, isolation from coworkers, entrapment in stereotypic roles, and tests
of loyalty" (p. 314). She concluded that the future is not bright: "It is likely
that the dynamics of tokenism will continue to operate, leaving policewomen
with a number of difficult choices in the face of the expectation that they
think like men, work like dogs, and act like ladies" (pp. 314–323).

Teresa Lynn Wertsch (1998) also examined the issue of women police officers and tokenism among one group of female police officers employed in a
medium-sized Pacific Northwest city. Of the twenty-four female officers in
that department, sixteen agreed to be interviewed. Wertsch found that tokenism, when combined with such factors as family commitments and organizational structures, plays a major role in determining upward mobility and
in serving to reduce the frequency of women's promotion to supervisory positions in police departments (pp. 25–26). According to this study, stereotypical categorization of the token into specific roles also created dissatisfaction
and frustration. Two women officers reveal this dissatisfaction in the following statements:

The guys can view you as a sex object instead of a professional. It makes me try harder to put up more fronts and play more of the macho, boy role rather than accept that I am a female. It makes me nervous and uncomfortable. You can't be meek or mild, too quiet. You can't be too loud or boisterous because then you would be a dike, too masculine. "That's why she can do the job because she's a dike," so the men automatically put you in a male role. If you're not good looking and act very masculine, they'll give you the job because you're a dike.

. . .

I wish it didn't have to be this way, but you're either a bitch, a dike, or a slut. It makes me frustrated because I don't know which I am. I'm not gay. I'm not a slut. I would probably fall more into the bitch category, which is the one that I have decided I would rather be in. (pp. 35–36)

Sexual Harassment in the Police Culture

One of the most unbelievable accounts of sexual harassment is what Romona Arnold, the first female officer in the City of Seminole, Oklahoma, police department, experienced. This case, which was decided on July 10, 1985, documented that in 1977 Arnold's problems began when she was transferred to the midnight shift under the supervision of Lt. Herdlitchka. He informed her that "he did not believe in women officers." He not only refused to speak with her and was hostile toward her, but "he told her that he would harass her until she quit or was fired" (*Arnold v. City of Seminole*, 1985).

The sexual harassment became stationwide when "demeaning cartoons and pictures were posted for public view within the police station with the plaintiff's name written thereon." Her son was arrested and taken to jail in June 1979. The charges against him were eventually dropped "because it was determined that the arrest and detention of plaintiff's son were totally unjustified. Lt. Downing advised plaintiff that the arrest of plaintiff's son was pure harassment." Officers with less service and seniority were promoted over her. When the department obtained new vehicles, male officers got them. She was informed that "as a woman, she didn't know how to take care of it." The windows of her car were rolled down when it was raining so that her seats would become wet. Her name was removed from her mail shelf, and the shelf was eventually removed altogether. Her husband, "a fireman for the City of Seminole, was told that if his wife filed a discrimination complaint, both husband and plaintiff would be fired" (*Arnold v. City of Seminole*, 1985).

On February 25, 1983, perhaps the most serious of all events in this sad account of police deviancy took place. Arnold received a call from Tommy Gaines, a known drug and alcohol addict, who wanted to see her. "He said it would only take five minutes and that it was urgent. When she arrived, Gaines told her that 'the County' had tapped his phone and was taping conversations." He also said, "In exchange for a reduced sentence," he "was to try to set plaintiff up in an illegal drug transaction." He assured her "that the Seminole Sheriff's office and the city police were involved" (*Arnold v. City of Seminole,* 1985).

The court decision concluded that "the plaintiff suffers from sexual assault stress syndrome caused by the sexual harassment and discrimination detailed herein; in addition, she suffers from physiological problems induced by stress and anxiety." As a result, she "has been unable to return to work at the Seminole Police Department essentially since January 1, 1984, due to the deterioration of her physical and mental health as outlined above."

Eighty plaintiffs have joined the growing class-action sexual harassment and discrimination lawsuit of *Tipton-Whittingham v. Los Angeles.* According to the *Los Angeles Times,* many of the Los Angeles Police Department's female officers felt that the 1994 inquiry into sexual harassment at the West Los Angeles Division was a failure of department leadership, because it did not follow through on this inquiry's recommendations. The inquiry reported sexist and racist remarks, male police officers who failed to back up female officers needing help, and so deeply ingrained mistreatment that policewomen had come to accept it as a part of life. The true scope of the problem will never be known because many female officers were reluctant to complain for fear of retaliation. As expressed by officer May Elizabeth Hatter, who has joined the Tipton-Whittingham case, "Management has thumbed its nose at this problem. . . . I had to prove myself every single day as a police officer. How can management just turn its back on me?" (Daum and Johns, 1994, p. 49).

There are a number of other tragic examples of sexual harassment. A two-week academy cadet was victimized when a firearms instructor approached her from behind, reached around, and grabbed her left breast as she was practicing. In repulsing the advance, she made it very clear that it was unwelcome and offensive. As a result, she failed her marksmanship test. This same instructor refused to send the cadet's broken firearm in for repair, claiming she could not shoot. He told the cadet the next day that she had "better learn to shoot" and called her "stupid" and "a dumb broad." Moreover, this same cadet was assaulted twice by a classmate who "pulled her against his body, and told her that he wanted to feel her body and that her body felt good" (*Watts v. New York City Police Dept.,* 1989).

A policewoman of color was working in the traffic division when she returned to her desk to find seven of her case files ripped and soda poured into her typewriter. She was harassed on other occasions when her personal vehicle was vandalized, including tires slashed, windshield wipers removed, and paint scratched. Furthermore, pornographic pictures were placed in her personal desk drawer and her male coworkers addressed her in sexist terms. Another disturbing incident involved items of her clothing, located in the officer's locker, which had a lime substance placed on them that caused severe burns to her back (*Andrews v. City of Philadelphia,* 1990).

A Caucasian policewoman in the same division was harassed with sexually foul and lascivious language. When she found sexual devices and pornographic magazines in her desk drawer, the males in the unit laughed at her. Officers also removed files from her desk, coworkers refused to help her with work, and she received obscene phone calls at her unlisted home phone number. After complaining to her supervisor about a case file removed from her desk, he warned her, "You know, you're no spring chicken. You have to expect this working with the guys" (*Andrews v. City of Philadelphia,* 1990).

A study done by R. Max Mendel and Elizabeth Shoenfelt (1991) demonstrates bias even in the appraisal process for new recruits. They surveyed a random sample of 226 police chiefs, serving populations over 80,000, to determine what administrative action they would use based on an actual arrest during which a male training officer was shot and after which his female trainee-partner was fired for cowardice. Mendel and Shoenfelt concluded that female trainees were significantly more likely than male trainees to be terminated for the same actions. This predisposition toward biased judgments of policewomen's performance not only questions disciplinary actions against female officers, but also contributes to why female officers are reluctant to report harassment.

Many of the harassment problems endured by female officers in large departments are likewise experienced by policewomen in small-town law enforcement, which makes up 85 percent of municipal departments in the United States. Curt R. Bartol and colleagues' (1992) study on stressors and problems in small-town police departments reported that 53 percent of female officers had been sexually harassed, predominantly by male supervisors; two respondents reported they had been sexually assaulted by male supervisors. Eighty-three percent felt that male supervisors frequently communicated negative attitudes about women in policing. One female officer wrote, "The most stressful factor is the belief that the attitude of male supervisors toward female police officers is not likely to change anytime in the near future or during my career as a law enforcement officer" (p. 240).

African American Women in Policing

Some evidence exists that African American women entering policing have to face a much different reception from African American males. The combination of the effects of race and gender expose African American women to multiple disadvantages, known as "double jeopardy" (Martin, 1994, pp. 383–384). According to some analysts, the African American's "unique social location at the intersection of different hierarchies has produced a distinct feminist consciousness different from that of white women." Martin continues, "White women have ample contact with white men and the potential for increased power by association with one of them. But they have limited their influence by internalizing an image of helplessness and allowing themselves to be 'put on a pedestal'" (p. 384). She concludes that "due to racism, black women have experienced far less protection and a far greater element of fear based on white hostility, physical separation, and intimidation" (p. 384).

Felkenes and Schroeder (1993) found that, during the police training academy experience, the dominant group of white male officers created and supported a culture that both implicitly and explicitly encouraged a wide range of discriminatory behaviors directed against minority women. It is no wonder, then, that minority women officers had higher rates of attrition and lower levels of satisfaction with the training. Subsequent to graduating from the academy, minority women officers continued to experience social discrimination, to face racist and sexist comments sent as computer messages from one patrol car to another, and to have to deal with the existence of openly racist and sexist cliques operating out of several bureaus in the Los Angeles Police Department.

Martin, in examining the interactive effects of race and gender in five large municipal police agencies, conducted in-depth interviews with 106 African American and European American officers and supervisors. One African American woman recounted:

> *Males didn't want to work with females, and at times I was the only female or black on the shift so I had to do a lot to prove myself. I was at the precinct 10 days before I knew I had a partner 'cause . . . (the men) called in sick and I was put in the station. The other white guys called the man who was assigned to work with me the 11th day and told him to call in sick . . . he came anyway. (p. 390)*

Martin's study also found that several African American women "observed differences in their treatment that reflect differences in the cultural images and employment experiences of black and white women" (p. 394). European American women, especially those who were physically attractive or attached to influential European American men, were more likely than African American women to be protected from street patrol by being given station house duty. When European American women were assigned to the streets, they were more likely than African American women to receive protection from both European American and African American males (p. 394).

This study also found that African American women's relationships to African American males were "strained by tensions and dilemmas associated with sexuality and competition for desirable assignments and promotions." Part of the explanation for these strained relationships was the competition "for position and promotions earmarked 'black' by affirmative action programs." Thus, within these five departments, African American women were, in a number of ways, the victims of "widespread racial stereotypes as well as outright racial harassment" (p. 394).

SUCCESS IN A DIFFICULT CAREER PATH

Women must decide how they will cope with their jobs because they are, at best, accepted at the fringes of the male's culture of policing. At the extremes of adaptation, women can decide to become either defeminized or deprofessionalized. "Defeminized" women become superefficient and see themselves as as good as or better than their male colleagues. Their competence, then, serves to mask their femininity. In contrast to competing with male colleagues, "deprofessionalized" women accept subordinate status and concessions granted to them (Hochschild, 1973, pp. 79–82).

Martin, in applying these extremes of adaptation to twenty-eight women patrol officers in Washington, D.C., renamed the two polar positions calling them "policeWOMEN" and "POLICEwomen." POLICEwomen focus on law enforcement, rather than service. They show a high commitment to the job and even criticize fellow female officers. Similar to male police officers, they wish to do specialist work and be promoted. PoliceWOMEN, on the other hand, emphasize the feminine. By accepting the male's invitation to function as a nominal equal, they are actually functioning as assistants or junior partners. They usually receive treatment and exemptions from work tasks that are inappropriate for a "lady" (Martin, 1980, p. 315).

More recently, Brewer (1996) observed two primary groups of women police officers in the Royal Ulster Constabulary in Northern Ireland. The first he labeled "Hippolytes." These women "interactionally manage the question of gender identity by retaining for themselves as much of their femininity as the bureaucratic regimen and the situation allows, and they resist the adoption and performance of occupational traits that are masculine" (p. 241). Described as loners, they avoided participation in the police occupational culture and were not looked on as effective as police officers. The "Amazons" were the polar opposites of the Hippolytes. Brewer reported that these officers used "aggressive humour and all the interactional and conversational devices associated with being 'one of the boys.' Being one of the boys is the defining characteristic of the way the Amazon type handle the problem of their female gender in the masculine occupational culture of the police station" (p. 242).

Regardless of what roles they pursue, women who survive in policing usually develop a thick skin. Men officers frequently pick on female officers, and if they discover their tender points, then they intensify their ribbing. One woman officer, in acknowledging that those sensitive to abuse could not survive an eight-hour shift, revealed her means of adaptation: "I've got a skin like a table. Nothing bothers me. I just made up my mind that I had to take it and live with it and just move on from there and that's what I did. Truly, truly nothing bothers me jobwise" (Fletcher, 1995, p. 162).

Another successful coping technique that women officers use is to utilize the talents they have on the job. Many women use their verbal skills to deescalate confrontative or potentially violent situations. Jeanne McDowell (1992) puts it this way, "cool, calm and communicative, they [women officers] help put a lid on violence before it erupts" (p. 70). Another woman officer expressed the importance of verbal skills a little differently:

So my theory is, you have to go in with your brain. I talk to people. And I talk to big guys and I talk to little guys and I talk to big women and I talk to little women. I talk to everybody. I think it comes in with this basic amount of respect for others as human beings. I don't take things person- ally. You can't. But a lot of people take things personally. As far as I'm con- cerned, the uniform walks into a situation all by itself. But it's not me. (Fletcher, 1995, p. 24)

Women, who are normally excluded from the culture of policing, must es- tablish their own supportive and nourishing network if they intend to survive on the job. These networks may be in the departments in which they are em- ployed or they may be state-wide or national networks of associations of po- licewomen (Heidensohn, 1992, p. 197).

Because of their superior interpersonal relationship skills, policewomen appear to handle stress better than their male counterparts. According to Pa- tricia Lunneborg (1989), 90 percent of the policewomen talked out their sources of stress, versus 45 percent of the policemen she surveyed (p. 99). Beer- mann and colleagues (cited in Blumenthal, 1994) also found that the "double burden" of the unequal division of domestic duties, particularly for those with children, did not result in more severe psychosocial or subjective health im- pairments. This extra burden, in fact, may be a source of stress relief as po- licewomen are forced to change roles from cop to mom. This allows them to leave the job behind, avoiding the "live to work" mentality that traps male officers as they become couch potatoes (resulting in withdrawal and numb- ing of emotions) or associate with other officers after work. Accordingly, "being married and having children is a protective factor against completed suicide for women—but not for men" (p. 3).

Women officers do experience the stressors of both low acceptance in the police agency and lack of access to the peer-group support structure of male officers. The importance of access to this peer-group support structure or po- lice culture is that it helps to mitigate the strain of occupation-related stress by providing a forum within which individual officers can safely ventilate (Lord, 1995, p. 631). J. G. Wexler and V. Quinn's (1985) examination of the occupation-related stress experiences of women officers in a major metropol- itan department in California found that women experienced a major stres- sor in attempting to demonstrate that they could be effective officers without compromising their femininity (pp. 98–105).

Many women police officers report that their jobs contribute to social and marriage problems. They claim that some men are too intimidated to date or marry a female cop (Kirschman, 1997, p. 203). They appear to be intimidated by assertive and self-confident women, whose work is a driving force in their lives, who sometimes are tougher and stronger than they are, and who are au- thority figures who strap on a gun to protect society and them. An officer re- flects on her dating experiences:

If you're a single woman cop and you meet a guy, it's a three-month thing. That's it. Three months. At first, they love the fact that you're a cop. Then you notice a change. What's the matter? They're intimidated, they're disturbed that you're capable and intelligent.

Well, try to understand. They work nine to five. They go home. You go out on midnights. You put on a gun so you can protect people. That's intimidating. They think they can handle it. But that's bullshit. They can't handle it. They're gone after three months.

Now I don't tell people what I do. (Fletcher, 1995, p. 187)

An Arizona State University study found the divorce rate of female officers to be twice that of the national average and three times that of male officers. In addition, female officers were almost twice as likely to be separated. Twenty-one percent felt that police work was definitely a factor in their divorce, and another 20 percent were undecided (testimony of Leanor Boulin Johnson, 1991).

Women officers also have a lower suicide rate than men officers. Explanations for this are that women are more likely than men to have stronger social supports; women seem to be more willing to seek professional help; and men are more humiliated by job-related life events, job loss, or problems. According to Susan Blumenthal (1996), former head of the Suicide Research Unit at the National Institute of Mental Health, "being married and having children is a protective factor against completed suicide for women but not men" (p. 3)

Policewomen generally are much less involved in deviancy than are policemen. For example, the Christopher Commission found that women officers handled suspects more successfully than men did as they are "less personally challenged by defiant suspects and feel less need to deal with immediate force or confrontational language" (Morrison, 1991, p. 84). Little evidence also exists that women officers are frequently involved in corruption. As Hunt (1990) suggests, an explanation for this might be that male officers tend to fear that "the moral woman would expose police involvement in corruption" (p. 14). Female officers, then, are likely to be excluded from both socializing events with male officers and from whatever corruption is taking place in the department.

LEGAL PROTECTIONS

In terms of having a successful and satisfying police career, women police officers need protection from the sexual harassment that traditionally has been present in most police departments.

Four categories of law cover sexual harassment in the workplace: (1) the United States Civil Rights Act of 1964 and 1991; (2) state statutes on fair employment practices; (3) common tort and criminal law; and (4) Statute 42 United States Code Section 1983 (Civil Rights Act of 1871).

United States Civil Rights Act

The Civil Rights Act of 1964 makes discrimination on the basis of race, color, religion, sex, or national origin illegal. Title VII of this act "prohibits employers from, among other things, discriminating on the basis of sex with respect to compensation, terms, conditions, or privileges of employment" (Rubin, 1995, p. 1).

Congress established the Equal Employment Opportunity Commission (EEOC) as the enforcing agency, but restricted its oversight to employers with fifteen employees or more and placed a back pay liability limitation of two years before the filing of charges (O'Linn, 1995, p. 2). In addition, Title VII did not apply to local governments, including police departments, until almost a decade later when Congress passed the Equal Opportunity Act of 1972 (Berg and Budnick, 1986, p. 314). Until then it was rare to see policewomen in a patrol function (Charles, 1982, p. 194).

By 1980, as a result of pressure from women's groups, the Equal Employment Opportunity Commission ruled that sexual harassment was a form of sex discrimination covered under Title VII and issued guidelines on discrimination because of gender (Petrocelli and Repa, 1994, pp. 1, 19). These guidelines did not have the force of law, but were acknowledged by the United States Supreme Court in its first ruling on sexual harassment, *Meritor Savings Bank, FSB v. Vinson, et al.* Sixteen years after the *Meritor* decision, Congress passed the Civil Rights Act of 1991 to correct some inadequacies in the Civil Rights Act of 1964.

The new law made possible a jury trial if punitive damages are alleged. Punitive damages are available under Title VII, providing the employer acted with reckless indifference or malice to federally protected rights. The limits on punitives range from $50,000 to $300,000 depending on the size of the workforce. If an employee is successful, the Civil Rights Act provides redress of reinstatement and promotion, back pay and benefits, a limited amount of money damages, injunctive relief to prevent similar harassment from taking place in the future, and a portion of or all of attorney's fees.

Fair Employment Practices (FEP)

Legal definitions of sexual harassment, as well as laws governing the enforcement of sexual harassment laws, vary from state to state. Although some states have no laws at all, most state Fair Employment Practices (FEP) agencies have powers similar to the EEOC's to seek remedies. In addition, various states' FEP laws provide remedies for recovering substantial monetary damages for personal injuries without limitations; other states have no remedy. Moreover, states vary widely on the amount of compensation they allow for damages. Only about half the states allow for punitive damages. Several states require that an administrative claim be filed with the enforcing agency before relief can be pursued under the FEP laws in court. Finally, counties and cities often have their own laws prohibiting sexual harassment and administrative agencies (Petrocelli and Repa, 1994). A complainant may find better relief filing with a state agency, but research and possibly legal advice is required to seek the best avenue for a remedy.

Tort Laws and Criminal Charges

A tort claim in state court may be the best solution for some victims; indeed, it may be the only remedy for victims who work for a small agency, whose governing entity's aggregate employment is fewer than fifteen employees (O'Linn, 1995). A tort is a "breach of duty, other than a breach of contract, for which the offender will be subject to legal responsibility" (*The New Lexicon Webster's Encyclopedic Dictionary of the English Language*, 1992, p. 1402). Common law torts include assault, battery, intentional infliction of emotional distress, wrongful discharge, and defamation (O'Linn, 1995, p. 5).

Providing a wider range of remedies than those available under the Civil Rights Act and most states' FEP laws, torts include both compensatory damages for the emotional and physical distress suffered from the workplace harassment and the possibility of large punitive damages aimed at punishing the wrongdoer (Petrocelli and Repa, 1994, pp. 2, 8). Unlike the Civil Rights Act, which pertains only to the employer, common tort actions can penalize the predator with punitive damages. The following are two examples of common tort claims based on sexual harassment: A woman who quit her job because of sexual harassment was entitled to unemployment benefits even though she voluntarily resigned. The court found that she had been subjected to severe sexual harassment and that any prudent person would have quit. She was awarded unemployment benefits and attorney's fees. The Court of Appeals in Atlanta ruled that a female who brought suit under Title VII against an employer for sexual harassment was properly permitted to bring state law tort claims. This woman was awarded $3,000 in back wages under Title VII, and a jury awarded her $10,000 for common law battery and $25,000 in compensatory damages for invasion of privacy under state law.

In addition to tort claims, criminal charges can be filed against the perpetrator for such actions as assault, battery, and sexual assault. As witnessed in the O. J. Simpson trials, filing criminal charges does not preclude taking civil action. In fact, the criminal action often precedes the civil one for the purpose of solidifying a claim or as a fact-finding measure.

Statute 42 United States Code Section 1983

Until the Civil Rights Act of 1991, there was more incentive to file under United States Code Section 1983 to obtain punitive damages and a jury trial. Unlike the Civil Rights Act of 1991, Section 1983 provides the opportunity to file for punitive damages against the offending party by establishing personal liability. Punitive damages allowed by Title VII are against the employer; Section 1983 can be against the predator (O'Linn, 1995). Section 1983 states:

> *Every person who, under color of any statute, ordinance, regulation, custom or usage, of any State . . . subjects, or causes to be subjected, any citizen of the United States . . . to the deprivation of any rights, privileges, or immunities secured by the constitution and laws, shall be liable to the party injured in an action at law."* (42 United States Code Section 1983; O'Neal v. DeKalb County, *1988*)

Mildred K. O'Linn, an attorney who specializes in the representation of law enforcement personnel and agencies in civil litigation, reminds law enforcement officers that "Statute 42 of the United States Code 1983 provides for civil remedies if an individual acting under color of law violates the civil rights of another individual." She adds that "if you are a peace officer, you are acting under color of law whenever you are on duty or off duty if there is a strong enough nexus or connection made between whatever your actions were and the fact that you are a police officer. Simply put," she says, "you are still acting under color of law if you are using the powers of your office. Under that statute, if you violate an individual's civil rights as a police officer in the form of sexual harassment, you can be sued under Section 1983" (interviewed in 1997).

In *Monell v. New York City Department of Social Services,* the court concluded that "sexual harassment can violate the equal protection provisions of the Fourteenth Amendment, thus creating a basis for an award of damages under Section 1983" (*Carrero v. New York City Housing Authority,* 1989). In addition, Section 1983 offers incentives for attorneys because employers can also be sued as persons (deep-pocket theory), and attorney's fees are recoverable pursuant to 42 U.S.C. §1988 (*Monell v. New York City Department of Social Services*).

THE COURTS AND FINDINGS OF SEXUAL HARASSMENT

Harassment violations were first considered by the court in 1972 in *Anderson v. Methodist Evangelical Hospital,* which required employers to maintain a work atmosphere free from racial and ethnic intimidation and insult (O'Linn, 1993, pp. 4, 14). Since that time, sexual harassment law has been rapidly evolving as courts interpret federal, state, and local antidiscrimination statutes.

According to Sarah E. Burns (1995), the most important unresolved issues concern the amount and kind of proof required to establish certain elements of sexual harassment claims and the employer's liability for harassment by nonsupervisory personnel (p. 193). Other important aspects concern the application of the law to the factual circumstances of a specific case, the evaluation of the parties' claims and proof, and the determination of proper damages. Nonetheless, courts have shown their disdain for sexual harassment practices:

> *Sexual harassment which creates a hostile or offensive environment for members of one sex is every bit the arbitrary barrier to sexual equality at the work place that racial harassment is to racial equality. Surely, a requirement that a man or woman run a gauntlet of sexual abuse in return for the privilege of being allowed to work and make a living can be as demeaning and disconcerting as the harshest of racial epithets.* (Henson v. Dundee, *1982)*

Sexual harassment has been categorized in two forms: (1) "quid pro quo" (something for something) harassment—sexual favors as a condition for receiving a tangible benefit, and (2) as a hostile work environment—an offensive environment that unreasonably interferes with the employee's job performance. The first two sections of the Equal Employment Opportunity Commission's definition of sexual harassment pertain to quid pro quo harassment; the last refers to hostile work environment.

Until the United States Supreme Court's ruling in *Meritor Savings Bank v. Vinson,* there was considerable debate in the lower courts as to whether harassment fell into the legal definitions of sexual discrimination (O'Linn,1995). The Supreme Court concluded:

> *The EEOC Guidelines fully support the view that harassment leading to noneconomic injury can violate Title VII. . . . Since the Guidelines were issued, courts have uniformly held, and we agree, that a plaintiff may establish a violation of Title VII by proving that discrimination based on sex has created a hostile or abusive work environment.* (Meritor Savings Bank, FSB v. Vinson, *1986)*

In addition the Supreme Court held that: ". . . The correct inquiry is whether respondent by her conduct indicated that the alleged sexual advances were unwelcome. . . ." (*Henson v. Dundee,* 1982).

According to some critics, the unwelcome standard places the plaintiff on trial similar to a rape victim. A plaintiff is "routinely required to explain why, if she was being subjected to sexual harassment, consistent with her claim of unwelcomeness, she failed to complain, remained politely silent, appeared flattered, joked, or even affirmatively participated in reciprocal slurs" (Burns, 1995, p. 194). In essence, she becomes the accused having to defend her actions. The proof of unwelcomeness "is usually determined by the sufferer's testimony corroborated by evidence that either she behaved as if the conduct were 'unwelcome' to her or the conduct was the kind likely to be obviously unwelcome or both" (Burns, 1995, p. 195). Proving or refuting a claim of sexual harassment can be very difficult, a he said/she said paradox centering on who is the most creditable person.

The Reasonable Woman Standard

The Ninth Circuit in *Ellison v. Brady* in 1991 focused the severity and persuasiveness of sexual harassment on the perspective of the victim, applying the "reasonable woman" standard:

> *We hold that a female plaintiff states a prima facie case of hostile environment sexual harassment when she alleges conduct which a reasonable woman would consider sufficiently severe or pervasive to alter the conditions of employment and create an abusive working environment.* (Ellison v. Brady, *1991*)

The circuit court felt that the "reasonable man" or "reasonable person" did not take into account the concerns women share. "For example, because women are disproportionately victims of rape and sexual assault, women have a stronger incentive to be concerned with sexual behavior than men" (*Ellison v. Brady,* 1991).

The decision of the Supreme Court in *Harris v. Forklift Systems, Inc.* two years later was its second on sexual harassment. The Court took the middle ground to resolve a conflict among the circuit courts, holding "that to be actionable under Title VII 'abusive work environment' harassment, the conduct need not seriously affect an employee's psychological well-being or lead to the employee to suffer injury" (O'Linn, 1995, p. 18). The Court did leave vague what standard the plaintiff needed to meet to prevail in such a claim (reasonable woman, reasonable victim, reasonable person standard). In using the test of an objectively reasonable employee, the Court did provide guidance, saying that the totality of the circumstances needed to be considered:

1. How often the conduct occurs;
2. How serious the conduct is;
3. Whether the behavior physically threatens the victim, or stops at offensive comments; and
4. Whether the behavior unreasonably interferes with work performance; and
5. The victims must perceive the environment to be abrasive in order for the conduct to be considered illegal. (*Harris v. Forklift Systems, Inc.,* 1993)

Anita Bernstein (1997) argues in an article in *Harvard Law Review* that sexual harassment can be better explained using the concept of respect. She defended the legal virtues of a legal rule that affirms respect, saying that these virtues

> *include the resonance of respect as a value among ordinary people, the history of inclusion based on human dignity that informs respect, the orientation of respect around the conduct of an agent (rather than the reaction of*

> *a complainant, the focus of current rules) and congruence with a tradition, found in many other areas of American law, of calling on citizens to render respect. (Bernstein, 1997, p. 446)*

This standard of respect is actually being used to guide behavior in many businesses. For example, the 3M Corporation's "Appropriateness Test" raises the following questions: "Would I be embarrassed to discuss my language and behavior at work with my family? Would a newspaper account of my language and behavior at work embarrass me or my family? Would I be embarrassed to discuss my language and behavior at work with my supervisors and members of management?" ("The Appropriateness Test").

Rosemarie Skaine (1996) provides more in-depth questions for men to ask themselves to aid in assessing their behaviors:

> *Would I mind if someone treated my wife, partner, girlfriend, mother, sister, or daughter this way? Would I mind if this person told my wife, partner, girlfriend, mother, sister, or daughter about what I was saying or doing? Would I do this if my wife, partner, girlfriend, mother, sister, or daughter were present? Would I mind if a reporter wanted to write about what I was doing? If I ask someone for a date and the answer is "no," do I keep asking? If someone asks me to stop a particular behavior, do I get angry and do more of the same instead of apologizing and stopping? Do I tell jokes or make "funny" remarks involving women and/or sexuality? (p. 401)*

SUMMARY

Policing has been reluctant to accept women police officers for several reasons. Law enforcement is perceived to be a man's job, and it is feared that its image of masculinity can be tarnished by the presence of women wearing police uniforms and carrying guns. The vulnerability of male police officers, so its defenders claim, is increased when men must depend on women for backup and support. There is also the concern that male camaraderie would be immeasurably harmed if a woman's presence interferes with men's talk in the locker room. In this age of sexual scandal, police supervisers are, of course, greatly concerned about the presence of women in the station house and on the street resulting in sexual alliances with married officers and contributing to the breakup of marriages of male officers.

Despite these concocted explanations for rejecting women as police officers, the most viable consideration is whether women can do the job. Research studies continue to indicate that female police officers have somewhat different skills from male police officers but that their competence is equal to that of male officers. These studies have specifically found that women can handle the crime-fighting, combat, rescue, peacekeeping, and social service aspects of police work as well as men. Studies have also found that men and women are equally capable of patrol work. In addition, there is strong evidence that men are in no greater danger with women as partners than they are with men as partners.

Yet the initial resistance to women entering this male-dominated world continues in too many departments. It is found in the appraisal process of new recruits, in supervisory attitudes and treatment, in attitudes of male line officers, and in promotional opportunities and career advancements. Policing may be gender resistant to women, but it is more resistant to an African American police officer. The effects of race and gender expose African American women police officers to "double jeopardy" (Martin, 1994, pp. 383–384). Particularly unfortunate is that African American policewomen not only experience the effects of race from white women and men, but their relationships with African American males on the police force are also often strained (p. 394).

The issue of sexual harassment affects women who work in the criminal justice system. It is a particular concern for women police officers, most of whom have experienced some form of sexual harassment at some point in their careers. The examination of sexual harassment in this chapter reveals that the term *sexual harassment* itself is multidimensional and has been expressed in various ways in law enforcement.

There is much that we do not know about sexual harassment in law enforcement. We do not know what the backgrounds of the offenders are. Are race and ethnicity factors? Are males from some groups more likely to harass women sexually than are males from other groups? Is education a factor? Are college-educated male officers more or less likely to victimize female officers? Is satisfaction in police work a factor? What is the relationship between job satisfaction and sexual harassment? Is emotional maturity a factor? How well adjusted are those who sexually victimize others?

Women police officers who have been pleased with their careers have generally pursued three adaptive strategies to the men's club they must deal with on a daily basis: First, they have attempted to be competent and do the best job possible. Second, on a departmental, state, or national level (and sometimes on all three), they have developed a supportive network with other women officers. Third, they have found positive reenforcements outside the job, such as family, friends, and hobbies, that permit them to balance the difficult experiences they often face on a daily basis.

REFERENCES

42 United States Code Section, 1983.
Andrews v. City of Philadelphia, 895 F.2d. 1469 (3rd Cir. 1990).
Arnold v. City of Seminole, OKL. 614 F.Supp. 853 (D.C.Okl. 1985).
Bartol, C. R., Bergen, G. T., Seager Volckens, J., and Knoras, K. M. (1992, September 1). Women in small-town policing. *Criminal Justice and Behavior* 19: 240.

Belknap, J., and Shelly, J. K. (1992). The new lone ranger: Policewomen on patrol." *American Journal of Police 12*(2): 47–75.

Berg, B. L., and Budnick, K. J. (1986). Defeminization of women in law enforcement: A new twist in the traditional police personality. *Journal of Police Science and Administration 14:* 314.

Bernstein, A. (1997). Treating sexual harassment with respect. *Harvard Law Review 111:* 446.

Blumenthal, S. J. (1994). Cited in Suicide and gender. *American Foundation for Suicide Prevention.*

Brewer, J. D. (1991). Hercules, Hippolyte and the Amazons—or policemen in the RUC. *British Journal of Sociology 42*(2): 231–248.

Burns, S. E. (1995). Issues in workplace sexual harassment law and related social science research. *Author's Abstract Journal of Social Issues 51*(1): 193.

Carrero v. New York City Housing Authority, 890 F.2d. 569 (2nd Cir. 1989).

Charles, M. T. (1982). Women in policing: The physical aspect. *Journal of Police Science and Administration 10:* 194.

Daum, J. M., and Johns, C. M. (1994, September). Police work from a woman's perspective. *The Police Chief,* p. 49.

Doerner, W. G. (1995). Officer retention patterns: An affirmative action concern for police agencies. *American Journal of Police 14:* 205.

Ellison v. Brady, 924 F.2d 872 (9th Circ. 1991): 878–879.

Feinman, C. (1986). *Women in the criminal justice system* (pp. 81–82, 95), 2nd ed. New York: Praeger.

Felkenes, G. T., and Schroeder, J. R. (1993). A case study of minority women in policing. *Women and Criminal Justice 4:* 65–89.

Fletcher, C. (1995). *Breaking and entering: Women cops talk about life in the ultimate men's club* (pp. xi, 24, 162, 187). New York: Harper Collins.

Gallagher, G. P. (1996, November and December). When will the message about harassment be acted upon. *The Law Enforcement Trainer 11*(5): 21.

Harris v. Forklift Systems, Inc., 114 S.Ct. 367 (1993).

Heidensohn, F. (1992). *Women in control? The role of women in law enforcement.* pp. 43, 52, 197, 200. Oxford: Clarendon Press.

Henson v. Dundee, 682 F.2d 897 (1982), p. 902, as cited in *Meritor Savings Bank, FSB v. Vinson, et al.,* 477, U.S. 57 (1986), p. 67.

Hochschild, A. P. (1973). Making it: Marginality and obstacles to minority consciousness. *Annuals of the New York Academy of Science 208:* 79–82.

Horne, P. (1980). *Women in Law Enforcement* (pp. xix–xx, 2–5, 10–11, 15–17, 23, 35–36, 52–55, 114, 140, 151, 192, 216), 2nd ed. Springfield, Ill.: Charles C. Thomas.

Hunt, J. C. (1990). The logic of sexism among police. *Women and Criminal Justice 1:* 3–30.

Johnson, L. B. (1991, May 20). Testimony in hearing before the Select Committee on Children, Youth, and Families, House of Representatives (pp. 41–42). Washington, D.C.: U.S. Government Printing Office.

Kanter, R. M. (1976). The impact of hierarchical structures on the work behavior of women and men. *Social Problems 23:* 415–430.

Kirschman, Ellen. (1997). *I love a cop: What police families need to know* (p. 203). New York: Guilford.

Lord, L. K. (1995). Policewomen. In *The encyclopedia of police science* (pp. 627–636), 2nd ed. William G. Bailey (ed.). New York: Garland Press. See also P. Horne. (1980). *Women in law enforcement.* Springfield, Ill.: Charles C. Thomas.

Lunneborg, P. W. (1989). *Women police officers current career profile* (p. 99). Springfield, Ill.: Charles C. Thomas.

Martin, S. E. (1994, August). "Outsider within" the station house: The impact of race and gender on black women police. *Social Problems 41:* 383–384, 389.

Martin, S. E. (1989). Female officers on the move? A status report on women in policing. In R. Dunham and G. Alpert (eds.), *Critical issues in policing: Contemporary readings* (pp. 313, 315, 321–322). Prospect Heights, Ill.: Waveland Press.

Martin, S. E. (1979). Policewomen and police*women:* Occupational role dilemmas and choices of female officers. *Journal of Police Science and Administration 7:* 314–323.

Martin, S. E. (1980). *Breaking and entering* (p. 315). Berkeley: University of California Press.

Martin, S. E., and Jurik, N. C. (1995). *Doing justice, doing gender* (p. 55). Thousand Oaks, Calif.: Sage Publications.

McDowell, J. (1992, February 17). Are women better cops? *Time:* 70, 72.

Mendel, R. M., and Shoenfelt, E. (1991, March 21). Gender bias in the evaluation of male and female police officer performance. Paper presented at the Annual Convention of the Southeastern Psychological Association, New Orleans.

Meritor Savings Bank, FSB v. Vinson, et al., 477 U.S. 57 (1986), p. 66.

Milton, C. (1972). *Women in policing.* Washington, D.C.: Police Foundation.

Monell v. New York City Department of Social Services, 436 U.S. 658 (1978).

Morrison, P. (1991, July 14). Women make better cops L.A. probers find. *Los Angeles Times.*

National Law Enforcement Officers Memorial Fund, Inc. (1997). Law enforcement facts.

The new Lexicon Webster's encyclopedic dictionary of the English language (p. 1042), Deluxe Ed. (1992). Danbury, Conn.: Lexicon Publications.

Newton, J. (1996, December 8). Harassment complaints continue to dog LAPD. *Los Angeles Times.*

O'Linn, M. K. (1995, January). Sexual harassment, handout prepared for the American Society of Law Enforcement Trainers Convention, Anchorage, Alaska, pp. 2, 4, 5, 14, 18.

O'Linn, Mildred K. Interviewed in 1997.

Petrocelli, W., and Repa B. K. (1994). *Sexual harassment on the job* (pp. 1, 2, 8, 19), 2nd ed. Berkeley, Calif.: Nolo Press.

Platt, A. (1969). *The child savers* (p. 76). Chicago: University of Chicago Press.

Reaves, B. A. (1996). *Local police departments* (p. 1). Washington, D.C.: Bureau of Justice Statistics.

Rubin, P. N. (1995, October). Civil rights and criminal justice: Primer on sexual harassment. *National Institute of Justice: Research in action.* Washington, D.C.: U.S. Government Printing Office, p. 1.

Schaper, D. (1997, January 28). More women in uniform could be a force for peace. *Newsday:* 32.

Schulz, D. M. (1993). Policewomen in the 1950s: Paving the way for patrol. *Women and Criminal Justice 4:* 5–30.

Schulz, D. M. (1995). *From social worker to crimefighter: Women in United States municipal policing* (pp. 4, 10, 134, 135). Westport, Conn.: Praeger Publishers.

Skaine, R. (1996). *Power and gender: Issues in sexual dominance and harassment* (p. 401). Jefferson, N. C.: McFarland.

Status of women in policing: 1998. (1999). Washington, D.C.: National Center for Women & Policing.

3M Corporation. The Appropriateness Test.

U.S. Dept. of Justice, 1996 survey published in *American Police Beat 3* (October 1996): p. 24.

Watts vs. New York City Police Dept., 724 F. Supp 99 (S.D.N.Y., 1989).

Webb, S. L. (1991). Step forward: Sexual harassment in the workplace. What you need to know! *Master Media:* 26–29.

Webb, S. L. *The global impact of sexual harassment.* New York: Master Media Limited, 1994.

Wertsch, T. L. (1998). Walking the thin blue line: Policewomen and tokenism today. *Women and Criminal Justice 9:* 25–26.

Wexler, J. G., and Quinn, V. (1985). Considerations on the training and development of women sergeants. *Journal of Police Science and Administration 13:* 98–105.

7

WOMEN IN THE LEGAL PROFESSION

Women have made far more significant advances in the legal profession than in law enforcement (Rollins, 1996). Women now make up almost a third of the profession, and most law schools have an almost equal enrollment of both sexes. In recognition of the contrast between women's accomplishments in law enforcement and law, a headline in *Working Woman* (1996) proclaims, "Law and Order! Women Sit on the High Court, But on the Beat, It's a Man's World." Although this headline exaggerates women's success in breaking down the barriers in the practice of law, as we will see in this chapter women have made strides in this field that twenty to thirty years ago could only have been imagined.

Women have gravitated toward law in record numbers. Their rapid movement into the profession, in turn, has laid the groundwork for further possibilities. From the famous former prosecutors Marcia Clark and Janet Reno to Hillary Rodham Clinton, a nationally prominent attorney in her own right, to Supreme Court Justices Sandra Day O'Connor and Ruth Ginsburg, to law professors Lani Guinier and Anita Hill, women lawyers are in the limelight. And for every one who has achieved national prominence, many more across the country are quietly making a contribution to law and, through law, to the whole society.

Because in the Anglo-Saxon tradition, the judiciary plays a recognizably powerful role, women's success here is of no small consequence. The "feminization of the legal profession," as Menkel-Meadow (1995) optimistically terms it, is occurring not only in the United States but in several Anglo-Saxon and European nations as well. In Canada, for example, women represent 35 to 40 percent of new entrants to the bar. In England and Wales 20 percent of those called to the bar (to be barristers) are female (in Britain women are far more apt to be solicitors than barristers).

In Norway, over half of law students are female. Women are well represented in the legal profession in Russia, where the practice of law is highly bureaucratized, and in countries like China, where they are likely to work in public service. The proportion of women lawyers is smallest in Japan and India where traditional sex roles remain very strong. In Germany, women flock into civil service jobs because family and maternity leaves are substantial; approximately one-third of the judges are women, accordingly.

Women's recent progress notwithstanding, the fact is that women are concentrated in the lowest echelons of the profession. The consistent pattern, as Menkel-Meadow (1995) suggests, is that women are "pulled" into work for which they are thought to have special talent, such as domestic relations, and "pushed" or kept out of high-status work, such as private commercial matters. Universally, women are underrepresented in litigation, even in egalitarian Norway, where they are overrepresented in the lower ranks of central government. In the United States, significantly, almost all paralegals are women.

Women's remarkable advances in the legal profession, in short, are cause for celebration but not complacency. In the law, as elsewhere, status and income disparities still exist. The strong differentiatials between male and female are reflected in the statistics that 44 percent of new entrants to the bar are women but that women make up only 16 percent of partners in the nationally registered law firms, 10 percent of the American Bar Association's Board of Governors, and 8 percent of the federal bench (Goldhaber, 1998; Rhode, 1995).

What is true for women is true for minorities as well. Minorities represent about 7 percent of America's lawyers, yet only about 3 percent of partners of law firms are minorities (Mauro, 1998, p. 3A). Women of color are often isolated in law firms, and most leave before their seventh year. African American women gravitate toward work in the public sector and in small firms in big cities with a large African American clientele. The mass media depiction of the typical criminal court judge as an African American female does not reflect reality.

HISTORY OF WOMEN IN LAW

Women lawyers have come a long way, and most of the growth has occurred in the last ten to fifteen years. Besides Shakespeare's Portia who, disguised as a young man, brought a soft touch to the law in her famous "the quality of mercy is not strained" exhortation (Shakespeare, 1600/1970: 4.1.182), few literary or historical examples of women advocates in court exist. The first practicing lawyer in North America was Margaret Brent, who was asked by the governor of Maryland to be the executor of his estate. Brent became officially empowered by the Maryland legislature to serve as the governor's executor and lawyer and to settle claims by soldiers against his estate. So powerful was she in her day that colonists called her "Gentleman Brent" (Menkel-Meadow, 1995). After litigating 124 court cases on behalf of the governor's estate, Brent moved out of Maryland because she was denied the right to vote (Morello, 1986).

Not much was heard from women again on the issue for a long time, until the mid-1800s (Bernat, 1992). Before that time, women were prohibited from attending law school or otherwise qualifying to take the bar exam. Some evidence does exist that some women appeared before the local courts, especially out West to defend land claims. One such woman, an African American named Lucy Terry Prince, successfully defended a land claim before the U.S. Supreme Court before the Civil War (Morello, 1986).

During the 1830s and 1840s, women began to struggle for the right to own property and to work (Bernat, 1992). In Britain, women worked hard to reform marriage and divorce law and property rights. Under the principle of coverture, women could not own property in their own names or enter the legal profession (Menkel-Meadow, 1995). The professions were considered improper avenues for women because of their unique biological characteristics, which suited them to the home. Working-class women and the servant classes, of course, were under no such requirements to stay home. In both Britain and the United States, women's involvement in the abolitionist, suffrage, and temperance movements galvanized them to further ambitions.

The usual method of becoming a lawyer in the early days was through a clerkship under the auspices of a practicing attorney. Women who did study the law under this arrangement clerked with their husbands and fathers. The reasons that impelled women to enter law were somewhat different from those that drew women to corrections and law enforcement; pioneers in legal practice were not primarily reformers but were motivated more by practical and intellectual considerations (Feinman, 1994).

The first woman to be officially recognized as a lawyer in the United States was Arabella Babb Mansfield who was admitted to the Iowa State bar in 1869. The first female to graduate from a law school in the United States was Ada Kepley who graduated from the University of Chicago law school in 1870. An ardent suffragist, Kepley urged women to support temperance and seize political power. As long as discriminatory admissions policies continued, however, women could not get their hands on power. In eastern urban schools and at Ivy League colleges, women were denied admission well into the twentieth century (Bernat, 1992). The state laws were gradually changing, but in Britain, it was not until 1919 when the Sex Disqualification Removal Act was passed that the official barriers to women lawyers were lifted (Menkel-Meadow, 1995). Moreover, the legal profession continued to be exclusionary on the basis of class, race, ethnicity, and gender (Abel, 1995). The proliferation of the apprenticeship system kept "unsuitable" aspirants out. On the Continent, where the university was the entry route, women entered the legal profession earlier than they did in England, which relied on legal apprenticeship, as Abel indicates.

Admission to the bar presented a barrier to women in the United States. Before the summer of 1869, there was little hope that a woman would be permitted to practice law anywhere in the country (Friedman, 1993). Then, surprisingly, thanks to a progressive Iowa judge who was dedicated to women's equality, Arabella Mansfield was quietly admitted to the bar in Iowa. She never did practice law, however. One state away, in Illinois, Myra Bradwell (who studied law in her husband's law office) was seriously committed to a legal career. After performing brilliantly on the bar exam, Bradwell was still denied admission to the Illinois bar. Her appeal to the U.S. Supreme Court was denied not solely on the basis of gender, but also because as a married woman she could not sign contracts on behalf of her clients, a requirement for any lawyer. The Court's refusal to overturn Illinois's prohibition against women practicing law meant that women, by necessity, would be engaged in a state-by-state struggle for admission to the bar (Morello, 1986). Bradwell was to achieve her major impact on the legal field not through the practice of law but as editor of the highly influential *Chicago Legal Notes.*

It was not until 1918 that the American Bar Association began to accept women. Ultimately, it was the state legislatures, not the courts, that struck down the barriers to female practice. Women made up 1.1 percent of all lawyers in 1920, and between 1950 and 1970, women's percentage grew to a mere 3 or 4 percent.

This limited historical overview reveals a firm resistance to women's entry into the legal profession, as compared with their acceptance into social work, teaching, nursing, and even medicine. With regard to the latter, by 1971 women constituted 7 percent of American physicians, double their numbers in law (Menkel-Meadow, 1995). Although law is construed as masculine, perhaps thanks to its legacy of trial by combat, women could argue that their special qualities render them especially suited to caring for the sick.

The passage of Title IX of the Higher Education Act in 1972, which prohibited discrimination based on sex in the enrollment of students and hiring of faculty, was a landmark decision in terms of opening the doors to budding female attorneys (Martin and Jurik, 1996). Facing denial of federal funds if they continued to discriminate, law schools began admitting women applicants in unprecedented numbers and still do so today.

As women gained entry into law school in the 1970s, they continued to find many unexpected obstacles in their path. The reasons for the resistance to women in law can never be fully explained, but as Morello (1986) suggests, it is likely that it has to do with the law's close relationship to power in society. As in other male-dominated fields, such as the police or firefighting, many men felt that their masculinity and stature would be threatened if women were admitted to their ranks. For a portrait of Flora Stuart, the only woman who was practicing law in the courts of Bowling Green, Kentucky, in 1977, read the article from the *Bowling Green Daily News* archives in Box 7.1 on pages 184–185.

Shortly after the 1977 article on Flora Stuart was published, this young public defender was catapulted to early prominence with a case that was any feminist's dream: a young woman charged with manslaughter for performing an abortion on herself with a knitting needle.

"Miss Flora," as the judge called her, argued for her beautiful young client, the defendant, before a packed courtroom. Reporters from *Time* magazine and *Newsweek* were among those in attendance. Following a not-guilty verdict

BOX 7.1   Bowling Green's Only Woman Trial Lawyer: "I Wanted to Change Things"

It isn't easy to juggle college and a full-time job. Ask anyone who's tried it. But it's even more difficult to balance law school, part-time jobs, and a preschool age daughter and still keep your sanity. Especially if you're on your own.

Flora Stuart will tell you it can be done, and she should know. Now partnered with Kelley Thompson, Jr. in the practice of criminal law, she is living proof that it can be done with only minimal damage to the sanity.

"I haven't had any problems since getting to Bowling Green," she said last week. "The people have really accepted me and the judges have been very fair and seem to show no resentment to the fact that I am a woman practicing law and actually trying cases in court."

The cool, plant-lined office she now shares with Thompson is very different, however, from the classroom environment of her law school days. "Oh yes, I had trouble when I was in school," she said. "Some of the teachers resented us (the female law students) because we were a breaking point. We were new to them and a little like invaders. Now it's not so bad. We broke them in."

Ms. Stuart said she had the most problems when she helped found the Women Lawyer's Club at Northern Kentucky University, where she attended the Chase School of Law. The club was founded, she said, because some of the male law students refused to have anything to do with the few female students. I took the problem up with the dean and he supported me all the way. After that, I didn't have too much trouble." The club has grown from six members at its inception to more than 23 at last count.

The decision to enter law school was inevitable in one way and not so probable in another. Born in New Orleans, Ms. Stuart said her father is a certified public accountant and attorney, now living in Arkansas. Her mother is a real estate broker in Bowling Green.

Great-grandfather Clay Elliot was a judge on the court of appeals in Louisiana, so there was plenty of exposure to the field of law.

Ms. Stuart said she didn't decide to make law her career until her junior year in college. "When I was 14, we left New Orleans and moved to Chapel Hill, N.C. The move had a really profound effect on me.

"Living in Chapel Hill was like living in a completely different world. The discrimination against blacks became very apparent. In Louisiana at the time, blacks couldn't own land or vote. Moving was like coming out of the Dark Ages," she said.

After her family's move to North Carolina, Ms. Stuart said she became actively involved in politics and civil rights. "That was my entry into the political structure," she said. "By being involved I was becoming politically aware. It was later on, during my junior year in college, that I made the decision about my career. I guess I decided that law was one way of being involved in politics, and deep down, I was hoping I could change things, too."

Although the decision sounds like the beginning of a novel about the rise of a young girl to fame and fortune, there was more to be considered in making the decision than whether law school sounded like a "good thing." Ms. Stuart also had to consider providing for her daughter, Natalie, born during her first year at Western Kentucky University.

"Sure, I wanted to change the world but I also had to support my child," she said. Getting where she wanted to go meant being a waitress and modeling for art classes and applying for every scholarship in sight. With the help of scholarships and the money from various odd jobs, Ms. Stuart managed to put herself through law school and take care of her daughter.

The "lady lawyer" credits her family with helping her stick to her aspirations. "My

BOX 7.1 *Continued*

mother was very ambitious. My sister and I were raised with the goal of having a career—not just having babies." Now Ms. Stuart is the second woman lawyer in Bowling Green and the only woman practicing trial law. Her sister is a college professor with a Ph.D. Since arriving here in August to practice law, she has tried five cases in Warren Circuit Court, making her the only woman in the history of Bowling Green to try a case before a jury.

Although she specializes in criminal law and representing women in divorce cases, she did have one fling with a civil case two weeks ago in Louisville. "And I won!" she said happily.

Her cases so far have "been interesting, I'll have to admit." Most of them have dealt with drug offenses and shoplifting, but she says she is also interested in representing fe-

male clients in divorce actions. "I think it will be easier for a woman to communicate with another woman," she said. "I can understand the situation and relate better than a man." And being divorced with an eight-year-old daughter does help give a perspective that others may not have.

Right now, Ms. Stuart says she is content with being a partner in the firm of "Thompson and Stuart." Eventually, she would like to run for a judgeship. ("The U.S. Supreme Court, of course!" she laughed.) "I want to practice a good many years and then run for a judgeship not below the circuit court. Complicated legal problems fascinate me." It's quite an ambition, but for someone who entered law school as one woman out of six in a total enrollment of 220 and graduated as one of the three women who made it, it certainly isn't unattainable.

Source: Bowling Green (KY) Daily News, March 20, 1977, p. 30. By Teri Hurst, Women's Editor.

came guest appearances for the lawyer and her client on *Good Morning America* and the *Phil Donahue Show*. Today, Flora Stuart concentrates on personal injury cases; she has recently settled dozens of silicone breast implant lawsuits. She has what must be one of the few mother-daughter law firms in the country. In her words:

> *A second glance at the major law firms would immediately reveal the fact that the lead partners are mostly male. Women who join the firms now rarely move to the top. Finding a mother and daughter as a legal team is still rare, but it is not unusual to find a father and son duo practicing law together. Some attorneys (particularly from the earlier generation) still find it difficult to accept a female attorney as their full equal. Time will eventually melt away these extreme prejudices against our gender, but the battle is far from being won.*
>
> *Twenty-two years after I started my journey down the legal road, my daughter now practices law by my side. It is a different world from when I began. (Stuart, 1998, p. 1)*

The contrast between the professional challenges that mother and daughter have known symbolizes the differences in the world a woman lawyer faced in the 1970s and the world of today. Unlike her mother, Natalie Stuart attended a law school in which almost half the students were female and was taught by female as well as male professors. On graduation, a place in an established law firm was ready for her. In her hometown, her mother had already blazed the trail. Not only is there no shock on people's faces today as the younger Stuart begins her opening statement before the "ladies and gentlemen of the jury," but the judge is likely to be a female, as is the opposing counsel. Not all women, admittedly, have such a clear trail to follow, and for everyone with family obligations, the 60- to 70-hour weeks can be strenuous. The grind, coupled with the relentless competition, starts with legal education.

LAW SCHOOL SOCIALIZATION

Given what law professor Patricia Williams terms the "clearly stated authority" of the law, that body of "hypnotically powerful rhetorical truths," as a female African American teacher of law she had to wrestle with the appropriate introduction of race, gender, class, and social policy into the law school curriculum (Williams, 1991, p. 10). She also had to confront the legacy of the institutional racism, sexism, and classism at her university. Williams's iconoclastic book, *The Alchemy of Race and Rights,* is the product of that struggle. Law school's mask of impersonality and "hyperauthenticity," as Williams suggests, is a cover for rigidity and prejudice. Being in law school is described by Williams as being on another planet, and being a law professor as being in another galaxy.

The traditional law school experience is sufficiently rigorous and formidable to be the subject of numerous films, novels, and nonfiction books. Because the dictates of the bar exam in each state to a large extent decree the nature of the education that law schools must offer, the law school experience is relatively comparable across the states.

In a painstakingly documented article published in the *University of Pennsylvania Law Review,* Guinier, Fine, Balin, Bartow, and Stachel (1994) present a wealth of data on students, male and female, enrolled in law school. Entitled "Becoming Gentlemen: Women's Experience at One Ivy League Law School," this much-cited article convincingly presents the case that the law school experience of women differs markedly from that of their male peers. This study's findings are that women:

- despite having identical entry-level credentials to men are far less likely to excel academically
- in their first year are much more highly critical than their male peers of the status quo, of legal education, and of themselves as students
- as third-year students are far more complacent and less idealistic than they were earlier
- enter law school with commitments to public interest law and justice and leave, like the men, with corporate ambitions

- are alienated in class and report lower rates of class participation than men
- are inclined to complain of the change that has come over them and feel submerged in a foreign belief system (pp. 1–2)

One of the most pervasive values of legal culture inculcated in law school is the belief in individuation through hierarchical stratification, according to Guinier and colleagues. Such practices as rigidly ranking students against each other and ranking faculty and deans as well as upper-level students above lower-level students within the law school trains students for later hierarchical relationships and a winner-take-all mentality. For female law school recruits, learning to think like a lawyer, as Guinier and her associates suggest, means learning to think and act like a man.

The narrative data collected by these authors add a poignancy to the findings. In interviews, women law students told of eating disorders, sleeping difficulties, crying (35 percent reported crying from stress compared to none of the men), and failure to learn in the intimidating environment of hostile questioning. As one third-year law student described her experience,

> *Just look at the way many professors here conduct their classes. They call on men predominantly. . . . I think if you look at the people in our class who have formed relationships with professors, they are very much the same men who all of us despise in class. The ones who feel they can monopolize the class time. (p. 51)*

Another woman concurs, "Women's sexuality becomes the focus for keeping us in place. If someone was rumored to be a woman who speaks too much, she was a lesbian" (p. 14). All the female students seem to echo the sentiment that human compassion is a negative trait in budding lawyers.

Stone (1997) echoes the sentiments of Guinier and her associates that U.S. law students generally succumb to peer pressure to abandon dreams of public interest work in favor of more lucrative and less altruistic forms of practice. The uncertainty and loss of confidence that women suffer in law school no doubt crushes their resistance and leads to a turnabout in attitude. Compared to the American law school experience, however, the Australian equivalent, as Stone observes, is far less traumatic, and somewhat more hospitable to social welfare concerns. Female law students in Australia, therefore, are less demoralized than their American cousins and seemingly less malleable in the hands of their professors.

PATRIARCHAL NATURE OF THE WORLD OF LAW

The world of law is decidedly and unequivocally masculine. It is not masculine in a physical sense but in a psychological sense. To have a "legal mind" is to be logical, or left-brain dominant. The law, in its Anglo-American format, is necessarily a site of conflict. It provides a means of dispute, notes Harrington (1994), but the means are combative.

A brief overview of the Anglo-Saxon adversarial system will put the masculine, winner-take-all ethos of today's courtroom into historical perspective. "We are what we were," as the John Quincy Adams character in the 1998 movie *Amistad* so eloquently informed us. The origins of the adversary system hark back to trial by combat and before that and even more primitive, to trial by ordeal. Today the trial is the ordeal.

The rationale for our Anglo-American adversarial legal approach is found in its history. The history is one of ancient customs of judicial ordeal based on magical dogma. In the Middle Ages in England, the ordeals of fire, food, and poison required the accused to demonstrate the solicitude of some all-powerful spirit. With William the Conqueror, trial by battle was brought to the island. Eventually, no dispute existed that might not be submitted to the decision of the sword or club. Hired champions represented the interests of involved parties. According to Anne Strick (1977), trial by ordeal is alive and functioning in the United States; the judicial ordeal is now called the "adversary system" (p. 37).

The adversary model attempts to resolve differences through the opposition of two parties; the ultimate aim of cross-examination is to arrive at the truth (Gardner, 1982, p. 22). Whether this gladiatorial process is properly suited to the resolution of most family relations problems, such as divorce, or to provide justice to crime victims is another matter.

The "hired champions" who fought in combat on behalf of the accused or accusing party were all men. Victory depended on physical strength and quickness. Law schools today are the training ground for success in the juridical ring. Through the harsh discipline of law school, the minds of the students are molded into marvelous instruments of control, or such is the aim. Law students are trained in verbal argumentation, "to make the worse appear the better cause" (see Aristophanes, 423 B.C.) Strategies that are compelling and victorious in the courtroom may one day suffice in the political arena as well. Lau (1983) sees the patterns of legal thinking—the dichotomizing and aggressive argumentation—as having started far earlier than law school. In a comparison between the stereotypical masculine lawyer and the feminine social worker, Lau proposes that the characteristics may have a basis in dominant thought processes. The distinction may be biological, she contends, in that certain types of personalities are more attracted to certain types of professions. The qualities that make for a good lawyer are: competitiveness; the ability to find creative solutions to problems and to persuade clients to take them; a willingness to take risks but knowing when to pull back and compromise; acting talent for convincing juries that the implausible is plausible; excellent short-term memory for quick mastery of the facts in a complicated case; sharp attention to detail while never losing sight of the big picture; and, above all, the versatility to work with people of diverse class and ethnic backgrounds. That these traits are not gender specific is revealed in the success of women attorneys in this competitive field today.

LEGAL PRACTICE: STRUGGLES IN A MAN'S WORLD

In her book, *Women Lawyers: Rewriting the Rules,* Mona Harrington (1994) follows women into the world of work. At the law office, women are torn between requirements of "the mind" and of "the body" and between the need to dress professionally and to be considered feminine at the same time. How to wear their hair is a minor crisis in itself. Harrington paints a picture of the legal landscape as cutthroat and highly competitive.

A fascinating biography of Hillary Clinton by Brock (1996), appropriately entitled *The Seduction of Hillary Rodham,* gives some idea of the pressures facing a young radical feminist trying to break into an established Southern law firm:

> *The firm's secretaries, who resented having to work for a woman in the first place, made cruel comments about Hillary's appearance behind her back, to which she could not have been oblivious. The comments likely amplified her sense of alienation and rejection by the locals, whom she may accordingly have judged in her own mind all the more harshly as country bumpkins.*
>
> *"At first, she didn't wear stockings and the old ladies at the firm were horrified," said Hillary's former Rose secretary from the late 1970s. "She was a comic figure as a lady lawyer. Her hair was fried into an orphan Annie perm. She had one large eyebrow across her forehead that looked like a giant caterpillar. We laughed until we cried. She tried to look good when she went to court, and she would put on some awful plastic jewelry. She'd be wearing high heels she couldn't walk in. There wasn't one stereotypically womanly or feminine thing about her." The office staff considered Hillary's weight problem an endless source of amusement as well. "She was on a perpetual diet," the secretary said. "She would show up for work with a big bag of lettuce and eat out of it all day." (p. 81)*

Even when women achieve conformity to the standardized legal norms, their patterns of interaction separate them from their male colleagues. In a content analysis of conversations between male lawyers and male clients, female lawyers and female clients, male lawyers and female clients, female lawyers and male clients, and same sex and mixed dyads of lawyer and lawyer, Bogoch (1997) was able to systematically measure gender differences in interaction. The setting was a legal aid office in Israel. What Bogoch found is that when clients related to female lawyers as women rather than as professionals, the women felt compelled to emphasize their legal role to the client. For example:

> *Lawyer to client: Look Madam, I am not a social worker. I'm a lawyer and I can't, I don't have time to hear this whole story from the beginning. (p. 10)*

Male lawyers in similar situations did not feel the need to define their professional roles; they simply deemed the client's remarks as irrelevant and returned to the task at hand. Occasionally, female attorneys did step out of their professional conception of themselves to relate to the life world of the clients; women lawyers especially granted legitimacy to the emotions of male clients.

Many women, notes Harrington (1994), shun chronic engagement in battle and gravitate toward areas of the law where they can work on deals, as between companies. The "macho" ethic of the office subjects women to subordinate roles. The emphasis among the male attorneys on winning as the ultimate value, and among prosecutors on browbeating witnesses, is distasteful to many women. Several of the African American women Harrington interviewed developed severe stress-related problems after working as tokens in big law firms.

A major stumbling block for women is the relentless work ethic among what Harrington (1994) terms "working hero hours." Salaried legal associates and partners are expected to work 60- to 70-hour weeks. Many of the large law firms in the East have an annual 2,000 billable hour quota. This leaves no time for social life, family, or to "have a life." Accordingly, there is a continual outmigration of women from the big firms, the "warrior-lawyer's habitat," and into routine, in-house positions, such as in the realty department of an investment firm. The cloister aspect of the in-house position effectively removes women from the power structure. Other possibilities, however, such as joining a small law firm with a civil rights focus or teaching on the faculty of a law school, do give women a voice and provide a network of lawyers who can recognize themselves as a class. We will consider women's influence on the legal system later in the chapter, but the next section examines women on the bench or women judges.

Women on the Bench

The number of women on the bench in any generation is the product of the opportunities and experiences of women in law school and practice in earlier periods (Cook, 1983). When women are restricted to law specialties handled in the back room rather than the courtroom, to legal research rather than litigation, they are effectively kept out of the eligibility pool for judgeships. They are also prevented from establishing the kind of reputation that could lead to judicial appointment.

At the 1998 conference in St. Louis of the National Association of Women Judges, an organization that has grown from 100 members in 1979 to more than 1,300 members today, current and former chief judges shared their stories. The stories typically concerned opposition to women in such positions of leadership by "in-your-face" male colleagues. Resistance to the female judges took many forms, ranging from locking one woman in her chamber room to inflicting verbal abuse on others (Lhotka, 1998).

In Milwaukee, also in 1998, the State Bar of Wisconsin honored the state's first 150 women lawyers, lawyers who broke through extraordinary legal and cultural barriers to achieve their right to practice law. Few of these women, however, went on to become judges. Not too many years ago, according to Janz (1998), the only robes women were permitted to wear were bathrobes.

Today, approximately 25 percent of U.S. judges are women. According to the National Center for State Courts, seventy-seven women are seated as supreme court justices; this is almost double the number from 1994 (Rybak, 1998). Women are often assigned to jurisdictions that are traditionally considered the speciality of women, such as municipal or domestic courts in which, according to Feinman, women judges have little status and are provided few contacts so essential for those seeking a political career. (Admittedly, Judge Judy Sheindlin [1996], the author of *Don't Pee on My Leg and Tell Me It's Raining* and frequent guest on television talk shows, got a lot of mileage out of her position presiding over family court.) Judges in domestic relations court (where many women judges work) do have wide discretion, but these courts—which handle matters such as divorce, child custody, and adoption arrangements—are at the lowest end of the judicial status totem pole. Although severely limited by court procedures and case law, not to mention mandatory sentencing laws, trial judges still possess an influence that extends beyond what they do in the courtroom. In the words of one Kentucky female circuit judge, "What you all do in the back halls and your informal conversations with male judges really has an influence on how they treat women in the courtroom" (Cross, 1999, 1B). Through such influence at equal status levels, women judges can help their male colleagues have greater sensitivity both for the kinds of pressure female attorneys face in the courtroom and for female victims and offenders who appear before the court. They also can help male judges have greater awareness when it comes to such matters as sexual harassment and job discrimination.

It is in the multijudge appellate courts, including state and federal supreme courts, however, where women can have the most impact. Here, as Feinman suggests, a woman can ask questions, raise issues, present data, and influence the progress of the discussion or debate. Therefore, it is significant that women are now being appointed to state and federal appellate courts in unprecedented numbers. One might expect that those women will help move public policy in the direction of greater sex equality. The two women on the U.S. Supreme Court, Sandra Day O'Connor and Ruth Bader Ginsburg, are, of course, among the most influential women of our time.

But do women on the bench bring a different touch to justice? Does gender affect judicial decision making at all? Studies of judges' attitudes and observations seem to indicate that they do, and not only in the United States.

Among the research findings: Florida statewide samples of over 300 male and female judges revealed that women who dispense justice are more aware than their male counterparts of biased treatment of women in the courtroom (Stepnick and Orcutt, 1996); young female judges have a heightened awareness of sexual harassment in the courtroom (Padavic and Orcutt, 1997); a New Zealand study revealed that female, compared to male, judges were twice as likely to believe that a female expert witness would be taken less seriously than a man and that the law reflected male interests and concerns predominantly (Bain, 1997); a Canadian study of decision making of women on the male-dominated Supreme Court of Canada found that the two women judges were more likely than the men on the court to be willing to "rock the boat" and write minority opinions (Tibbetts, 1999).

As more women take their place beside men in "courts of last resort," a new dynamic is emerging, according to an article in *The Christian Science Monitor* by Ryback (1998). "We do not feminize the bench, we humanize it," the California superior court judge is quoted as saying in this article (p. 1). Often focused on different issues from their male counterparts, women are subtly changing courthouse culture and the tenor of American jurisprudence. This fact is confirmed by the newly appointed female supreme court justice in Minnesota, Chief Justice Kathleen Blatz. A longtime supporter of children's issues, Blatz has a master's degree in social work as well as a law degree. Her self-description includes this accomplishment: "Loves to bake and is renowned for her peach cobbler" (Rybak, p. 1).

RACE, CLASS, GENDER

To review one of the major assumptions of this book, the oppressions found in gender, class, and race are very much related to the careers of women lawyers.

Gender and Discrimination

Despite the generally favorable climate and the unprecedented opportunities for women in the law today, a legacy of discrimination remains. Although more women now hold faculty and administrative positions in law schools than in earlier decades, they are still accorded relatively low prestige if, as teachers, their main focus is on "women's issues" as opposed to business and corporation law (Feinman, 1994). Furthermore, female law students study case law from the male point of view; only men's opinions are cited. Legal issues that are important to women, such as marital rape, wife beating, and family law, meanwhile may be dealt with only superficially, as Feinman further suggests.

Survey results reported by MacCorquodale and Jensen (1993) indicate the depth and scope of gender bias in the legal profession. Males surveyed seemed relatively unaware of gender bias. Women were very aware of tokenism, preferential treatment by the judges and other lawyers, and inquiries addressed toward women to verify their professional status.

According to a survey of 220 female attorneys working in a midwestern city, many women reported that their gender helped them get hired (Rosenberg, Perlstadt, and Phillips, 1993). But respondents reported that discrimination existed in salary, promotion, and assignments. Approximately two-thirds of the women reported being addressed as "honey" or "dear" and receiving remarks about their appearance. Young women were especially susceptible. One-fourth of the lawyers reported being sexually harassed in the courtroom.

Rainmaking is a term that refers to the amount of business a member of a law firm can generate. More than anything else, rainmaking is the barometer of success in the legal world today. Critics complain that law is less driven by altruism and more driven by profit than it formerly was.

Still largely excluded from old boys' clubs, female lawyers are at a clear disadvantage, socially and professionally, compared to men. Legal experts explain that women's other obligations, such as family pressures, prevent them from entertaining or traveling (Deutsch, 1996). Women rarely participate in team sports or other male-type bonding activities. To help compensate for their lack of connections, some female lawyers are forming clubs, such as the Eleanor League of Detroit, members of which meet every month and routinely refer business to each other.

At the national level, as Feinman indicates, women are taking a very active role in annual meetings of the American Bar Association. They also have been instrumental collectively in establishing state and federal task forces on women and gender bias in the courts. Sexual harassment is a part of this bias, which is being thoroughly investigated.

Sexual Harassment

Following the Clarence Thomas–Anita Hill hearings, sexual harassment and discrimination claims filed with the Equal Employment Opportunities Commission increased 71 percent. Among the litigants were partners and associates in major law firms. Unwanted touching and other forms of sexual harassment were among the charges.

Like sexual demands on an unwilling wife, sexual harassment of women by male colleagues expresses the ancient rule that women should be sexually available to men. The existence of sexual harassment means that the woman who objects may put her career at risk; this form of activity reminds the professional woman that she is not really an equal (Harrington, 1994). Above all, sexual harassment is an abuse of power, sometimes by an older man inflicting unwanted attention on a younger, often unmarried woman. Typically, the harasser flatters himself that the woman enjoys his attentions. Most women are familiar with such examples of abuse of power in the form of sexual games and innuendos. Another form of harassment, *gender harassment,* is less obvious and less related to the perceived sexual attractiveness of a woman. Gender harassment entails *belittling* a woman as a woman, as a means of putting her down and preserving the status quo. Although prohibited under federal law by 1980, and by the Civil Rights Act before that, tradition decreed that sexual bantering and teasing were natural to relations between the sexes and that only male-bashing, prudish women would raise a fuss over teasing or "sweet talk."

The Equal Employment Opportunity Commission (EEOC) regulations passed in 1980 followed a survey that produced hard data on the extent of sexual harassment within the federal government. The two aspects of sexual harassment that were discussed in the previous chapter are quid pro quo, which implies a trade-off of sexual favors for job benefits, and the creation of a hostile work environment through offensive sexual conduct. These categories are the basis for sexual harassment suits. As Schultz (1988) notes, however, the law tends to equate workplace harassment with sexual pursuits, to the utter disregard of nonsexual forms of harassment. We need to attend to the larger social structures of workplace gender discrimination in which both sexual and not-so-sexual forms of harassment flourish (Schultz, 1998). Clearly, a greater commitment has to be made at the management level of law firms to encourage and provide an environment that is more receptive to women (Merlo and Pollock, 1995). Despite the years of entrenched resentment and discrimination against women who join the legal fray, the contributions of such women on the periphery of the power structure (and sometimes very much within it) have been considerable.

Synergistic Nature of Race, Class, and Gender

Race, class, and gender, as previously noted, are not simply additive forces; the effect of membership in more than one of these categories is synergistic. A woman, for example, who is both African American and working class inhabits a world in which the forces of gender, race, and class intersect with each other through the social and economic structure (Anderson and Collins, 1995).

The fact that approximately half of all African Americans grow up in poverty restricts their life chances; it also stigmatizes the members of that race as lazy and uneducated. We need to recognize that the intersection of race, class, and gender is not limited to those at the bottom of the social ladder. In the professions, especially prestigious professions such as law, one is expected to have the bearings of gentry. This includes a polished manner of speech and dressing like a lawyer in a subdued, not flashy, style of dress (Reidinger, 1996). A desirable attribute of a lawyer is the ability to bring business into the law firm. Bringing in poor clients charged with petty crimes may be considered a minus more than a plus.

In the legal profession, to be a person of color, lower class, and a woman is to have three strikes against you before you start. The path to law school is extremely difficult for persons without educational and financial advantages. The low-income college student must obtain loans and work his or her way through college. This ordinarily means less study time and a lower grade point average. The privileged student, on the other hand, has the luxury of study time and the lack of heavy financial debt. Then come the expensive crash courses in LSAT (Law Scholastic Aptitude Test), an exam that appears to be culturally and gender biased. Affirmative action programs help compensate for gender and racial discrimination in our society but not for class.

In her study, "The Plexiglass Ceiling: The Careers of Black Women Lawyers," Simpson (1996) examined the ways in which race and gender intersected to shape the career transitions of 238 African American women lawyers. Respondents worked in municipal and federal government predominantly, but also in private practice and law firms. Fifty-four percent had college-educated parents. Racism and sexism in law were first evidenced in law school. Of the respondents, 87 percent said discrimination was rampant. Alumni from a prestigious northeastern school recalled that the dean of students said that admitting blacks had lowered their academic standards. Ninety percent of respondents stated that they had been excluded from student study groups. This pattern of discrimination was further evidenced at the job entry level. Opportunities to practice in high status, powerful, and financially remunerative sectors of the profession were found to be few and far between for these African American attorneys.

In the University of Pennsylvania study described earlier (Guinier et al., 1994), attrition rates, or movement from job to job, were studied as an indirect gauge of career satisfaction. Almost 90 percent of the respondents moved from their first job to another entry-level position. Government lawyers showed the most stability. Respondents felt that "not being a white male" limited their chances of promotion tremendously. Questionnaire and interview results revealed that although affirmative action policies and programs dramatically increased the number of African American women lawyers, a "Plexiglass ceiling" limited their career choices.

A major economic obstacle confronts most law school graduates. Following law school, these graduates, like others, must pay for an expensive crash course to prepare for the bar exam and take a legal assistant job while awaiting bar exam results. Assuming favorable results, the newly admitted member of the bar may bear a debt of easily well over $100,000.

In summary, given the structural conditions of the legal profession, it is very difficult for women of any ethnicity or background to assume positions of leadership. And yet, entering into the ranks of the powerful (whether through marriage or career) is the only way to have an impact. This is what is happening today, slowly and surely, as women acquire the language and tools of their successful brothers.

MASS MEDIA IMAGES

"The first thing we do, let's kill all the lawyers" (Shakespeare, 1590/1970 *King Henry VI, Part II*, 4.2.86). This sentiment from the sixteenth century is echoed today in newspaper articles, joke books, and comments by the general public concerning the alleged greed of attorneys. Whether or not everybody is suing everybody, this is often the public image. And it is true that the United States has the highest number of lawyers per capita of any country (the count is expected to climb to one million by 2000) and the greatest number of legal cases (Gubernick and Levine, 1996).

The low public image of lawyers is pervasive. Newspaper articles and magazine accounts decry (or proclaim) the unprecedented number of attorneys opting out of the profession. The number of law school graduates taking non-legal jobs has about doubled between 1990 to 1996—from 6 to 11 percent (Gubernick and Levine, 1996). "Many Lawyers Sentenced to Life of Misery" declares one headline (Dolan, 1995). What has happened to the profession? As Gubernick and Levine suggest,

> *Law was once a respected profession. That was some compensation for the hard work and long hours. No longer. The antics and outrageous lawsuits launched and sometimes won by trial lawyers, and their corrupting influence on public life, have driven public regard for lawyers to new depths. (p. 75)*

"No fee unless you win." This phrase, used in legal advertising to entice winning personal injury cases, sums up the contingency fee arrangement in a nutshell. Lawyers sue on behalf of injured clients when the claim is against a company or individual with assets. Lawyers collect one-third to forty percent of the damages; usually such cases are settled out of court. If the case comes to court, as a civil case, the level of proof required is lower than that in a criminal case. The winning civil case against O. J. Simpson in the death of his wife illustrates how justice can be achieved monetarily when criminal justice cannot. The flaw in this system as it operates in the United States is that innocent people can be sued for damages and win, and yet still be socked with exorbitant legal expenses.

In the past female attorneys concentrated on the divorce and family law, legal aid work, wills, and criminal law cases nobody wanted. Personal injury settlements were handled by men. Today, in states where lawyers advertise without restriction, assertive women can market their services through ads in telephone books, on the radio, and on television. Whether from reticence or complacency, however, few women have taken advantage of the possibilities for acquiring business through the use of the media.

In personal correspondence, Stuart (1998) recalls her success in marketing her services in the state of Kentucky:

> *Being somewhat of an anomaly and minority has had its advantages. My own firm, consisting of all female attorneys, started many years ago and now includes my daughter. We describe ourselves as being the "family law firm that cares about people." What better way for an office of all females to express the compassion we have for our clients? I have even been known to shed a few tears with my clients (imagine a male attorney shedding tears). Our clients love it! (p. 2)*

Television and Film Portrayals

We have been talking about the mass media. One of the main ways the general public forms impressions of a particular profession is through fictional accounts, especially through television portrayals.

Harrington (1994) conducted a study of Hollywood and television dramas involving women lawyers. One major theme during the plots in many of the shows is the women's attempt to maintain their feminine qualities in a world of power and intrigue. Harrington calls these the mind/body stories. The women who become too cold and calculating are sure to be punished in the end.

The plot of *Presumed Innocent* concerns the just desserts women victimizers of men receive. The movie begins with the murder of an attractive power-seeking prosecutor who, we learn as the plot unfolds, deserved her fate. The TV drama *L.A. Law* carried a similar warning to career women who manipulate men to get ahead. A tough, successful middle-aged attorney who has waged a successful sex-discrimination suit gets killed in a freak elevator accident.

Other images of women lawyers parallel yet contradict these images of women who successfully fight for justice through their clients, such as in *The Accused* and *The Client.* Similarly, lawyer heroines expose corruption in *Class Action* and *Music Box,* although at considerable personal cost. But on the whole, Harrington concludes, the ranks of the new heroines do not include a cadre of dissident lawyers. Fictional lawyers, unlike their real-life counterparts, seem relatively unaware of both cultural biases in the legal system and the need for social change. A refreshing new development is the role of Lindsay Dole, played by Kelli Williams, a full partner who makes a pile of money and is known for her courtroom smarts; or DA Helen Gamble, played by Lara Flynn Boyle, who is as feminine as they come but can be as hard as nails; or the intelligent, self-identifed fat woman, Camryn Manheim, in the role of feisty attorney Ellenor Frutt, who fights for the underdog and has healthy romantic relationships of her own. The show is ABC's *The Practice* which premiered in the fall of 1998 (Graham, 1998).

STRENGTHS OF WOMEN ATTORNEYS

How are women lawyers using their authority to help individual women? How are they advancing the equality of women generally?

Whether the influx of women into the legal profession will transform the profession—feminize it—or whether the legal profession will transform women into clones of men who "think like a lawyer" is a hotly debated issue. Some theorists argue that women bring to the law a "different voice" that will enable such values as caring, empathy, and mediation to become more central to legal practice (see Anleu, 1992; Harrington, 1994; and Menkel-Meadow, 1995). Others proclaim that the bastion of the law is so imbued with male values such as value-free objectivity, abstract rights, and adversarial know-how that there is little scope for women to make a difference. Anleu refers to the former arguments as the "cultural feminist approach" and the latter as the "radical theorist approach." Both approaches offer a one-dimensional view of women, according to Anleu; women's differential locations within the settings need to be taken into account. Established female attorneys may thrive in their own law firms. Stuart (1998), in a semihumorous vein, provides the following account:

> *My practice blossomed because women wanted a female attorney who could empathize with their plight—especially in divorce cases. Much to my surprise, men also began hiring me so they could have "a woman on their side." I later began handling bankruptcy cases in Federal Court and the creditors called me the "Bankruptcy Queen."*
>
> *Presently, we have established the only female law firm in our community. The name of my firm is Stuart, Stuart and Broz (Broz is the last name of a female partner in my firm). We often get addressed as Stuart, Stuart and Brothers! Through the years, some of my male clients have come up with such endearing names for me as "country child" (he wrote a poem for me). My favorite name was "pretty whipper snapper." Just this year, 1998, an opposing attorney with whom I was reviewing a case addressed me as "Listen Lady." (p. 2)*

Let us now return to the question of whether women who enter law school lose their ideals through rigorous socialization or whether they emerge from their education with their principles unscathed. In truth, this is not an either-or proposition. As women or other minorities or working-class people enter the power structure, they can still hold onto their original values and goals. True, legal training socializes women to be advocates, to engage in gladiatorial-type contests for hire, and to be tough in negotiation. On the other hand, to paraphrase Audre Lorde (1984), the master's tools alone will never dismantle the master's house (p. 123). In other words, acquiring the legal knowledge and credentials may be a necessary but not sufficient condition for effecting social change. Real power and change, as Lorde argues, come with bonding (on the basis of race, class, and gender) and a militance in acknowledging rather than denying our differences. If we merge with the power structure, on the other hand, we will suffer a loss of identity. Borrowing Lorde's metaphor, we can conclude that only through acquiring the master's tools and gaining access to the power structure will we be able to dismantle the master's house. The risk is that in joining the rich and powerful, lawyers who set out to change the world will lose sight of their original goals.

Ronnie Podolefsky (1998), a feminist activist turned lawyer, has seen how economic pressures and materialism can divert even the most idealistic law students from their original course. See Box 7.2 for an interview with Podolefsky, a specialist in employment discrimination and one of the three National Organization for Women (NOW) board members chosen from the Midwest to serve on the NOW board of directors.

BOX 7.2 Interview with Ronnie Podolefsky, Attorney at Law

Katherine van Wormer (KvW): What made you decide to go to law school?

Podolefsky: Law school seemed a natural progression for social activism. I had always thought law boring and didn't even consider becoming a lawyer until the 1990s when I became very involved in feminist politics. I'd typically be arguing a legislative issue as Iowa NOW (National Organization for Women) president, and an opponent, always a male attorney, would pull the trump card: "We know 'the law,' you do not," he would say. I decided to supplement my knowledge and the appearance of legitimacy. I thought, "Well, heck, I'm as smart as these guys. I can go to law school, too."

My activism continues now that I have a law degree and am currently a NOW national board member. However, practicing law has impacted the character of my activism. While I remain an activist apart from my law practice, and the area of my practice is largely the area of my activism, the majority of my time is spent in my practice. As a result, a client's interests, rather than abstract social issues, must determine the focus of my work. Unlike activism, I generally can't take a case to the press or to a street demonstration. Since I must consider ethical restrictions of client confidentiality and judicial process, I keep a self-imposed silence.

KvW: So can lawyers make a difference, or does the law change people who try to do so?

Podolefsky: Lawyers can make a difference in the world—in civil rights, discrimination law, immigration law. In the area of sexual harassment, for example, busi-

nesses today are more likely to enforce antiharassment policies than they were a few years ago. This trend gained momentum only after *plaintiffs' attorneys* began winning significant damage awards against businesses that did not have or enforce such policies. While we might not change employers' hearts, we can begin by changing their conduct, and litigation is one way to do this.

I saw many go into law school to change society who then discarded that goal before graduation. For one thing, law students can incur huge debts while in school. After graduation, their priorities shift from social justice goals to finding jobs that pay well, going through mental gymnastics to justify and live with the decision. Some set aside their dreams, instead taking jobs requiring that they defend the company against the worker, the powerful against the weak. One female graduate excitedly told me a large firm had offered her a position *routinely* defending a client police department against sexual harassment claims. She was very excited about the salary and the less-than-dull nature of the subject matter. I asked if she felt like a sellout. She conceded that the jury appeal of her attractive female presence at the defense table was likely a consideration in recruiting her for this particular position, but insisted that everyone is entitled to representation. The irony leaves me more than uncomfortable.

KvW: Will having more women in law bring a more feminine touch to the law?

Podolefsky: The polarized concepts of feminine and masculine impose an artificially constraining lens on legal doctrine. I'm also generally uncomfortable with

(Continued)

BOX 7.2 *Continued*

essentializing genders. At the same time, it would seem that women as a class bring to the practice of law their unique life experiences *as women*. This can and has influenced the law in countless areas, from reconceptualizing legal definitions of rape to feminist deconstruction of federal tax law.

KvW: How do you think you will be able to help empower women?

Podolefsky: By facilitating meaningful access to and influence on the legal system. When women bring issues of discrimination to an attorney, attorneys must listen with a legal ear informed by, among other things, feminist jurisprudence and critical race feminism. My sense is that countless women with good claims under existing laws are denied legal protection because they are unable to engage a lawyer who "gets it" and respects the legitimacy of their harms. I wonder how many women give up after a lawyer says "You don't have a case" and never pursue the matter further.

In the larger scheme of things, this has implications beyond the individual. Our case law is built on precedent created when a court decides an issue. Each new decision is then based on those before it. Under this system, case law may never be fairly informed by women's experiences if a significant cross section of women's cases never get to court.

I also provide mentoring and encouragement for others to work in this area of law. Discrimination law is very complex and imprudently underestimated by lawyers who dismiss it as fringe. When I interviewed for jobs my last year in law school, interviewing at-

torneys asked which area of law I was interested in. Consistently, I answered "civil rights and discrimination law." Each interviewer smiled solicitously and said, "That's very nice, but which area will you practice to pay the rent?" This form of discouragement is value-laden, distressing, and ill-informed.

KvW: I understand you've worked with Muslim women from Bosnia?

Podolefsky: Yes. When working with immigrant groups, cultural sensitivities are critical. An ethnocentric legal system, from police to prosecutors, attorneys to courts, can seriously obstruct justice. For instance, recent Bosnian refugees may come from politically opposing regions. Police employment of a translator from one region to interrogate a defendant from the opposing region can dangerously compromise the interrogation and the rights of the defendant. As another example, laws that appear neutral may in fact not offer equal protection to our refugee populations. While refugee women in the United States may invoke the protection of U.S. domestic violence laws, this may be meaningless. Iowa law requires that the primary perpetrator must be arrested. The result for a noncitizen can be very harsh: after arrest, a noncitizen may then face deportation to his country of origin. In some cases, this is tantamount to a death sentence. Effectively, noncitizen victims are discouraged from ever calling the police.

KvW: One final question: have you been discriminated against as a female attorney?

Podolefsky: Yes. I have had male attorneys and even judges act dismissively, treat

BOX 7.2 *Continued*

me as less than an adult. On one particular occasion, I called a judge for some information. "Oh, I remember we've met," he said. "You were that cute little thing." This was extremely unprofessional and certainly not something he would have said to a male attorney. It di-

minishes the professionalism of the environment offered me as compared to that offered my male colleagues. Another judge actually called me Ms. Lewinsky in the courtroom, a tasteless attempt to make light of my difficult last name.

(This interview took place on November 30, 1998, in Cedar Falls, Iowa.)

SIGNIFICANCE OF WOMEN'S ENTRANCE INTO THE LAW

When women make their presence felt in a formerly all-male preserve, whether in the military, in prison, or in substance abuse treatment, the social climate changes: The effect is humanizing and even salutary (see Champion, 1998, p. 325). In an article entitled "Jurisprudence and Gender," Robin West (1998) argues that women bring to the legal culture a sense of literal connectedness with others and a linking between family and work that permeates the atmosphere. Jack and Jack (1989), in their study of the changing values of men and women lawyers, found the traditional male-female divide: men focusing on competition and winning, and women favoring cooperation and compromise; men reasoning formally and abstractly, and women reasoning contextually and holistically. As women intrude on an all-male preserve, such as a traditional law firm, the social climate changes. Conversations among colleagues are more personal than in male-only establishments. Personal experience and personal values relevant to legal work become integrated; the social norms shift to allow for ongoing conversations about one's family and recreational life (Harrington, 1994). The level of friendliness and intimacy at a cogender law office are palpable.

Another interesting effect of women's entry into legal work is revealed in Shore's (1997) study of the relationship of gender balance at work, family responsibilities, and workplace characteristics among male and female attorneys. Data for a survey of more than 500 male and female attorneys revealed that work-related drinking diminishes as contact with women peers becomes more frequent. The extent to which both men and women had household and child-related responsibilities after work also influenced the extent of workplace drinking.

Politically, women's presence in law has had an impact, even beyond their numbers. To gauge this impact, we have to look to the opposition. Conservative critics such as Weiss and Young (1996) inveigh on the courts and legislatures to resist efforts by feminists to limit individual rights under the guise of protecting women as a class. Weiss and Young's tirade about the "harm" feminist activists have done is oddly encouraging:

> *In the past decade, feminist legal theory has become a formidable presence in many of America's top law schools. Feminist activism has also had a major impact on many areas of the law, including rape, self-defense, domestic violence, and such new legal categories as sexual harassment. However [the purpose of] the new agenda is to redistribute power from the "dominant class" (men) to the "subordinate class" (women), and such key concepts of Western jurisprudence as judicial neutrality and individual rights are declared to be patriarchal fictions designed to protect male privilege. (p. 1)*

The writers further express their concern over the effects of feminist pressure regarding "loose and subjective" definitions of harassment and rape, "dangerous moves to eviscerate the presumption of innocence in sexual assault cases," and the "license to kill" that battered wives enjoy with regard to their allegedly abusive spouses (p. 1).

Law school, as Weiss and Young imply, is a powerful, transformative experience. Widely regarded as an ideological training ground, law school historically has been the domain of aggressive white males. Today, change is under way. Tightly enforced affirmative action programs at universities have resulted in an influx of minorities and women into the teaching arena. It is in this arena of law school that the feminist voice is increasingly heard.

What is the feminist legal theory to which Weiss and Young refer? And what is the nature of its impact? Sharyn Anleu (1995) describes feminist legal theory as a "transformative potential [that] derives from women's experiences of exclusion" (p. 395). These experiences create an outsider's critical perception, which engenders empathy for other subordinated and oppressed groups. In contrast to traditional legal theory, which stresses value neutrality, feminist theorists promote consciousness-raising as a central element in empowering the client. Through consciousness-raising, students are made aware of sexism, racism, and classism and of how some inequalities can be rectified through resourceful use of the law and courts. Feminist litigation is taught as one means of addressing human rights violations against women. Consistent with this perspective, law school professors and lawyers tend to recommend alternative, disputed resolution procedures, especially in family law and child welfare where the avoidance of adversarial conflict is an advantage to all parties. In regard to wife battering and rape, on the other hand, as Anleu indicates, women's groups tend to be adamant about the use of criminal penalties; they see little scope for mediation in light of inequalities in bargaining power between men and women.

SUMMARY

The members of the first generation of women lawyers tended to be white, upper-middle- to upper-class, and the daughters or wives of lawyers, and they devoted all their energy to gaining the right to practice. They won tolerance rather than acceptance by playing conventional female roles and by being nonthreatening. Myra Bradwell, who worked toward legislative reform crucial to women, was an exception. The suffrage movement from the 1890s to 1920 and the postsuffrage era saw a little more legislative activity, but compared to other professions such as medicine or correctional administration, women have been largely excluded from the male legal power structure.

Thanks to federal laws from the 1960s, many of the traditional barriers against women's entry into the legal field, including law professorships, have been broken. Today, we are seeing a rise in a new class of professionals, women trained in knowledge of the law, who refuse to be treated as second-class citizens. The creation of specialized women's groups such as the Commission on Women in the Profession of the American Bar Association, the National Women's Lawyers Association, the National Association of Women Judges, and regional networking groups helps compensate for the reluctance of established attorneys to mentor new female recruits. Professional networking among women has helped to catapult some among their ranks to positions of national prominence and provide other women with the psychological support they need for professional growth. For all women in society, the gain is tremendous. For victims of crime, especially of sexual and physical abuse, for women seeking a divorce or needing to write a will, and for female offenders, female advocacy can provide a rare sense of protection. Male clients, similarly, can benefit from a warm, personal touch.

Discrimination against women in the legal profession persists nevertheless. In this chapter, we reviewed evidence that continues to show that our judicial arena retains its status as a battleground between opposing forces and still tends to be stratified by gender, race, and class and that women in law firms are less likely to become full partners during their careers, to earn as much money as their male peers, or to thrive in the highest-paid legal specialties. Moreover women, compared to men, express more dissatisfaction about their treatment in the courtroom and by other lawyers. Sexual harassment is the norm, especially for younger attorneys.

Despite the barriers erected to keep women out of the practice of law and, ultimately, lawmaking, many women have found a niche for themselves in this august and challenging field. Although only a small percentage of the female attorneys see themselves as social activists, those who do are developing new models for the practice of law and new arguments to guide their legal briefs. In short, in the practice of law, many women are finding fulfillment as they adopt the "tools of the master" for their clients' ends, perhaps not to "dismantle the master's house" as Lorde (1984) envisioned but, less drastically, to remodel and renovate it—and then to add some personal, finishing touches.

REFERENCES

Abel, R. (1995). Revisioning lawyers. In R. Abel and P. Lewis (eds.), *Lawyers in society: An overview* (pp. 1–38). Berkeley: University of California Press.

Anderson, M., and Collins, H. C. (1995). *Race, class, and gender,* 2nd ed. Belmont, Calif.: Wadsworth.

Anleu, S. L. (1992). Women in law: Theory, research, and practice. In B. R. Price and N. Sokoloff (eds.), *The criminal justice system: Offenders, victims, and workers* (pp. 359–371). New York: McGraw-Hill.

Anleu, S. L. (1992). Women in law: Theory, research, and practice. *The Australian and New Zealand Journal of Sociology 28:* 391–410.

Bain, H. (1997, June 26). Discrimination widespread in judiciary, say women judges. *The Dominion* (Wellington, New Zealand): 3.

Bernat, F. P. (1992). Women in the legal profession. In I. Moyer (ed.), *The changing roles of women in the criminal justice system,* 2nd ed. (pp. 307–321). Prospect Heights, Ill.: Waveland.

Bogoch, B. (1997). Gendered lawyering: Difference and dominance in lawyer-client interaction. *Law and Society Review 31*(4): 677–712.

Brock D. (1996). *The seduction of Hillary Rodham.* New York: Free Press.

Champion, D. (1998). *Criminal justice in the United States,* 2nd ed. Chicago: Nelson-Hall.

Cook. B. B. (1983). The path to the bench: Ambitions and attitudes of women in the law. *Trial 19*(8): 48–57.

Cross, A. (1999, March 31). Women of the bench convene. *The Courier-Journal* (Louisville, Ken.), p. 1B.

Danner, N. (1998). Three strikes and it's women who are out: The hidden consequences for women of criminal justice policy reforms. In S. L. Miller (ed.), *Crime control and women: Feminist implication of criminal justice policy* (pp. 1–14). Thousand Oaks, Calif.: Sage.

Deutsch, C. (1996, June 2). Female lawyers join forces. *The Des Moines Register,* p. 1.

Dolan, M. (1995, July 13). Many lawyers sentenced to life of misery (from the *Los Angeles Times*). *Waterloo Courier,* p. 2a.

Feinman, C. (1994). *Women in the criminal justice system,* 3rd ed. Westport, Conn.: Praeger.

Friedman, J. M. (1993). *America's first woman lawyer: The biography of Myra Bradwell.* Buffalo, N.Y.: Prometheus Books.

Gardner, R. (1982). *Family evaluation in child custody litigation.* Cresskill, N.J.: Creative Therapeutics.

Goldhaber, M. D. (1998, December 21). Women's numbers rise at the bigger law firms. *National Law Journal,* pp. A1, A11.

Graham, J. (1998, August 26). For Manheim, practice is perfect. *USA Today,* p. 3D.

Gubernick, L., and Levine, J. (1996, November 4). Make lox, not law. *Forbes:* 68–76.

Guinier, L., Fine, M., Balin, J., Bartow, A., and Stachel, D. L. (1994). Becoming gentlemen: Women's experiences at one Ivy League law school. *University of Pennsylvania Law Review 143*(1): 1–110.

Harrington, M. (1994). *Women lawyers: Rewriting the rules.* New York: Alfred A. Knopf.

Hunt, J. (1990). The logic of sexism among police. *Women and Criminal Justice 1:* 3–30.

Jack, R., and Jack, D. C. (1989). *Moral vision and professional decisions: The changing values of women and men lawyers.* New York: Cambridge University Press.

Janz, W. (1998, October 28). Women lawyers had to overcome society's verdict. *Milwaukee Journal Sentinel,* p. 1.

Lau, J. A. (1983). Lawyers vs. social workers: Is cerebral hemisphericity the culprit? *Child Welfare 62:* 21–29.

Lhotka, W. C. (1998. October 10). Women jurists discuss challenges from male colleagues. *St. Louis Post-Dispatch,* p. 8.

Lorde, A. (1984). *Sister outsider: Essays and speeches.* Trumansburg, N.Y.: Crossing Press.

MacCorquodale, P., and Jensen, G. (1993). Women in the law: Partners or tokens? *Gender and Society 7*(4): 582–593.

Martin, S. E., and Jurik, N. C. (1996). *Doing justice, doing gender: Women in law and criminal practice occupations.* Thousand Oaks, Calif.: Sage.

Mauro, T. (1998, August 5). Report: Minorities not reaching top legal levels. *USA Today,* p. 3A.

Menkel-Meadow, C. (1995). Feminization of the legal profession: The comparative sociology of women lawyers. In R. L. Abel and P. S. Lewis (eds.), *Lawyers in society: An overview* (pp. 221–280). Berkeley: University of California Press.

Merlo, A., and Pollock, J. (1995). *Women, law, and social control.* New York: McMillan.

Morello, K. B. (1986). *The invisible bar: The woman lawyer in America 1968 to the present.* New York: Random House.

Padavic, I., and Orcutt, J. D. (1997). Perceptions of sexual harassment in the Florida legal system: A comparison of dominance and spillover explanations. *Gender and Society 11*(5): 682–699.

Palmer, N. (1991). Feminist practice with survivors of sexual trauma and incest. In M. Bricker-Jenkins, N. R. Hooyman, and N. Gottlieb (eds.), *Feminist practice in clinical settings* (pp. 63–82). Newbury Park, Calif.: Sage.

Podolefsky, R. (1998, November 30). Women in law. Presentation at University of Northern Iowa Department of Social Work, Cedar Falls, Iowa.

Reidinger, P. (1996). Dressing like a lawyer: Whether in a law office or courtroom, what you wear may be almost as important as what you say. *American Bar Association Journal 82:* 78–81.

Rhode, D. L. (1995, July 31) Career progress, yes: Equality, not quite yet. *The National Law Journal 17*(48): A21–A22.

Rollins, J. H. (1996). *Women's minds/women's bodies: The psychology of women in a biosocial context.* Englewood Cliffs, N.J.: Prentice-Hall.

Rosenberg, J., Perlstadt, H., and Phillips, W. R. (1993). Now that we are here: Discrimination, disparagement, and harassment at work and the experience of women lawyers. *Gender and Society 7:* 415–433.

Rybak, D. C. (1998, March 12). Minnesota gets a new benchmark. *The Christian Science Monitor,* p. 1.

Scanzoni, L., and Scanzoni, I. (1998). *Men, women and change: A sociology of marriage and family,* 3rd ed. New York: McGraw-Hill.

Schultz, V. (1998, May 25). Sex is the least of it: Let's focus harassment law on work, not sex. *The Nation:* 11–13.

Sheindlin, J. (1996). *Don't pee on my leg and tell me it's raining: America's toughest family court judge speaks out.* New York: HarperCollins.

Shore, E. R. (1997). The relationship of gender balance at work, family responsibilities and workplace characteristics to drinking among male and female attorneys. *Journal of Studies on Alcohol 58:* 297–313.

Simpson, G. (1996). The Plexiglass ceiling: The careers of black women lawyers. *Career Development Quarterly 45*(2): 173–188.

Skaine, R. (1996). *Power and gender: Issues in sexual dominance and harassment.* Jefferson, N.C.: McFarland.

Stepnick, A., and Orcutt, J. D. (1996). Conflicting testimony: Judges' and attorneys' perceptions of gender bias in legal settings. *Sex Roles: A Journal of Research 34*(7–8): 567–579.

Stone, A. (1997). Women, law school, and student commitment to the public interest. In J. Cooper and L. G. Trubek (eds.), *Education for justice: Social values and legal education* (pp. 56–87). Aldershot, England: Ashgate.

Strick, A. (1977). *Injustice for all: How our adversary system of law victimizes us and subverts true justice.* London: Penguin.

Stuart, F. (1998, December). Personal reminiscence, unpublished communication with van Wormer.

Tibbetts, J. (1999, January 21). Gender colours judges' views: Study calls women on Supreme Court outsiders. *The Ottawa Citizen,* p. 4A.

Weiss, M., and Young, C. (1996, June 19). *Feminist jurisprudence: Equal rights or new paternalism? Policy analysis.* Washington D.C.: Cato Institute.

West, R. (1998). Jurisprudence and gender. *University of Chicago Law Review 55*(1): 1–73.

Williams, P. J. (1991). *The alchemy of race and rights.* Cambridge: Harvard University Press.

Woodman, S. (1995, November/December). On the run from the law. *Ms:* 38–42.

Working Woman. (1996, November/December). Law and order: Women sit on the high court, but on the beat, it's a man's world. *Working Woman 21*(11): 53.

8

WOMEN IN CORRECTIONS

Prisons have few friends. They have been described as dark, dingy, deteriorating, and depressive dungeons where the senses are deprived and the human spirit is destroyed by endless monotony and regimentation. Because this description is often all too accurate, dissatisfaction with prisons is widespread. Small cages, stone walls, and multitiered cellblocks make them seem oppressive and unfit for human habitation. They are too frequently the scene of brutality, violence, and racial unrest. Furthermore, although these institutions purport to cure offenders of crime, their record in that area has not been encouraging (Morris, 1974, p. ix). Few would share the vision of the Reverend James Finey, chaplain at Ohio Penitentiary in 1851:

> Could we all be put on prison-fare for the space of two or three generations, the world would ultimately be the better for it. Indeed, should society changes places with prisoners . . . taking to itself the regularity, temperance, and sobriety of a good prison, the goals of peace, light, and Christianity would be furthered . . . Taking the world and the next together . . . the prisoner has the advantage. (Nagel, 1974, p. 1)

The reasonable person might ask: Why would women ever want to subject themselves to working in such a toxic environment? Women work in prisons for the same reasons that women become police officers. The pay is reasonably good, particularly with overtime; the job provides security; jobs are available; and they feel that they can do some good. But the fact is that women work in corrections in many capacities. They are employed as probation and parole officers and supervisors; residential counselors and supervisors in community-based corrections; correctional counselors; jail officers; correctional officers; and correctional administrators, including wardens and superintendents. As women have received resistance in policing and law practice, so has the world of corrections, especially institutional corrections, been reluctant to receive women within the walls of prisons.

One of the problems of examining the careers of women who work in corrections is that so little research has been done in this area, with the exception of the female correctional officer who is working in a prison for male inmates. Accordingly, the major emphasis of this chapter is women who are correctional officers in men's prisons, but, based largely on Bartollas's experiences and observations, the other women working in corrections will receive some attention.

HISTORY OF WOMEN IN CORRECTIONS

The history of women in probation and parole goes back to the early part of the twentieth century when there was an ever-increasing demand in juvenile probation for trained social workers to serve as probation officers. These social workers, trained under the medical model, began to treat juvenile probationers as disturbed children who needed psychiatric therapy. The philosophy and administration of probation thus retained the older concern with helping children adjust to their environment and added a new concern with helping them resolve their emotional problems. In addition to a greater interest in treating children's problems, twentieth-century probation theory also included the idea of more responsibility for the delivery of services to probationers, a greater consciousness of standards, and a desire to upgrade the probation officer and restore the volunteer to probation services.

This history of providing rehabilitative services was part of the rising *parens patriae* movement in juvenile justice and was also influenced by the Progressive reformers who were committed to the "child-saving" crusade (Platt, 1976). It sought out those who could provide treatment services to children and, not surprisingly, were willing to turn to women who had been trained as social workers. Aftercare in juvenile justice took longer to develop than juvenile probation, but, it too was treatment oriented and remained so until the 1980s. As a result, women were also welcomed in aftercare services. Thus, although women in policing and law careers encountered opposition and resistance, women interested in juvenile probation experienced far more receptivity.

With their greater acceptance in juvenile probation, the way was paved for the receptivity of women in adult probation and parole as well. Indeed, as revealed later in this chapter, it was only in the late 1970s and 1980s that the rehabilitative emphasis in adult probation and parole changed to a "get-tough" approach in which individuals were held accountable for their actions.

Women in community-based residential corrections programs also benefited from the reintegrative philosophy developed in the late 1960s and early 1970s. At that time the spirit was one of reform. The area of mental health had undergone a period of deinstitutionalization in the 1960s, during which greater numbers of mental patients were kept in the community rather than placed in large institutions. The turbulence brought on by the Vietnam War, urban riots, and disturbances on college campuses as well as the widespread questioning of traditional values by youth countercultures fostered a receptivity to new solutions. The bloody prison riots that erupted between 1971 and 1973 also helped support the conclusion that there must be a better way.

Federal funding, finally, provided the catalyst that linked correctional reform with social and political realities, thereby creating a huge array of community-based programs throughout the United States. For example, from the inception of the Law Enforcement Assistance Administration (LEAA) in 1967 through July 1975, $23,837,512 of the Safe Street Act federal monies was matched with $12,300,710 from state and local funds for grants devoted solely to residential aftercare programs for adults. Thus, guided by reintegrative philosophy, advocated by a number of blue-ribbon commissions, and supported by federal dollars, community-based programs sprouted in nearly every state. Jobs were available in these programs. Ex-offenders were hired in some programs, and women also received an acceptance that was denied them in more security-oriented institutional contexts.

Community-based corrections began to decline in popularity even more than it had gained public approval. In the mid-1970s, as the mood of the nation suddenly changed to a "get-tough with criminals" approach, publication of official statistics and media coverage of street crime convinced the public that the crime problem had gotten out of hand. By then women were firmly entrenched as part of the landscape of community-based corrections.

Some women in residential programs worked in programs for women, as either line staff or counselors. Others were employed in facilities that were co-correctional, serving both a male and a female population, and some were able to attain jobs as counselors for male-only residential programs. By the late 1970s, it was not unusual, especially in privately administered facilities, to find women who were directors of residential facilities. Debby Lidster, director of the Talbert Halfway House of Women, in discussing her career in community-based programming, gives some good advice to new counselors (quoted in Bartollas, 1981):

> *To work with these women, you need to know where they're coming from—where they dope out and where they're picking up their tricks. You also have to know what they're talking about. If someone comes to you and says "I'm using half a tea a day or eight and two shot," you better know about it. Unless you take the time to learn, you'll show your ignorance, and if you show your ignorance, you won't communicate. (p. 119)*

Despite the greater receptivity of women in probation and parole and residential programs, the path of acceptance in jails and prisons was certainly different. The history of women in institutions, as previously stated, can be traced to demands by benevolent groups outside the criminal justice system for prison, jail, and police matrons. In the 1820s, volunteer Quaker women, joined by upper-middle-class women, were motivated to reform female inmates and blamed their poor living conditions on neglect and sexual exploitation by male keepers.

From 1825 to 1873, reformers achieved occasional success in acquiring matrons for women. Eliza Farnham, a feminist and head matron of the women's section of Sing Sing from 1844 to 1848, was one such success. She adopted the reform program of Elizabeth Gurney Fry, which was to make the environment of the prison more like a home and interaction between staff and inmates more like a family. Farnham upheld the conviction that environmental conditions caused criminal behavior and, therefore, that a change in the environment would change behavior. She ended the silence system, as she grouped the women together for purpose of educational instruction. She also established a library of secular books. In teaching the women to read and write, she instructed them in U.S. history, geography, astronomy, physiology, and personal hygiene. She expected the women to work and encouraged them to become involved with handicrafts. She had the women's wing of the prison decorated with maps, pictures, flowers, and lamps, and she had a piano brought in to provide music. Yet Farnham was not reluctant to employ discipline if it was needed, and solitary confinement was applied for recalcitrant inmates (Feinman, 1994, pp. 43–44).

Farnham was replaced in 1848 for being too liberal, but this did not stop reformers from lobbying for the better treatment of women in corrections. Eventually, reformers were able to convince a male legislature to establish a separate women's prison and to hire women superintendents and matrons. The first prison for women staffed by women opened in Indiana in 1873. By 1913, other reformatories had opened in Farmingham, Massachusetts; Bedford Hill, New York; and Clinton, New Jersey. In 1927, the Federal Institution for Women opened in Alderson, West Virginia; in 1932, the House of Detention for Women opened in New York City, representing the first separate jail for women (Feinman, 1994, p. 44).

Until the 1970s, women were hired strictly to work in prisons for women. Working in male prisons was not viewed as a job for a woman. Still, there were several positions of responsibility for women in male and female corrections. For example, Kate Barnard was the Commissioner of Corrections for Oklahoma from 1907 to 1915, Katherine B. Davis was the Commissioner of Corrections for New York City between 1914 and 1918, and Clara Waters served as the warden of Oklahoma State Reformatory in 1927 (Merlo and Pollock, 1995, p. 98).

WOMEN PROBATION OFFICERS

Probation is the most widely used judicial disposition for dealing with juvenile and adult offenders. Persons sentenced to probation are subject to conditions imposed by the court and are permitted to remain in the community under the supervision of a probation officer. Conditions of probation vary from jurisdiction to jurisdiction and from individual to individual, but they generally include payment of fines, restitution to victims, community service, periodic imprisonment, enrollment in drug or alcohol abuse programs, gainful employment, and cooperation with a citizen volunteer.

Probation emerged from a treatment model in the early part of the twentieth century. It was spearheaded by white, women probation officers who had been trained as social workers. This emphasis on rehabilitative services was altered somewhat in the late 1960s and early 1970s, as reintegrative philosophy became widely accepted in probation services across the United States. Many women probation officers became deeply involved in providing services to probationers to help them adjust to community living. Box 8.1 presents an example of how one woman probation officer influenced the life of a client.

In the 1980s and 1990s, the goals of probation swung to risk assessment and increased surveillance models. In an attempt to convince the public, as well as policy makers, that probation could be "tougher" on criminals, probation administrators began to emphasize a number of strategies that would better ensure public acceptance of probation. The most widely used of these

---

BOX 8.1   Probation Can Make a Difference

One success story I remember is a 17-year-old black girl who had been arrested on first-degree robbery and prostitution charges. She had never been referred before. What it came down to was there were two juvenile girls with two adult males who were their boyfriends, and they were in a bar trying to shake down this white guy. The girls got him up to their apartment, and they were going to get it on with him. Then their boyfriends came up and were real mad because he was with their women. The white guy said, "Take anything," and they took some money he had in his car. The robbery charge was dropped, but there was a finding of fact on the prostitution charge. She was placed on supervision until her eighteenth birthday. When I got her, the first thing we did was go out to the hospital's family practice center to have her checked and placed on birth control. But she was already pregnant. The

majority of time we spent together was concentrated on job, education, getting ready for the baby, and independent living skills. It wasn't a traditional probation case. We spent a lot of time together, getting ready for the future. Her mother was dead and her father was in the mental health institute. Several older sisters were already on ADC, weren't married, and were not models by any means. So, I felt like I'm the one she counted on. I took her to the hospital when she had her baby and was with her during delivery. It was a neat experience. She asked me to be the godmother for her baby. She's very motivated to make something out of herself. She is now 19, has her own car, and keeps an apartment fairly well. She has either gone to school or worked since before she had the baby. With what she has had to work with, it's amazing she is doing so well.

Source: Interview by Linda Dippold Bartollas in 1985 in the Midwest.

strategies have been the combination of probation and incarceration, financial restitution and community service programs, classification systems, intensive probation, and electronic monitoring and house arrest.

This change in goals in adult probation has adversely affected job morale and involvement. The demise of ideology contributed in large measure to the increased rates of burnout for both women and men adult probation officers. Yet, beyond dealing with the demise of ideology and the increased burnout rates, there are probably at least three reasons that women probation officers do not usually experience the rejection and harassment that they have faced in policing jobs and, to a lesser degree, in law careers. First, male probation and parole officers have not developed a culture, which is found in the men's club of policing and the "good old boys' network" in large law firms. Second, there is a long history of treatment in probation and even parole, and professionally training social workers, including both women and men, have been welcomed with open arms to be line probation officers and supervisors. Third, probation, especially, has never been known as a male occupation and, accordingly, male probation officers do not usually see a problem with women being hired in the office.

G. Wunder's (1969) survey of West German male and female probation officers revealed that female officers believed that their work with male clients was successful because they were able "to establish contact rapidly and to communicate effectively." Both male and female officers in this study acknowledged that female offenders were substantially more difficult to work with than male offenders. Younger female officers also believed that younger male clients had difficulty in accepting the authority of a women, and the majority of female officers agreed that male sex offenders were inappropriate clients for supervision by a woman (pp. 91–107).

Another study of female probation officers to sexual assault felons in a metropolitan Ohio county in the years 1978 to 1981 found that male probation officers made more serious sentencing recommendations for sexual assault offenders than did female officers (Walsh, 1984). When given thirteen different criminal acts to consider, male officers ranked rape as the most serious and female officers ranked it eighth. Equally as surprising, female officers tended to view rape as a victim-precipitated crime, but male officers did not. Perhaps even more noteworthy, the average sex offender processed by male officers received about six more months of imprisonment than those offenders processed by female officers (Walsh and Anthony, 1984, pp. 371–388).

Anderson and Spanier's (1980) study of juvenile probation officers in Pennsylvania found that officers with a higher level of education were less likely to label acts as delinquent than were officers with less education and that officers who were treatment and service oriented were less likely to label juvenile acts as delinquent than were those officers who responded to lawyer role models. Consistent with the first two findings, those officers who made rehabilitative recommendations were less likely to label acts as delinquent than were those officers who did not (pp. 505–514).

A 1995 study examined the role of gender in determining the offense seriousness by male and female probation officers in England and Wales. In a review of 169 presentence reports, it was found that the officer's gender was an insignificant factor in terms of the degree to which officers considered aggravating and mitigating circumstances in determining the seriousness of the offense (Nash, 1995, pp. 250–258).

Hayes (1989) examined whether female probation officers in England and Wales were held back as a consequence of their socially ascribed gender roles or because of indirect discrimination by the probation services. They concluded that what restricted promotion and management as choices for women were the women's philosophical disagreements about the present style of probation service management (pp. 12–17).

In sum, some preliminary understanding has been developed concerning the female probation and parole officer's role expectation and performance and gender inequality in probation and parole services. Yet this understanding only scratches the surface of perceiving the challenges and obstacles of probation and parole for women officers, the comparison of rates of burnout between men and women officers, the effect of the "get-tough" crusade on work attitudes of women officers, the similarities and differences between how women and men officers handle clients and the sentences they recommend, and the actual dynamics of gender equality or inequality in probation and parole services.

WOMEN JAIL OFFICERS

During the 1980s and 1990s, there was a dramatic increase in the number of women correctional officers working in U.S. jails (Pogrebin and Poole, 1997). In 1995, women constituted a larger percentage of correctional officers in jails (24.2 percent) than they did in either state (18 percent) or federal (11.0 percent) correctional institutions (Maguire and Pastore, 1996, pp. 91, 94).

Despite recent advances in employment in this nation's jails, women have not been welcomed in the jail setting. As Pogrebin and Poole (1997) expressed it, the jail job "is perceived to be a highly sex-typed male job requiring qualities of dominance, authoritativeness, and aggressiveness. Female qualities of nurturing, sensitivity, and understanding are thought by many male jail officers to be unnecessary and even problematic (p. 41). It is not surprising, then, that Pogrebin and Poole found from their semistructured interviews with 108 women deputies that women experience problems stemming from sexism and sexual harassment by their male coworkers (p. 41).

Belknap's study of thirty-five women correctional officers working in a large metropolitan jail also revealed that women experienced discrimination and sexual harassment. Of this sample, 40 percent indicated that they chose a career in corrections because they wanted to become police officers; 40 percent responded that they were attracted to the money and benefits. In their support for gender equality, 94 percent of the respondents further indicated that they believed that men and women were equal and that they should receive more opportunities. But when asked about their advancement opportunities, 89 percent of these officers believed that they fared poorly compared with male officers. In this study, 31 percent of the women reported that sexual harassment had been an issue for them while working in the jail. White women (45 percent) were more likely than African American women (13 percent) to report sexual harassment, and younger women (47 percent) were more likely to report sexual harassment than older women (13 percent). In addition, these women correctional officers believed that their behavior toward inmates was more respectful than that of men but that their actions were devalued in comparison to the men's more aggressive approaches.

Stohr, Mays, Beck, and Kelley's (1998) study of sexual harassment incidents in seven women's jails revealed that 22 percent reported that they had been victims of sexual harassment. In explaining the low level of harassment victimization compared with that in other correctional settings, these researchers concluded that it was probably significant that women were in a majority and occupied some of the midlevel management positions. This is so because it provides "support for the hypothesis that harassment will be reduced as women achieved more situational and achieved power in the criminal justice workplace" (pp. 147–148).

WOMEN WARDENS

Women have been superintendents of women's correctional institutions since late in the nineteenth century, but today increasing numbers of women are seeking for and being appointed wardens of men's prisons.

Early in the chapter, we discussed Eliza W. B. Farnham, head matron at New York's Sing Sing Prison, and the reforms that she instituted between 1844 and 1848. The first women administrator in U.S. corrections actually preceded Farnham, for Mary Weed was named principal keeper of the Walnut Street Jail in Philadelphia in 1793.

Other early leaders in women corrections were Clara Barton, who served as superintendent of the Massachusetts Reformatory Prison for Women at Farningham in 1882; Kate Barnard, who was elected to be the first Commissioner of Charities and Corrections in Oklahoma in 1907 and served for two terms; Katherine Davis, who was superintendent of the Bedford Hills prison from 1901 to 1914; Mary Bell Harris, who became the first superintendent of the Federal Women's Prison at Alderson, West Virginia; Kate Richards O'Hare, who was first an inmate sentenced for violation of the Federal Espionage Act and then, following her pardon, eventually became assistant director of the California Department of Penology; Mable Walker Willebrandt, who oversaw the administration of federal prisons from 1921 to 1929; and Dr. Miriam Van

Waters, superintendent of the Massachusetts Reformatory for Women from 1932 to 1957 (Morton, 1992, pp. 76–82).

More recently, Elaine Hunt was appointed Louisiana corrections commissioner in 1972, but she died four years later before she could implement many of her reforms. In the 1980s, Ward Murphy in Maine, Ali Klein in New Jersey, and Ruth L. Rushen in California became directors of state systems. In 1990, Alaska, North Dakota, South Dakota, and Puerto Rico had women commissioners of adult corrections, a record number. In 1992, Kathleen M. Hawk was appointed director of the Federal Bureau of Prisons and became the sixth director of the Bureau of Prisons since its establishment in 1930. Women have also made some inroads in terms of administrators of male institutions, but the road has not been easy. By 1997, women represented about 10 percent of wardens and superintendents of the 900 statewide correctional facilities for men (Marks, 1997, p. 1). Camille Graham Camp was one groundbreaker who in 1977 became warden of the Maximum Security Center in South Carolina. She was responsible for the state's most violent inmates and was the first woman to head such a facility (Morton, 1992, p. 86).

Women have found an early and still present reception as superintendents of women's prisons, and a number of women have been appointed as chief administrators of aspects of or even total correctional systems. But to be appointed as warden of a prison for men has been a much more inaccessible career goal. Part of the difficulty is that women's acceptance in men's institutions has been extremely problematic. It is still believed, particularly by the old-timers, that women do not belong in a men's prison. On a different level, promotions to warden generally require a stint as assistant warden of operations of a men's prison. It is no simple matter for a woman correctional officer or woman correctional counselor to overcome the barriers to gender equality and to receive the promotion to head of security or assistant warden of operations of a men's prison. Old-timers, especially, charge that women may be there because the courts insist on it, but that does not mean that we have to trust institutional security to a *woman*.

Pamela K. Withrow (1992), who has served as warden in more than one men's prison, talks about her journey up the career ladder of corrections. In the midst of optimism in Michigan concerning the hiring of women in corrections, she notes that this movement took a backward step in 1987, when an inmate raped and murdered a female officer at the State Prison of Southern Michigan. In the early 1990s, she states that optimism was much less for women in the corrections profession. Women, she adds, continue to experience resistance from male coworkers, and the perception is still alive that prisons are too dangerous for women to work in. She contends, based on her conversations with a number of women corrections workers in Michigan, that women stay in corrections for a number of reasons. They like the interaction with others, especially the opportunity to work as a team; the wages and benefits; the opportunity to test their physical and mental abilities; the challenge of working with staff and inmates; and the fact that the job is fun and never monotonous (p. 90). Women also feel that they bring certain advantages to correctional institutions:

- A women's body language is nonthreatening.
- Being a woman reduces the number of critical incidents because women have to stop and think before getting physical. A low-key approach sometimes best controls a situation.
- Women can calm down hot situations. Male staff sometimes can't or won't back down.
- Women often hear things others present do not because they have good listening skills. Sharing these perceptions may help improve operations.
- Women can benefit from affirmative action, where available.
- Women receive a certain amount of respect simply because of their gender.
- Women are not as concerned with dominance and destructive power games.
- When a woman supervisor does make herself heard, staff really hear.
- Women more often are able to see inmates as people. (pp. 91–92)

Kathleen M. Hawk (1992), director of the U.S. Bureau of Prisons adds, "I recognize that many women have suffered trials in the field of corrections over the years and that their perseverance certainly opened many doors for my generation." But she claims that in her years in the profession, being a woman "has been nothing but a plus" (p. 132).

Tekla Dennison Miller (1996), a former warden and author of *The Warden Wore Pink,* gives another twist to women's acceptance: "You have to be terribly strong, not just to deal with the offender population, but also to deal with the negative attitudes of the employees. Many people say it's changed, but it's still there."

The Reverend Jannie Poullard, the first woman warden of New York City's Brooklyn House of Detention and the J. A. Thomas Center on Riker's Island, claims that women are still held to a higher standard and still must work harder to gain equal recognition. She says, "If they're males, it's automatically assumed they're responsible, in charge, and can manage males or females." But "a woman, on the other hand, no matter how qualified she is, always has to prove she can do the job equally as well" (Marks, 1997, p. 1).

A sexual harassment suit settled on November 30, 1997, revealed that the sexual harassment present so widely in law enforcement and in men's prisons with women's correctional officers can also affect women who are wardens. In this suit filed by Linda George, a former associate warden, she charged chief deputy warden Augustine Infante with touching her breasts in front of a prison Equal Employment Opportunity investigator, grabbing her by an ankle, following her off prison grounds in a manner "somewhat like stalking" and telling her she had "the hottest seat in the prison." The settlement on this suit was $6.57 million; including $2 million in damages, $1.8 million paid to private defense attorneys, $1.7 million in fees and expenses to plaintiff attorney, and $353,955 already awarded to Linda George (Wisely, 1998, p. 15).

In sum, the success of some women administrators and wardens of men's prisons has been impressive, and a convincing argument can be made that men's prisons need the talents and skills that women bring to the leadership of prisons. Morton, who has recently completed a national study of women wardens, adds: "They tend to be reform oriented. They all talk about changes they've made to make things better for their staff and to find additional programming for the inmates. Morton also contributes that this has been the traditional role women have played in the criminal justice system, but they rarely had the authority to implement their ideas (Marks, 1997, p. 1). Nevertheless, the number of women wardens will be limited until women gain greater acceptance as correctional officers and correctional counselors in men's prisons and are promoted to supervisory and administrative positions in greater numbers. It is this career path from which wardens are chosen by central offices.

THE CORRECTIONAL COUNSELOR

The correctional counselor is the basic treatment officer in many adult correctional institutions. Counselors generally agree that they should serve four functions in adult correctional institutions, as:

1. A social change agent who is involved with opening up a closed and coercive system;
2. A resource developer who provides the link between community and institutional services;
3. A therapist who helps prisoners relate successfully to the community; and
4. An advocate who ensures to the greatest possible extent that inmates are not deprived of their rights. (Ivey, 1974, pp. 137–138)

Expectations of counselors range from the professional role they studied in college to the formal job description of the federal and state correctional systems to the role that institutional staff and inmates expect them to assume. The expectations of security staff and inmates are well documented in the letter in Box 8.2 on pages 218–219, which describes how it feels to be a female counselor in a male correctional institution. This letter certainly reflects the lack of authority and status that both male and female correctional officers have in correctional settings. Counselors may bring the concept that they are professionals to the prison, but it does not take them long in a maximum-security facility to realize that they have no formal authority at all and little informal power or status. Because they have no formal authority to deal with institutional problems, they can only make inquiries or recommendations to those in line positions. For example, if a resident has no sheets, a counselor

BOX 8.2 The Woman Counselor in a Male Institution

I would first like to talk about the role of counselors at Joliet. Initially, the counselors are sought out by a resident who cannot get any satisfaction from the security staff. Security will often tell the resident to "see his counselor," thereby creating the image that the counselor can do anything. When the counselor tries to explain to the resident the limitations of his role, it is viewed by the resident as failure and results in distrust of the counselor.

When a counselor does establish a working relationship with a resident, it is extremely difficult to maintain because the resident starts to depend on the counselor for everything. It is very hard to be a "friend" and still maintain a working relationship.

When I first started working at this maximum-security facility, which is primarily designed for young, immature, unsophisticated offenders, it was a very frightening experience. I was certain that every resident I saw was in for *at least six* brutal murders. Although I no longer believe that all the residents are murderers, there is still an element of fear—particularly when I run into large groups of residents. A female is "eyeballed" nearly every time she walks the yard. This, along with the "hoots and howls," is a bit disconcerting. It is also very disturbing to walk across the sidewalk in front of the Segregation unit. Residents in Segregation are very *vocal* to women (to say the least). Of the eight counselors here at Joliet, four of us are female and we do not all experience the same fears.

The female counselors are expected to "walk" the gallery at least once a week. A gallery consists of forty cells, each housing two residents. Before a woman goes onto the gallery, it is standard procedure for an officer to announce that there will be a woman on the gallery. Here at Joliet, the 7–3 A.M. shift cellhouse sergeant will do anything in his power to keep female counselors off the gallery. Since several officers feel this way, it is always a trial to have to go to the gallery.

From my observations, the residents on the gallery react the same way to male and female counselors. By this I mean that certain residents will follow the counselor along the whole gallery just to pester him. The difference in treatment comes about in what the residents are pestering the counselor about. For the female counselor, often the resident just wants to talk to a woman. Some will ask for the same thing over and over again just for the contact with a female. Many residents are quick to protect the female counselor from peers they deem "troublemakers." Others try to manipulate the female by being overly polite. A few residents will tell the female counselor that she is the "best" counselor here, even though he just met her and she may not have spoken a word.

It has been my experience that the resident thinks he will be able to manipulate the female counselor far easier than he could the male counselor. From my observations, I see the female counselor as more aware of the possibility of being manipulated and therefore not falling prey to the residents' games as easily as the males.

The residents' manipulation is particularly obvious when there is an all-female Program Unit. The Program Unit hears minor disciplinary infractions. Some residents turn on the charm to the females deciding their tickets and some become loud and aggressive in an attempt to frighten the women. Although I cannot say this with authority, I feel that if you were to compare male and female Program Unit decisions, they would be about the same.

In terms of job longevity I cannot really express an opinion because the female counselors here at Joliet have all been here the same amount of time. As a group the female

BOX 8.2   *Continued*

counselors tend to group together to discuss cases with each other more than with male counselors.

One of the main problems I see as a counselor is dealing with residents who are on the "make." These residents suggest meeting the female when they get out and how they could show her a "good" time. It's difficult to judge how to handle this type of resident. I hate to be writing disciplinary reports (I think this feeling is shared by all counselors here); yet, this type of behavior cannot be tolerated. So far I have simply told the resident that if it happens again, he'll be on his way to Stateville [a maximum security facility in Illinois that is known to be one of the toughest prisons in the nation]. This seems to keep them quiet for a while.

Our job responsibility which I feel is much harder on the female than on the male is going onto the Segregation gallery. The residents scream and shout obscenities (in unison) and there is really nothing that can be done. The resident is already in Segregation status so another ticket could only be useful if it caused a transfer.

There was a lot that I wanted to say, but I guess I summed it up the best way I could. It may help you to know that when I started this job I was informed that as counselors we are not here to rehabilitate the resident. We are also not to be concerned with reorientation either. Our main goal is to make the residents' institutional time go as smoothly and productively as possible.

Take care,

Tina Loos

Source: Ms. Loos wrote this letter to Clemens Bartollas in response to an inquiry about the role and problems of being a female counselor in a male institution. Used with permission.

cannot order the appropriate correctional officer to distribute them. If a resident wants to enter an educational program, a counselor often does not have the power to authorize his enrollment.

The low status of the counselor is directly related to his or her marginal position in the prison environment. Security is the number one priority of every prison. When security breaks down, everything stops, including treatment programs; nor do counselors meet with inmates during a period of lockdown, or deadlock. Although a counselor may be given information in confidence, he or she is expected by the authorities to immediately report any breach of security to a custody officer. The counselor who is informed by an inmate that he smoked a joint the previous night is expected to find the source of the marijuana, to ascertain whether there is any more in the institution, and to pass this information on to one of the custody staff.

Counselors in maximum-security institutions work in a violent atmosphere. Inmates generally assault only other inmates, but sometimes they strike out against staff. Many counselors now have their offices in a cellhouse rather than in the administration building, and those who still do have an office "up front" must usually spend most of their workweek in the cellhouse.

Thus, counselors are placed in a vulnerable position, and they know that if a riot occurs, they may be taken hostage, injured, raped, or killed.

Stages in Counselors' Correctional Careers

Correctional counselors generally go through several stages in their careers. These stages were developed during training sessions with correctional counselors at the Illinois Corrections Training Academy during 1980. The following stages are more characteristic of male than female correctional counselors. Women do not appear to react as strongly to manipulation by inmates as do men.

1. Counselors initially come into the institution full of enthusiasm, for they are hopeful that they can make a valuable contribution to offenders' lives.
2. This euphoric state quickly gives way to confusion as counselors become aware of the practical realities of the job. Inmates create much of the confusion, for they are constantly putting pressure on new counselors. They are also attempting to manipulate or intimidate the neophyte who is not yet familiar with the rules and regulations that determine eligibility for such a program.
3. This third stage occurs when counselors feel let down or manipulated by inmates. When new counselors see that their reputations with other staff members have suffered because of inmate manipulation, they frequently adopt a more inflexible, punitive approach to their clients.
4. At this stage, counselors swing back to a more moderate position. Although they may not be as accommodating as they were when they first came into the institution, they become more flexible than at any time in the preceding six months or so. Counselors who maintain the punitive, inflexible stance of the third stage are frequently transferred, or at least encouraged to transfer, to other correctional facilities.
5. During this final stage, counselors settle down and try to do the best job they can for their clients. Yet, because they have become realists, they know that they are working for the system and so do not want to jeopardize their reputation by going overboard for offenders. They also are aware that many wardens and assistant wardens started out as counselors and they therefore realize the possibility of upward mobility. Thus, with some their anticipation of a successful career in corrections, along with a growing awareness of their importance to the organization, results in good morale and the desire to stay on the job.

The male correctional counselor may feel marginal to the hostile world of the men's prison, but the women's correctional officers feel even more marginal. Lynn Zimmer (1989) paints a picture of the correctional world facing the woman who desires to be a correctional officer, but, as Ms. Loos's letter clearly reveals, the same scenario faces women correctional counselors:

*Today, almost two decades after the integration process began, women in cor-
rections continue to work in a generally hostile environment where they face
opposition, discrimination, and harassment. These are problems the law has
helped to create through its failure to mandate equality for male and female
workers. They remain problems that the courts may be unable to resolve.
Prison administrators themselves have been reluctant to confront them, perhaps still hoping that the courts will yet exclude women altogether from correctional employment in men's prisons. There is little ground for such a hope
as the courts have, in recent years, moved toward a narrowing of male-female
distinctions even as they have resisted their elimination. What most prison
administrators have not done is look for ways to reduce inequality within the
restrictions established by the courts. Without such an affirmative effort by
prison administrators, there is little reason to be optimistic about the potential for substantial improvement in women's working conditions. (p. 56)*

In sum, the double marginality of the environment of the men's prison
for the female correctional counselor makes it difficult for her to feel overly
positive about her job. It is even more difficult for her to gain the respect of
staff and inmates so that she would be considered for higher administrative
responsibilities.

THE FEMALE CORRECTIONAL OFFICER

The basic role expectation of the correctional officer is that he or she is to prevent escapes, riots, and disruptive inmate behavior. But this function is ac-
complished in various ways, depending on whether the correctional officer is
assigned to a maximum-, medium-, or minimum-security institution.

In maximum-security and most medium-security cell houses, the correctional officer is required to open and close the steel-barred door allowing entrance and exit; to conduct an inmate count several times a day; to distribute
medicine, mail, and laundry; to supervise maintenance activities; and to answer the telephone. The guard must see that inmates are fed, either in the cellhouse or in the central dining facility, to which they must be escorted. The
inmates' daily showers must also be supervised. If violations of rules occur,
the cellhouse guard must write disciplinary tickets. During the day shift, the
majority of the correctional officers are assigned to guard work areas, such as
the metal factory, the furniture factory, the yard gang, the canteen, or another
prison industry.

Correctional officers in maximum-security institutions also guard the tow-
ers and gates. Although faced with loneliness, often uncomfortable tempera-
tures, and boredom, the guard in the tower must nevertheless keep inmates
under constant surveillance. If a problem arises in the yard, the guard on the
tower must resolve it. If an inmate attacks another prisoner or a correctional
officer or dashes for the wall, the use of deadly force may be necessary.

The correctional officer at the gate is expected to search, check, and stamp the hands of all outsiders as they come into the prison. There are several gates in most maximum-security prisons, and a guard is assigned to each. Inmates are required to have a pass and to be "patted down" at each gate. Protected from the violence of prison life, the gate guard is also in the advantageous position of being highly visible to administrators and to outsiders. Thus, when promotions are made, the gate guard often has an advantage over those in the cellhouse and on the tower.

Officers in segregation units have many of the same responsibilities as officers in cellhouses, but they have the additional task of guarding inmates considered more disruptive than those in the general prison population. The job of these officers is more difficult today than ever before, for disruptive inmates no longer can be denied their constitutional rights. Nor is it wise to use brutality against inmates, because they can be awarded damages in a civil suit against their keepers. Thus, in view of the limitations placed on correctional officers, the pandemonium that exists in many of these units is not surprising.

Toxic Environment

The prison environment for both male and female correctional officers is toxic. Several studies have revealed that the arrival of female correctional officers has met with considerable resistance from male correctional officers (Peterson, 1982; Zimmer, 1986, pp. 156–159; Owen, 1985). Horne (1985) has stated this very strongly:

> *Negative male attitudes towards women in corrections have been the most significant factor in hindering the advancement of female CO's. No solid proof supports this male bias against female CO's, but none is needed, since males run the corrections agencies. The feeling was, and still is, among the majority of male officers, that "prison work is a man's work." (p. 51)*

However, Lawrence and Mahan's (1998) study of men and women officers working in men's prisons in a Midwestern state found that women officers did not face the resistance suggested by previous studies, but the resistance came chiefly from more experienced men officers. These researchers did note that this continued resistance is likely to provide an obstacle to the advancement and promotion of women officers in men's prisons.

Warden Pamela K. Withrow's (1992) conversation with women's correctional officers revealed a number of disadvantages women saw in working in men's prisons:

- Women often are not taken seriously. They have to work harder and do more before being able to increase staff respect for their abilities. This means having to prove themselves over and over every day—not only their abilities, but personal worth.

- If a woman is seen as an affirmative action appointment and makes a statement or gives an order, eyes may shift to supervisory men present for confirmation, even if the woman outranks them.
- Women are always on display. This visibility is not an advantage when a woman makes an error.
- Stereotypes live. Women get asked to type, take notes, or check punctuation and grammar even when they are custody staff.
- Informal networking—golf outings, fishing, hunting, and other traditionally male pursuits—excludes women.
- Tokenism is aggravating. Women may be assigned to the control center or the front desk so they will be visible to important visitors.
- In a tense, noisy situation, a woman's voice may not be audible or may lack the power to command.
- Sexual harassment and abuse of gender is widespread and difficult to combat, especially if the victim does not want to be seen as a snitch.
- Instead of sharing information, male coworkers let women figure things out for themselves and seem to hope they won't.
- When women want to be included, it seems they have to choose between using profanity or professional language. They also have to choose between conduct that may violate personal standards (such as barhopping) or seeming to be aloof. . . .
- There is pressure for women to seek advancement whether that is their goal or not. Also there is pressure to attend social functions that sometimes verges on sexual harassment.
- Women sometimes must develop multiple personae. A woman feels like an actress as the day progresses.
- Women and men have communication styles that often do not mesh, making the work harder than it already is.
- Male staff sometimes use "PMS" as an explanation for any action by a woman they don't like or agree with.
- Less-qualified male staff will sometimes complain that women get promoted over them because of their gender. (p. 92)

Jurik (1985), in an examination of barriers confronting women employed as correctional officers in a state department of corrections in the western United States, found that several organizational barriers have prevented greater acceptance of women correctional officers. One organizational problem is that the reforms initiated by the department created the perception of increased danger in the prison environment. This perception has contributed to the feeling that women are unreliable in such a violent setting. These fears about women's unreliability seem to be rooted in three popular beliefs about women: (1) the "greater physical weaknesses" of women make them incapable of functioning in dangerous situations; (2) the "mental weaknesses" of women prevents them from handling the strain of working in the prison; and (3) the sexual identity and behavior of female officers cast the fear that they will become emotionally involved with inmates (pp. 378–379).

Walters (1993) surveyed correctional officers at four facilities concerning their attitudes toward their jobs. As part of this study, male correctional officers were asked about their attitudes toward working with women correctional officers. The variables that were found to be significantly related to a "pro-woman" correctional officer attitude were the quality of the working relationship with women officers, custody orientation, job satisfaction, educational level, and prison type. But no significant relationships were found between a pro-woman correctional officer attitude and race, length of service, security level, rank, marital status, stress, or age of male respondents.

Crouch and Alpert (1982) studied occupational socialization among prison guards in three recruit classes trained at the Texas Department of Corrections between mid-June and the end of July 1979. They point out that research generally indicates that guards have an increased aggressive or punitive attitude toward inmates over time. However, when the variable of sex was examined, it was found that "women guards become much more tolerant and nonpunitive over time, while their male counterparts become increasingly punitive and aggressive" (pp. 169–170).

Gross, Larson, Urban, and Zupan (1994), in a study comparing work-related stress in male and female correctional officers, found that there were statistically significant differences between gender and stress outcomes for male and female correctional officers. Women were more likely to be absent more frequently and to have taken sick leave more often than men, but the latter finding, especially, may be due in part to greater family responsibilities.

A female correctional officer in a men's prison usually finds that the stress of working in a violent environment is coupled with conflict with male coworkers. But even assuming that problems with male coworkers can be resolved, the role confusion or uncertainty of the job may cause her to seek out or be assigned to low-contact positions (Zimmer, 1986). This, in turn, results in dead-end work assignments or limited promotional possibilities (Jurik, 1985).

Jenne and Kersting (1996) compared how male and female correctional officers deal with volatile inmate situations with male inmates. They found that female officers usually respond to aggressive incidents in the same manner as male correctional officers. Indeed, in some cases, female correctional officers even handle some encounters more aggressively than male correctional officers do. Jenne and Kersting claim that these results debunk the assumption or notion that women are incapable of handling situations that require an aggressive response.

Jurik and Halemba (1984) compared the job satisfaction of male and female correctional officers working at the same prison facility in a western state. They found that female correctional officers tended to be more highly educated than male correctional officers, come from more professional backgrounds, and have a much greater likelihood to be divorced or separated. In contrast, the majority of male correctional officers had previous law enforcement or military experience, but none of the female correctional officers had military experience and only about a third had previous police experience. But despite such demographic differences, Jurik and Halemba discovered that "women exhibited largely the same attitudes toward their work as did male officers," but that "female respondents, more often than men, cited intrinsic reasons for employment in corrections" (p. 564).

Privacy–Equal Employment Dilemma

Affirmative action measures have resulted in more minority officers, with the result that the percentage of racial minorities among officers is now equal in many states to that of the minority population of the state. But it was not until the enactment of equal employment legislation—specifically Title VII, which prohibited sex discrimination in hiring by state and local governments—that doors began to open for women in men's prisons.

Three criticisms have been directed toward women working as correctional officers in men's prisons: First, women are not fit for the job; for example, they are not strong enough, are too easily corrupted by inmates, or are poor backup for other officers in trouble. Second, women are a disruptive influence; that is, inmates will not follow their orders or will fight for their attention. Third, the presence of women violates inmate privacy, especially when women are working in shower areas or conducting strip searches of inmates (Hawkins and Alpert, 1989, p. 359).

Dothard v. Rawlinson (1977) and *Gunther v. Iowa State Men's Reformatory* (1979) have been the most important U.S. Supreme Court cases examining whether women are qualified to work in men's prisons. The former was an Alabama lawsuit filed by Diane Rawlinson, a recent college graduate in correctional psychology who was denied a job as a correctional officer because she was five pounds below the minimum weight requirement. Her class-action suit challenged the state's height and weight requirement; the suit also charged that a department of corrections' regulation preventing female officers from "continual close proximity" to prisoners in maximum-security prisons for men (known as the no-contact rule) was discriminatory. The Supreme Court, in a 5–4 decision, overturned a lower court decision that had invalidated the no-contact rule. The Court was unwilling to let women work in maximum-security prisons for men in Alabama because of the danger of sexual attack and because the extra vulnerability of women to attack would weaken security and endanger other prison employees.

However, in *Gunther v. Iowa,* the Court dismissed security issues as a reason for limiting women's employment as guards in that state. The *Gunther* decision defined that job requirements to strip search male inmates or witness them in showers constituted an attempt to prevent women from working as correctional officers.

These and other cases demonstrate that the courts have generally established procedures that both guarantee women the right to employment and protect inmate privacy as much as possible. In the *Forts v. Ward* decision (1978), the circuit court held that "equal job opportunity must in some measure give way to the right of privacy" (p. 1099). The background of this case was that female inmates at the Bedford Hills Correctional Facility in New York contended that their right to privacy was violated because male correctional officers were assigned to duties in hospital and housing units. As a result, the women inmates argued, male correctional officers were able to observe them while they were sleeping, showering, dressing, undressing, and using the toilet facilities. In the *Torres v. Wisconsin* decision (1988), prison officials used the bona fide occupational qualification (BFOQ) defense for restricting male correctional officers from working in the living units of a women's prison. The case went through two appeals processes, but eventually the rights of female inmates were determined to take precedence over the equal employment rights of male correctional officers (Maschke, 1996, p. 32).

Departments of corrections can maintain inmates' right to privacy by administrative policies preventing women from doing some types of searches, such as strip searches. The installation of modesty half-screens, fogged windows that permit figures to be seen, or privacy doors on toilet stalls offer another solution to privacy issues. Security does not have to be sacrificed, and these modifications can be made to the physical environment at little cost.

Comparison of How Female and Male Correctional Officers Do Their Jobs

Several studies have compared male and female correctional officers (Alpert, 1984, pp. 441–455 and Peterson, 1982). They have generally found that men and women do not differ on the quality of their job performance. This does not mean that they are equal in all tasks. Although men may be able to handle physical assault better than women, women may more effectively defuse an incident before violence erupts (Peterson, 1982). Leo L. Meyer, a former warden in the Illinois correctional system, describes the role of women officers in a male medium-security institution (quoted in Bartollas, 1981):

> *We probably have more female officers than any other correctional center because of the transfers from mental health. Two are lieutenants, and one of them just passed the NRA [National Rifle Association] test for instructor in firearms. I think she is the first woman in history to do this. A female who wants to be a warden has a real good opportunity. I say one thing about females, they're dependable and they seem to try harder. In terms of qualifying for their firearms test: Their scores are better than some men, and many have never shot a gun before. (p. 300)*

Various studies have found that women correctional officers are more treatment oriented than are their male counterparts (Jurik and Halemba, 1984; Crouch, 1985). Women also tend to supervise inmates with a more personal interaction style than men officers. For example, women will frequently ask inmates to perform certain tasks, rather than commanding them to do so (Pollock, 1995, p. 107). Zimmer (1986) adds that inmates claim that women officers explain orders more fully, while male officers tend to bark orders and resent any attempt by inmates to get a fuller explanation.

SUMMARY

This chapter examined the role of women working in corrections. Although the empirical examination of women probation and parole officers, women jailers, correctional counselors, and even wardens of men's prisons is thin, every indication is that women continue to experience the problems faced throughout policing careers and legal professions. These problems are particularly highlighted with women who attempt to become correctional officers in men's prisons. Consistent with the men's club in policing, women correctional officers face the time-worn "truth" that women do not belong in a men's prison. Women correctional officers have faced stiff resistance and, at times, physical intimidation and sexual harassment. But some women correctional officers, as with women correctional counselors and correctional administrators, have survived and even thrived in men's prisons.

What is fortunate about women's survival in corrections is the impact that they can bring to the toxicity of correctional environments. The early entrance of women in probation and parole had a considerable impact on humanizing the profession. It can be argued that much of the ideology of probation and parole throughout most of the twentieth century is attributable to the influence of its early women leaders. In some sense, this same tendency seems to be occurring in correctional systems that employ women wardens. There seems to be a consistent difference in how women and men correctional staff approach inmates, handle problems, defuse violence, and respond to crises. These disparities, over time, can make major differences in the quality of institutional life.

REFERENCES

Alpert, G. P. (1984). The needs of the judiciary and misapplications of social research: The case of female guards in men's prisons. *Criminology 22:* 441–455.

Anderson, E., and Spanier, G. (1980). Treatment of delinquent youth: The influence of the juvenile probation officer's perceptions of self and work. *Criminology 17:* 505–514.

Bartollas, C. (1981). *Introduction to corrections.* New York: Harper and Row.

Belknap, J. (1991). Women in conflict: An analysis of women correctional officers. *Women and Criminal Justice 2:* 89–115.

Crouch, B. M., and Alpert, G. P. (1982). Sex and occupational socialization among prison guards: A longitudinal study. *Criminal Justice and Behavior 9:* 159–176.

Dothard v. Rawlinson, 433 U.S. 321, 1977.

Feinman, C. (1994). *Women in the criminal justice system,* 3rd. ed. Westport, Conn.: Praeger.

Forts v. Ward, 471 F.Supp. 1095 (S.D.N.Y. 1978).

Gross, G. R., Larson, S. J. Urban, G. D., and Zupan, L. L. (1994). Gender differences in occupational stress among correctional officers. *American Journal of Criminal Justice 18:* 219–234.

Gunther v. Iowa State Men's Reformatory F2d 1079 (8th Circ., 1979).

Hawk, K. M. (1992, August). BOP programming administrator sees opportunities for women. *Corrections Today 19:* 32, 34.

Hawkins, R., and Alpert, G. P. (1989). *American prison systems: Punishment and justice.* Englewood Cliffs, N.J. Prentice-Hall.

Hayes, M. (1989). Promotion and management: What choices for women? *Probation Journal 36:* 12–17.

Horne, P. (1985). Female corrections officers: A status report. *Federal Probation 49:* 46–54.

Ivey, A. E. (1974). Adapting systems to people. *Personnel and Guidance Journal 53:* 137–138.

Jenne, D. L., and Kersting, R. C. (1996). Aggression and women correctional officers in male prisons. *Prison Journal 76:* 442–460.

Jurik, N. C., and Halemba, G. J. (1984, Autumn). Gender, working conditions and the job satisfaction of women in a non-traditional occupation: Female correctional officers in men's prisons. *The Sociological Quarterly 25:* 551–566.

Jurik, N. C. (1985). An officer and a lady: Organizational barriers to women working as correctional officers in men's prisons. *Social Problems 32:* 375–388.

Lawrence, R., and Mahan, S. (1998). Women correctional officers in men's prisons: Acceptance and perceived job performance. *Women and Criminal Justice 9:* 63–83.

Lidster, D. (1979, March). Personal interview.

Maguire, K., and Pastore, A. (eds.). (1996). *Sourcebook of criminal justice statitics 1995.* Washington, DC: U.S. Government Printing Office.

Marks, A. (1997, April 23). Women break into some of the toughest men's prisons. *Christian Science Monitor:* 1.

Maschke, K. J. (1996). Gender in the prison setting: The privacy-equal employment dilemma. *Women and Criminal Justice 7:* 23–42.

Merlo, A. V., and Pollock, J. M. (1995). *Women, law, and social control.* Boston: Allyn & Bacon.

Miller, T. D. (1996). *The warden wore pink.* Brunswick, Minn.: Biddle Publishing.

Morris, N. (1974). *The future of imprisonment.* Chicago: University of Chicago Press.

Morton, J. B. (1992). Looking back on 200 years of valuable contributions. *Corrections Today 18:* 76–87.

Nagel, W. G. (1974). An American archipelago: The United States Bureau of Prisons. Hacksensack, N.J.: National Council on Crime and Delinquency.

Nash, M. (1995). Aggravation, mitigation and the gender of probation officers. *Howard Journal of Criminal Justice 34:* 250–258.

Owen, B. (1985). Race and gender relations among prison workers. *Crime and Delinquency 31:* 147–158.

Peterson, C. B. (1982). Doing time with the boys: An analysis of women correctional officers in all-male facilities. In *The criminal justice system and women,* edited by B. R. Price and N. J. Sokoloff. New York: Clark Boardman.

Platt, A. (1976). *The child savers,* 2nd ed. Chicago: University of Chicago Press.

Pogrebin, M. R., and Poole, E. D. (1997, March). The sexualized work environment: A look at women jail officers. *The Prison Journal 77:* 41–57.

Pollock, J. M. (1995). *Women in corrections: Custody or the "caring ethic."* In A. V. Merlo and J. M. Pollock (eds.), *Women, law and social control* (pp. 97–116). Needham Heights, Mass.: Allyn & Bacon.

Stohr, M. K., Mays, G. L., Beck, A. C., and Kelley, T. (1998). Sexual harassment in women's jails. *Journal of Contemporary Criminal Justice 14:* 135–155.

Torres v. Wisconsin Department of Health & Social Services, 838 F.2d 944 (7th Cir. 1988).

Walsh, A. (1984). Gender-based differences. *Criminology 22:* 371–388.

Walters, S. (1993). Changing the guard: Male correctional officers' attitudes toward women as co-workers. *Journal of Offender Rehabilitation 20:* 47–60.

Wisely, W. (1998). $6.5 million spent in California sexual harassment suit. *Corrections Today 60:* 15.

Withrow, P. K. (1992, August). Workplace reality: Women staff tell it like it is. *Corrections Today:* 88–92.

Wunder, G. (1969). Zur Situation der Bew Ahrungshelfer: Algemeines zur Arbeitssituation der Bew, *Bewahrungshilfe-Germany 16:* 91–107.

Zimmer, L. (1989). Solving women's employment problems in corrections: Shifting the burden to administrators. *Women and Criminal Justice 1:* 55–75.

Zimmer, L. (1986). *Women guarding men.* Chicago: University of Chicago Press.

9

SUMMARY AND NEW DIRECTIONS FOR THE FUTURE

We have presented and examined five feminist themes in this text. First, gender, class, and racial analysis was used to examine the experiences of women offenders, victims, and practitioners in the criminal justice system. Second, the effects of the multiple oppressions of gender, class, and race have been given consideration. Third, this book has focused on the social construction of knowledge and how the role of women has been influenced by male-oriented social constructionism. A number of myths concerning female offenders, victims, and practitioners have been unearthed. Fourth, social context, especially the social context of patriarchal society, has been heavily emphasized. On a micro level, subcultures within the wider society have been developed by women to escape the oppressiveness of the wider society. Finally, the theme of empowerment has received some emphasis in nearly every chapter.

THEME OF GENDER, CLASS, AND RACE

The fundamental theme of this book is that women, especially troublesome ones, are subjected to various forms of discrimination, exploitation, and criminalization. The women who are most likely to experience such oppressions also are poor and from minority groups. With female delinquents, it is their sexual behavior that brings them to the attention of juvenile authorities. It can be argued that much of the state's response is a criminalization of young women's survival strategies (Schaffner, 1998).

Gender is further related to the themes of domination and subordination. Women in a patriarchal society experience inequality of many resources but chiefly of status and power. Placed in subordinate categories, they become more vulnerable to victimization. Wife battering, incestuous attacks of female adolescents by fathers or father substitutes, and rape are crimes of domination against women that take place in situations of inequality.

Class can be another form of exploitation experienced by females. It can increase the likelihood of entrance into homelessness, unemployment, drug use, survival sex and prostitution, and even more serious delinquent and criminal acts. In adolescence, lower-class girls are high risks to have unsatisfactory experiences at school, to lack educational goals beyond high school, to experience higher rates of physical and sexual abuse, to deal with pregnancy and motherhood, to be involved in drug and alcohol dependency, to confront the risk of AIDS, and to lack supportive networks at home. Lower-class adult women are more likely to be victimized than are middle- and upper-class ones and to be subjected to domestic abuse. Equally important, lower-class women are less likely to receive the benefits of chivalry.

Racial oppression of women further receives documentation throughout this text. Both minority girls and women are often forced by their minority status and poverty to deal early and regularly with problems of abuse, drugs, and violence. In addition, they are likely to be attracted to gang membership.

Some evidence also supports the belief that girls and women of color enjoy the benefits of chivalry much less than do white girls. They tend to be viewed as more dangerous to society and to require jail incarceration and long-term institutionalization.

Moreover, there is evidence that African American rape victims are reluctant to go to rape crisis centers or to report their rapes to the police. A large part of this reluctance relates to larger needs and concerns in their lives, including poverty, homelessness, unemployment, difficulties in feeding their children, racism, and fear of the police.

THEME OF MULTIPLE OPPRESSIONS OF GENDER, CLASS, AND RACE

The tendency is to think about gender, class, and race in such a way that they are each examined and the total effect is equated to be the sum of each on offenders, victims, and workers in the justice system. Spelman notes that "it isn't easy to think about gender, race, and class in ways that don't obscure or underplay their effects on each other" (Spelman, 1989, p. 115). As a result, what has been most typically done is to focus on gender and sexism and then to ponder about how gender and racism are related to race and racism and to class and classism, but, as Spelman observes, this "obscures the way in which race and class identity may be intertwined with gender identity" (Spelman,1989, pp. 112, 115). Lewis (1977) has added that because feminist theories of women's inequality "focused" exclusively on the effects of racism, this has been of "limited applicability to minority women subjected to the constraints of both racism and sexism" (p. 339). In Chapter 3, which examined women in prison, it was seen that it is not possible to separate the violence and discrimination against women based on their gender from issues of race, class, and ethnicity. These effects are exacerbated if women are African American or Latina and even more if they are living in poverty.

Daly (1993) summarizes this argument by saying "that unless you consider all the key relations of inequality—class, race, gender (and also age and sexuality)—you have considered none" (p. 65). She added that "unless you consider the inseparability of these relations in one person, you do not understand what we are saying" (p. 65). What all this suggests is that both female delinquents and adult women suffer the consequences of multiple oppression as more than some form of simply additive experience and that the whole of gender, race, and class is greater than its individual parts.

THEME OF MALE-ORIENTED SOCIAL CONSTRUCTION OF KNOWLEDGE

The major theoretical works on crime have been written by male criminologists about men and boys. Alarmingly gender blind, they added females as a type of footnote. Clearly, from the very beginning, the study of crime and the justice process has been shaped by male experiences and understanding of the social world (Daly and Chesney-Lind, 1988).

In the debate that has taken place between *sex,* which is a biologically based category, and *gender,* which refers to the socially constructed meanings that are associated with each sex, it has been argued that the claimed difference between women and men represents a political and social decision rather than a distinction given in nature (Rothenberg, 1998, p. 9).

The feminist movement, in offering a framework for viewing male-on-female violence, was to turn the conceptualization of rape upside down. For the first time, sexual assault was redefined from the victim's perspective. Rape was seen as the violence it is. Through the efforts of the antirape movement, it would soon become clear that such violence against women was one more mechanism for male social control (Schechter, 1982).

Such feminists as Brownmiller and Griffin helped conceive of rape not in either-or terms but as a series of acts along a continuum. Far from being an isolated event that could be rooted out from the society at large, the crime of rape was now seen as only the logical extension of what was already there. Brownmiller defined rape as "a conscious process of intimidation by which all men keep all women in a state of fear" (Brownmiller, 1975, p. 5).

In considering the crime of rape, a number of rape myths were examined and refuted. These included:

- Most rape claims are false; women feel guilty about sex and redefine the situation later.
- Rape happens only to bad women such as prostitutes.
- Unconsciously women want to be raped.
- Most rape is committed by a stranger down a dark alley.
- When women say no, they mean yes.
- Women's wearing of seductive clothes causes rape.

- Rapes are impulsive acts committed by men who are unable to control their passions.
- Rapes are black-on-white crimes.
- Rape is caused by male deviance and pathology.

IMPORTANCE OF SOCIAL CONTEXT

In Chapter 1 began a theme that ran throughout the book: U.S. society and many others have been affected by gender in the distribution of power, wealth, and opportunities. What is so disturbing about the social construction of gender is that males have assumed the power and control over women. This is what the term *patriarchal society* ultimately means. Women who live in such a society will be subordinate to the males.

For the past three thousand years, the power of patriarchy has been pervasive. It "has influenced our basic ideas about human nature and about our relation to the universe—'man's' nature and 'his' relations to the universe, in physical language" (Capra, 1988, pp. 29–30). It is a system that only recently has been challenged and whose doctrine seemed to be so universally accepted that it seems to be one of the laws of nature (p. 29).

The laws of society have represented one of the means by which women have been oppressed under patriarchy. The belief that women had to be protected from the sordid nature of life led to restricting them from working and earning a living on an equal basis with men, keeping them from owning property for much of the history of this nation, excluding them from jury duty, and punishing in a severe way those who violated what a woman should be.

The sexual harassment of women has emerged in the context of their employment in legal and criminal justice agencies. This context has been promoted by the cultures of the "men's club" of policing, the "good old boys" of law agencies, and male esprit de corps in correctional institutions and probation and parole agencies.

The kinds of violence that take place in intimate relationships also reveals the importance of social context in this nation. In understanding the violence of intimate relationships, including wife and partner abuse, marital rape, and child abuse, the issues of authority and control by men over women must be carefully explored. Indeed, a man's right to chastise his wife was affirmed in the doctrine of the church as well as in early Roman law and English common law. Even into the twentieth century, domestic violence was considered a private matter, not one for intervention by the state.

An examination of women offenders in correctional institutions reveals the sad story of one form of social injustice after another. Race, gender, and class intersect in the women's prison. One could easily make the argument that the antifeminist and antiwelfare movements are being played out in the prisons of the United States. The war on drugs has taken its toll on poor minority women and on their children, who are destined to grow up in foster homes while their mothers serve their time. The new "get-tough-on-crime" laws have brought their effect to bear disproportionately on persons without political and legal leverage in society.

Rape is a tool of dominance, power, and control. Rape in some situations, such as in war or by gangs, is an act of male bonding. Historically little sensitivity has been shown toward rape victims. In past centuries, a man who wanted a woman, raped her and brought her into his tribe (Flowers, 1987). In our most recent past, the rape victim's behavior before the claim of rape, her behavior during the sexual encounter, and her relationship to the perpetrator all were often taken into consideration by legal officials in deciding whether a "real" rape occurred. Indeed, until the 1970s, the law in most states recognized that a rape occurred only when a man forced a woman to have sex under the threat of injury, when she had resisted strenuously, and there was outside corroboration. As part of the misfortune of rape, a woman who engaged in sex outside marriage, even against her will, was considered a "fallen" woman and was frequently blamed for her own victimization (Donat and D'Emilio, 1992).

Subcultures also become important in shaping behaviors of offenders, victims, and workers in the justice system. In the subcultures of some college campuses, men socialized into these subcultures regard sex in terms of gaining possession of a woman. According to Schwartz and DeKeseredy (1997), "the frustration caused by a reference-group-anchored sex drive often results in predatory sexual conduct" (p. 35).

The subculture of males in law has traditionally resulted in women being concentrated in the lowest echelons of the profession. Recently, women have made remarkable advances in the legal profession, but in the law, as elsewhere, status and income disparities still exist. The subculture of males in both policing and corrections has resisted the entrance and acceptance of women. Law enforcement, according to the perspective of the policing subculture, is a men's club and women are not wanted. Correctional staffs, especially in men's prisons, have been quick to say that women do not belong in men's prisons and have provided stiff and consistent opposition to the acceptance of female correctional officers.

EMPOWERMENT OF WOMEN INVOLVED WITH THE JUSTICE SYSTEM

In searching for solutions, this test has drawn on empowerment at all levels—personal, interpersonal, economic, educational, and political. For example, the rape reform and domestic violence intervention movements have made progress on several fronts: the legal one, women's group counseling centers, rape crisis centers, women's shelters, and other crisis intervention programs for victims. Police officers also have become more sensitized to the feelings of women who have been sexually abused. Women's entry into policing, corrections, and the law has had a tremendous impact on those fields, bringing a feminist perspective to issues of women and violence. The close relationship between substance abuse and women offending has encouraged a wide variety of treatment programs for women who have substance abuse problems.

FUTURE TRENDS

Many trends and events of the twentieth century transformed the criminal justice system and the roles of women within it. Broadly, these events have been expressed as chivalry for white women of a certain class; harsh punishments for African female offenders; first a stress on rehabilitation and then a cynicism toward rehabilitation; a war on drugs and on drug users; and a conservative backlash against women on welfare and women convicted of crime.

There is a truism that says we can't know where we are going until we know where we have been. What we learn from the past is that the pendulum swings in one direction, then comes back to swing the other way. So how long will it take to reverse the present conservative trend?

We can say one thing for certain: things may have to get worse before they get better. In all probability, this will mean more executions, harsher drug laws, more lethal weapons for the police, fewer rights for prisoners, and more politicians securing public support by capitalizing on the public's fear of crime, a fear largely generated in the mass media. Another truth worth pursuing is that changes at any level of the system will have repercussions throughout the system as a whole.

Over the past decades, the most significant change that portends well for the future is the increasing diversity of the population. This diversity is slowly being reflected in law, the legislatures, and the judiciary. Feminist women have worked for legal reform with some notable successes. Among these are the criminalizing of marital rape in many states and reforms in rape law, such as shielding the past sexual history of victims and removing corroboration requirements. The filing of lawsuits against state departments of corrections has improved career opportunities for women and minority staff as well as vocational training options for female inmates. As increasing numbers of women are appointed to the bench and join prosecution teams, we can expect to see greater protection for victims and prison inmates (another kind of victim) in the future.

The greatest single factor in producing social change and humanizing the criminal justice system at the turn of a new century, in short, may well be the voice of female authority. As women gain in political influence, areas for anticipated change relevant to criminal justice are:

- swifter punishments for male batterers; greater protection for battered women, legally and economically
- more protection for incest victims and less stress on reunification of violent and sexually abusive families

- legislation to provide extensive counseling services to child rape victims to prevent traumatization
- further improvements in rates of conviction of rapists as a result of advances in DNA testing and enhanced victims' rights
- less litigation and increased use of alternative forms of conflict resolution, such as mediation and conferencing between opposing parties
- greater focus on substance abuse, mental health, and medical treatment needs of female offenders
- increased funding for child halfway-house parenting programs for offenders
- as an alternative to imprisonment, much greater use of intensive community supervision programs
- within prison, strict rules restricting male guard access to female inmates
- improved educational and vocational opportunities for women in prison
- an end to mandatory minimum sentences and a return to an individualized approach to justice
- changes in the laws meting out harsh sentences to women convicted as conspirators due to their close associations with drug dealers
- a reversal in "welfare reform" laws so that women will have and be able to maintain more independence from men, if they so desire

Much more research is needed to explore the link between women's victimization in society—sexually, economically, and personally—and their criminality. Research is also needed to show how substance abuse and other addictive behavior figures into the equation.

In the future, we can expect to hear a great deal more about empowerment and a solutions-based (as opposed to problems-based) strengths approach in the criminal justice field. Already, the strengths approach is making inroads into the criminal justice field for work with adolescent offenders. Whether this will be the new paradigm for criminal justice practice, as Clark (1998) predicts, remains to be seen.

REFERENCES

Brownmiller, S. (1975). *Against our wills: Men, women, and rape.* New York: Bantam.

Clark, M. D. (1998, June). Strength-based practice: The ABC's of working with adolescents who don't want to work with you. *Federal Probation 62*(1): 46–53.

Daly, K. (1993). Class-race-gender: Sloganeering in search of meaning. *Social Justice 20:* 56–71.

Daly, K., and Chesney-Lind, M. (1988). Feminism and Criminology. *Justice Quarterly 5:* 497–538.

Donat, P., and D'Emilio, J. (1992). A feminist redefinition of rape and sexual assault: Historical foundations and change. *Journal of Social Issues 48:* 9–20.

Flowers, R. B. (1987). *Women and criminality: The woman as victim, offender, and practitioner.* New York: Greenwood Press.

Lewis, D. K. (1977). A response to inequality: Black women, racism, and sexism. *Signs: Journal of Women in Culture and Society 3:* 339.

Rothenberg, P. S. (1998). *Race, class, and gender in the United States: An integrated theory,* 4th ed. New York: St. Martin's Press.

Schaffer, L. (1998, November). Female juvenile delinquency: Sexual solutions and gender bias in juvenile justice. Paper presented to the Annual Meeting of the American Society of Criminology in Washington, D.C.

Schechter, S. (1982). *Women and male violence.* New York: Macmillan.

Schwartz, M. D., and DeKeseredy, W. S. (1997). *Sexual assault on the college campus: The role of male peer support.* Thousand Oaks, Calif.: Sage.

Spelman, E. V. (1989). *Inessential woman.* Boston: Beacon Press.

INDEX